Egypt's Past and Potential: Nationalism, Neoliberalism, and Revolution

Derek Alan Ide

Hampton Institute Press

Hampton Institute Press

www.hamptoninstitution.org

Copyright © 2014 Hampton Institute Press
All rights reserved.
ISBN-10: 0991313607
ISBN-13: 978-0-9913136-0-0

To my mother, Kim
who always taught me to fight for what I believe in
And my father, Bruce
who taught me there is usually more than one way to do it

CONTENTS

Preface and Acknowledgements   ix

Introduction   1

Part I – Nationalism to Neoliberalism

Chapter 1 – Undemocratic Political Institutions   18
Political Repression and Colonialism
The Role of the Military
A Permanent "State of Emergency"
Repressing Political Liberties
A Massive "Omnipresent Security Apparatus"
Absence of a Democratic Political Structure

Chapter 2 – Declining Economic Conditions   35
The Struggle for Economic Autonomy under the Ottomans and the British
Nasser, Nationalism, and Economic Development
The Contradictions of Arab Nationalism
Sadat's *Infitah* as the Quintessential Neoliberal Model
Mubarak as Neoliberal Poster Boy
Schisms within Elite Circles
Despondent Economic Conditions at the Outset of Revolution
Egyptian Neoliberalism and the Capitalist World Order
Economic Disparity and the Paucity of Mubarak's Social Base

Chapter 3 – Egypt as US Client State   68
Egypt's Unique Position in the Imperial Power Structure
Egypt's Historic Role in the Colonial and Post World War II Order
Israel and Egypt: Primary and Secondary Sources of Regional Hegemony
"Normalizing" Relations with Israel as a Means of Securing Hegemony
Egypt's Imperial Functions under Mubarak

Mubarak Doing Israel's Bidding
The Complex Dynamics of the Arab Uprisings and Imperial Interests

Chapter 4 – Revival of Popular Movements   95
The Growth of a Modern Working Class in Colonial Egypt
Egypt's First Mass Movement: the Society of the Muslim Brothers
Workers and Brothers after the Military Coup
Politics of Contention in the 2000s
Labor Militancy in the 1990s and 2000s
The Groundbreaking Strike at Mahalla
The Significance of Mahalla and the Birth of Independent Trade Unionism
Socialists Reach Out to the Muslim Brothers
A Loose Alliance Forms

Part II – Labor and Revolution

Chapter 5 – Labor Enters the Scene:
"Take Tahrir to the Factories"   119
The Weeks before January 25th
Workers as Individuals and the Emergence of Independent Trade
    Unionism
February 8: "Normalizing" Economic Relations and Labor's Response
The Working Class and its Economic Threat to the Regime
Mubarak Desperately Holds On
Mass Strikes and Mubarak's Resignation

Chapter 6 – Labor Activity and Military Rule:
"Let the Revolution in Egypt Be Permanent!"   134
"It is the Fate of All Revolutions that This Union of Different Classes
    Cannot Subsist"
The New Pejorative of the Military, the Media, and the Brotherhood:
    Ihtijajat Fi'awiyya
Mid-February: Taking Tahrir to the Factories
Working Class Organization: The Proliferation of New Political Parties
The Movement towards Independent Trade Unionism
Making the Revolution Permanent

Pacification, Repression, and Resistance
A New Era for Trade Unionism: The Egyptian Federation of Independent Trade Unions

Chapter 7 – Action and Reaction:
"The People Want another Wheel of Production"   162

The Collapse of State Security and Continuation of Popular Struggles
The Social Revolution Lags Behind the Political
"There Are So Many Strikes That We've Lost Count"
Making Strikes Illegal: The Military Pushes Back
Alternative Political Parties Grow: the Democratic Labor Party
The Experience of the Democratic Labor Party
Contentious Labor Action Under the Anti-Strike Law

Chapter 8 – April 2011 and Beyond:
"The Union is a Shield and Our Sword is the Strike"   183

April to August (2011): Obstacles for Egyptian Labor
The Mass Strike-wave of September: "A Shift from the Defensive to the Offensive"
Gains Thus Far
EFITU Rapidly Expands in Spite of Challenges
The First Schism in the New Movement: The Egyptian Democratic Labor Congress
Labor and Party Politics in the Egyptian Elections
The Muslim Brotherhood in Power
Economic Protests Explode During Morsi's Tenure
Morsi: Mubarak with a *Zibiba*

Conclusion   210

Resources   230

Preface and Acknowledgments

Writing a book is at the same time a profoundly solitary and collective experience. It is the summation of all an individual's thoughts, ideas, and analysis into what is hopefully a cohesive narrative that can stand up to rigorous examination. Yet, it is also a culmination of the all the discussions and debates of countless people who have in some way contributed to the author's analysis, either forming it, refining it, or providing a juxtaposition to it. Here I will briefly explain the reasoning behind the structure of the book, as well as its intentions and its limitations. I will also provide acknowledgements for all those who had a hand in helping bring this work to fruition.

This project was a long-time in the making. My first introduction to Egypt was at a conference in the summer of 2008. There I had the opportunity to hear Mamdouh Habashi and Saber Barakat, both long-time socialists and trade union activists, outline their analysis of the Egyptian political scene. This was immediately after the tremendous anti-Mubarak demonstration and strike of April 6, 2008 in al-Mahalla al-Kubra, following on the heels of a year-and-a-half upsurge in labor militancy across the country. I sat near the front row, immensely inspired by the struggle, even if I did not realize at the time how formative that experience was for me. It was three years later, as the uprising against Mubarak was in full swing, when I wrote about Egypt for the first time. That article formed the foundation for this book. Since then, Egypt has been my primary area of study, both academically and independently.

I hope it is clear from the outset that in writing this I do not mean to suggest ways forward for the left in Egypt, a paternalistic enterprise first world leftists who are removed from the immediate struggle sometimes engage in. Nor do I assume to know something Egyptian leftists and activists do not. On the contrary, this book starts from the premise that we, leftists in the United States and the rest of the First World, have an immense amount to learn from the revolutionary struggles that have taken place in Egypt. Indeed, it is my contention that in order for us to make any sort of revolutionary transformation in our own societies we must study and learn from the largest revolutionary movements of our time.

A brief note on both the purpose and organization of the book is in order. There is a significant amount of written material on Egypt, and in no way should this book be considered a definitive work on Egyptian history. In essence, I have attempted to provide a review of some of the most pertinent literature, synthesizing an array of academic and left-wing analysis into one coherent narrative. I hope this process has been facilitated by the organization of the book, which I have split into two parts, each with four chapters. The first part of the book is organized into thematic chapters, allowing the reader to delve into the various "spheres" of Egyptian history: the political forms of modern Egyptian society (chapter one), the economic development models and their impacts upon the population (chapter two), the crucial geopolitical realm which situates Egypt within a broader imperial framework (chapter three), and the various social movements that have shaped Egyptian history (chapter four).

The second part is organized chronologically, as it deals with the events immediately before and directly after the ousting of Mubarak in 2011. However, the second part of the book has its own thematic. I did not attempt a comprehensive political and economic account of events after the revolution. Instead, this book simply posits that the working class has played, and continues to play, a formative role in the revolutionary process. Therefore, the emphasis in the last four chapters is primarily upon the role of the labor movement and the working class in the post-Mubarak era. The fifth chapter analyzes with the role of labor immediately prior to and during the ouster of Mubarak. The sixth and seventh chapters roughly deal with February and March respectively, providing a detailed analysis of the various developments that occurred during the decisive period immediately after Mubarak's downfall. The eighth chapter switches gears, and instead of a detailed analysis of events provides a broad overview of the political and social developments from April of 2011 until the military coup overthrowing Mohamed Morsi in July of 2013.

I have attempted to eliminate and minimalize any flaws or errors in my research, but it is possible that some have escaped me. Thus, while I stand by the general trajectory outlined in Part II, there may be small errors that must be accounted for and rectified in the future. I have not relied solely or even primarily upon my own research. Instead, I have also drawn on the newly established scholarship that has dealt quite convincingly with the new wave of working class activism in Egypt during the revolution. In this way, I hope that my small contribution helps provide a cogent timeline and framework within which the role of the working class in Egypt can be understood.

For full disclosure, I believe it is appropriate that the reader has an accurate account of the limits of this work. The analysis presented in this book is restricted in obvious ways: I have never visited or lived in Egypt, I have only basic Arabic reading and writing skills, and I claim no particular degrees or expertise in the field. While I am currently pursuing postgraduate studies in Middle Eastern history, the bulk of this book was written prior to my entrance into graduate school. Although my thoughts and analysis have been shaped by discussions with Egyptian friends and political acquaintances, conversations are no substitute for experience. With these limits fully in purview, my intention with this book was to take available literature and shape it into a cogent, organized analysis. I leave it to the reader to judge whether I have accomplished this task. My real stake in this project is that, as someone born into a working class family, the lives and politics and future of working people are profoundly important to me. Watching the tumultuous events in Egypt over the past three years has been both immensely inspiring and at times discouraging. As someone who identifies with the hopes and aspirations of the millions of working class Egyptians fighting for a better future, I understand that their struggle for liberation is intricately bound up with my own. I hope the following pages do justice to their cause.

Despite the breadth and scope of this book, I have done my best to make it as easy and accessible to the widest layer of people possible. It is not a particularly esoteric or hefty theoretical work. My hope is that even those without a cursory knowledge of Egyptian history could pick up the book and develop a general outline of the country's history, politics, and economics from the 20th to the early 21st century. Paraphrasing Edward Said, I have tried to avoid the "private-clique consciousness" of critical theorists who have abandoned trying to reach a large or mass audience. I hope that readers draw inspiration from the various social movements that have punctuated and shaped modern Egyptian history. As such, this book is not intended to be an academic contribution to the scholarship. It is meant instead to be a book for individuals, activists, and organizations who are interested in changing the world.

As for acknowledgements, I must give thanks first and foremost to Rania Abu Alhana, who was a constant source of encouragement even in times of doubt. She also helped by providing a significant amount of editing, working with me on translations, and doing some of the complicated economic calculations for chapter two. Hours of discussion on the topics present in this book also helped refine my analysis. Colin Jenkins deserves enormous credit as well, not only for his enthusiasm about the project and his help editing, but also for being the nexus through which the Hampton Institute was built and continues to function, making this book a possibility in the first place. I also must thank the team from the Hampton Institute, who have made my experience there such a good one. A few people in particular deserve mention, including Andrew Marshall for his excellent analysis of Egypt and the useful contributions his writing made to this book, Devon Bowers who helped edit chapter one, and Jason Williams who gave me access to the tools to help with grammar and style. I also must thank Samaa Moosa for her provocative and thoughtful commentary on the introduction, chapter one, and chapter two. Similarly, Zeinab Khalil deserves thanks for her editing the introduction, and catching so many of the errors I had left behind. Melvin Barnes, always a voice of moderation, often forced me to reassess my analysis and fine tune it while providing useful comparative commentary from his field of expertise. For those who provided commentary or feedback in one form or another, or simply words of encouragement after reading early drafts, I thank you as well. Among others, that includes Yehudi Asamoah, Lamiya Khandaker, Lis-Marie Alvorado, and Spencer Ponce. I thank Hossam El-Hamalawy for providing me with the list of sources which made the research for chapters six and seven possible. I thank all those unnamed and unmentioned with whom I have ever spent time discussing (and likely debating!) the history, economics, politics, and current events of Egypt with. There are too many to name here, but whether we agreed or disagreed, those discussions and (often heated) debates were important in shaping my analysis and this book. Last, I thank all of my family and close friends who have in one way or another supported me along the way. Thank you. You should know who you are.

Needless to say, any and all errors are my own. I take full responsibility for what comes in the following pages.

Introduction

"Those who make revolution half way only dig their own graves." These words from the French revolutionary, Louis de Saint-Just, echo loudly today. It has been nearly three years since the uprising in Tahrir Square and across Egypt, yet the revolution remains a half-made one. For those who suffer the most in Egyptian society, the poor, the exploited, the urban proletariat and the rural *fellaheen*, [1] the graves that were being dug prior to 2011 continue to proliferate. The reason for this is simple: the transformation that happened in Egyptian society was, by and large, one that affected the political superstructure and not the economic base. There was no fundamental shift in economic production and distribution, no large scale restructuring of the social order, and too little organizational infrastructure capable of moving society in such a direction.

As this book went to print, events in Egypt continued to develop. Only a few months prior, a new phase had opened up in the ongoing revolution. A transient mass movement helped facilitate a military coup against Egypt's first elected president, Mohamed Morsi, in early July of 2013. This movement was reminiscent, despite its partially dissimilar social base and ideological orientation, to that which brought down the decades long dictatorship of Hosni Mubarak in 2011. In a period of 30 months Egyptians overthrew two separate regimes. For the outside observer it seemed that, despite the brutal military coup that followed, Egyptians had developed a profoundly democratic, collective impulse that rivaled any in history.

The following pages will trace the development of this impulse and place it in historical context. This book posits that Egypt's uprising in 2011 and the revolutionary process that followed resulted from decades of changing and declining social, economic, and political variables. These variables are intertwined in a complex web of domestic and geopolitical considerations. I attempt to reinforce the idea, manifest most clearly in the 2013 uprising against Morsi, that without a fundamental transformation of Egyptian society the conditions which sparked the uprising will not only remain unchanged but could be exacerbated.

Egypt's relevance on the global and regional scale cannot be underestimated. With nearly 85 million inhabitants, it holds enormous weight as the country holding the largest population in the Arab world. Aside from its demographic mass, it also rests at a pivotal geographic intersection where Northern Africa, the Arab East, the Gulf, and sub-Saharan Africa all converge. This is not to mention its possession of the Suez Canal, a site where colonial powers have been challenged and imperial aggressors have waged wars. Egypt in many ways has also acted as the political and cultural capital of the Arab world. Subsequently, what happens in Egypt is felt far and wide.

While understanding Egypt's revolution as half-made is important to grasp the essence of revolutionary change, the value of the uprising itself is immense. For weeks millions of people took to the streets in what was of the most popular, democratic, and collective struggles for liberation in human history. While calculating the actual number of demonstrators who engaged in the revolutionary process is not exact science, the mass character of the Egyptian movement is without doubt. Some observers claim that on one day alone nearly two million people occupied Cairo's Tahrir Square and the surrounding area, while on February 1st it was estimated that between six and eight million people flooded Egyptian streets and squares in Cairo, Alexandria, Mansoura, Suez, and other cities. By the end, some estimates suggest that 15 million participants took part in the uprising over the course of the 18 day struggle, a toll greater than the number of people that partook in the downfall of all the Eastern European regimes in 1989.[2] While these numbers may be optimistic or inflated, there is a profound depth and mass to the uprising that is without precedent.

A plethora of historical comparisons have been made between Eastern Europe in 1989 and the Arab World in 2011. Yet, as Noam Chomsky has pointed out, these juxtapositions rest on "dubious grounds." The uprisings of 1989 "plainly conformed to economic and strategic objectives" of the West and, therefore, were "a noble achievement" in the eyes of the world's imperial rulers. On the other hand, "western power remains hostile to democracy in the Arab world for good reasons."[3] Such "good reasons" lie at the heart of the unbridgeable chasm that separates these two historic periods of struggle. Namely, the revolutions overturning the Stalinist regimes bolstered western imperialism while the Tunisian and Egyptian revolutions threatened it.

In Egypt, this uprising represented the first mass struggle by the Egyptian population since what has been dubbed the "Bread *Intifada*" in 1977. At the time, millions of people hit the streets across major cities for two days protesting Sadat's nascent *Infitah* or "open door" economic policies, part of which meant massive cuts to food subsidies and an enormous increase in the price of basic staples for millions of Egyptian citizens. At the start of 2011, however, things were different. *Infitah* had been in progress for decades, and the tempest of economic, political, and social tensions that had been gathering finally erupted. Hossam El-Hamalawy noted in October of 2010, "Something is in the air. It could be Mubarak's Autumn of Fury,[4] as I and increasingly many people around me sense. Not a day passes without reading or hearing about a strike. No one knows when the explosion is going to happen, but it seems everyone I meet or bump into today feel it's inevitable."[5] This commentary from El-

Hamalawy, himself a long-time activist and opponent of the Mubarak regime, could not have been more prophetic. Only three months later Egyptian civil society exploded in an unprecedented uprising against the authoritarian regime of Hosni Mubarak. From January 25th to February 11th a heroic battle was waged to oust a dictator whom the United States had propped up for thirty years. Millions of Egyptians, galvanized by the revolution of the Tunisian people only a few days prior, called for fundamental political change and an end to Hosni Mubarak's decades-long rule. Mubarak was the unifying, hated symbol of authoritarianism and political corruption throughout Egyptian society. Participants in the revolution, while running the gamut ideologically, were united in their call for Mubarak to step down and their demand of free and fair elections.

The Egyptian uprising dismantled the claim that "ordinary Egyptians want democracy but will not fight for it."[6] The revolution was the culmination, first noted in 2005 by Mona El-Ghobashy, of the contest between "two traditions and two logics: the logic of political deferral at the level of government and the logic of political movement at the level of society."[7] Although the gears of revolution had been turning for years in Egypt, it was an outside catalyst, an upsurge by the oppressed in another part of the Arab world that galvanized the Egyptian masses to impose themselves onto the course of history. Egypt's tinderbox had been prepared; Tunisia was the spark that set it aflame.

The people of Tunisia overthrew their long-time dictator Zine al-Abidine Ben Ali in mid-January. Inspired by the revolutionary struggle there, and propelled to take action against an increasingly anti-democratic state and declining economic conditions, Egyptians organizers called for Tuesday, January 25, 2011 to be their first day of action. Dubbed the "Day of Rage" among the Egyptian people, the 25th marked the beginning of what turned out to be the most wide-spread and popular movement in Egyptian history. Organizers chose the 25th because it coincided with National Police Day, an official holiday Mubarak had instituted in 2009 to purportedly celebrate the achievements of "security and stability" achieved by the police. January 25, 1952 also marked the day when the British army, then occupying Egypt, brutally murdered 50 Egyptian police officers and took over a police station with tanks and soldiers.[8] Mubarak utilized this courageous historical moment as a propaganda tool to justify severe repression and placate the widespread hatred of the state police. Thus, the symbols of anti-colonial resistance were transformed into symbols of oppression. The iron fist was shrouded in anti-imperialist rhetoric. At the time no one knew for sure what would come of the call to mass action. "We were used to people putting out calls for mass days of action," explained Sameh Naguib, a member of the Revolutionary Socialists and participant in the January 25th uprising, "only to have 100 or 200 people show up, and quickly get routed by the security forces."[9]

The planned protest was originally organized through online social media networks, mostly in the form of Facebook events, before the regime shut down internet access on January 28th. Organizers included a broad intersection of Egyptian society, with the Muslim Brotherhood and some officially recognized and legal political parties tailing behind the rest of the population and reluctant to join in the initial uprising. Far exceeding the expectations of some organizers, tens of thousands of people showed up in Tahrir square on January 25th and solidarity demonstrations sprung up in other cities. Quickly, however, the protests turned violent in the following days as police attacked demonstrators through a variety of "riot-control" measures. By February 1st the highest estimates place the number of anti-Mubarak demonstrators in Tahrir Square, which was to become the focal point of the revolution, at over one million. Reports suggest that hundreds of thousands of people also marched in Mansoura and Alexandria, with tens of thousands of people in many other major cities. Over the course of the next ten days, pitched battles would be fought in the streets of Tahrir and elsewhere between demonstrators and state security forces. Plain-clothes officers acting on Mubarak's behalf infiltrated and attacked protestors. With each new conflict, the demonstrators realized their own collective power and beat back the forces that tried to break them, winning back Tahrir Square and defending it time and again.

Although it is true that young activists sparked this movement through social networking, the movement itself drew in people of all ages, including men and women, workers, peasants, journalists, lawyers, students, secular leftists, and members of the Muslim Brotherhood. Even one of Egypt's wealthiest businessmen, Naguib Sawiris, joined protestors and called for Mubarak's dismissal. While this was motivated primarily out of self-interest, as Sawiris represented the "nationalist capital" faction of the elite who felt threatened by the influx of foreign investors inching out domestic businessmen like himself, it points to the looseness of the front that was being formed.[10] As popular revolutions tend to do, the convergence of a singular demand united broad swathes of people who normally diverged economically or ideologically. Echoing the increased solidarity between the younger rank-and-file Muslim Brotherhood members and the new generation of leftist revolutionaries that had emerged in the years prior to 2011, one account recalled the movement's unique nature:

> You will know what it means when you see the leftist artist standing beside the Muslim Brotherhood activist and chanting against the Mubarak regime. It is the first protest in the history of Egypt that gathers every colour of the

political spectrum for one goal: the departure of Mubarak and his regime.[11]

Shouts of "Muslim, Christian, we're all Egyptian!" articulated the importance of religious solidarity, especially for the Coptic Christian minority in Egypt. On Friday, February 4th an enormous crowd entered Tahrir Square and in a remarkable display of solidarity Christian protestors formed a human chain around the Muslims who kneeled to worship during Friday (*jum'ah*) prayer, preventing any attacks by Mubarak's forces. This transcendence of religious difference between Muslim, Christian, and secular leftist was just one facet of the solidarity that the uprising cultivated during the early stages. The extremely diverse, profoundly broad movement brought in essentially every element of civil society. While these conditions never last, and schisms never fail to emerge, this unity was enough to force the removal of Mubarak from power.

Eventually, some of the legal opposition groups such as the center-left *al-Wafd* and *al-Tagammu* parties, and even momentarily the Muslim Brotherhood, noticeably late in joining the uprising, attempted to engage in negotiations with the Mubarak regime. Yet, as one protestor, Nasser Abdel Hamid put it, "the grounds for negotiations are not acceptable to us. We have seen a trend of groups who do not represent public opinion trying to speak on our behalf." Furthering this idea, another protestor Amr Ezz explained, "On the ground parties have no tangible power. People here have no faith in old opposition figures who talk and talk but have done nothing for the people." Ahmed Douma, a 22-year-old activist spoke positively of the popular power in the streets, "The people who were capable of achieving this revolution can prevent it from being stolen. Influence is proportional to power on the streets, and I think that the people are more powerful than the political parties."[12]

By the 10th of February, workers had begun engaging in strikes, crippling important sectors of the Egyptian economy. Mubarak and his family fled the capital and were reported to be in the relatively prosperous and politically calm Red Sea resort area of Sharm el-Sheikh. A slew of resignations and escape attempts followed. Minister of culture Gaber Asfour had already resigned when former finance minister Youssef Boutros Ghali fled to Beirut. Hossam Badrawi, the recently appointed secretary of the National Democratic Party (NDP), resigned from his position in the party due to Mubarak's refusal to step down. The regime was crumbling and the Egyptian people knew it. Egyptians moved quickly to further their revolution, with organizers calling for millions of people to take to the streets on the 11th of February. Although it is hard to tell exactly how many people responded to the call, enormous protests continued with hundreds of thousands participating in Cairo. Demonstrators surrounded the presidential palace and parliament, taking over the state television building, a key symbol of the regime's power. Hundreds of thousands of people came out in Alexandria, Suez, Mansoura, and Ismailia. Large demonstrations also took place in Mahalla, Shebin el-Kom, El-Arish, Sohag, Minya, and many other cities and towns.[13]

Finally, after 18 days of sustained collective action, recently appointed Vice President Omar Suleiman announced in a brief televised address to the nation that Mubarak would be "stepping down" and handing over power to the Supreme Council of the Armed Forces (SCAF). The SCAF, composed of a governing body of 21 senior military officers who ostensibly met only during "times of national emergency," would play a formative role in the years to come. The military leaders understood that unrest could not be quieted without immense force or the removal of Mubarak. They quietly opted for the latter, politically sacrificing the president. Mubarak had been forced out by the power of the people and February 11th became a day of celebration. Car horns went wild and cheers lasted for hours in Tahrir and across Egypt. Fireworks were set off in the middle of the square. People exchanged embraces with one another on the streets, even those who never personally knew each other before. Others jubilantly exclaimed *"Mabrook, Mabrook,"* congratulating one and celebrating their victory. Anjali Kamat, reporting from Cairo, wrote the day after Mubarak's resignation:

> After their long night of jubilation, the revolutionaries returned to the square Saturday [the day after Mubarak's ouster], armed this time with brooms, garbage bags, and a newfound sense of national pride. Thousands swept the dusty streets in and around Tahrir square, pausing at different intersections to recall the bloody battles with state security and thugs unleashed by Mr. Mubarak's regime. Others applied a fresh coat of paint to the pavements while talking about the freedoms they wanted to enshrine in their rejuvenated country.[14]

For many Egyptians, uncertainty was preferable to the bleak existence promised under the old order. February 11th remains emblazoned in the minds not only of the Egyptian people, for whom this struggle was so pertinent, but everyone around the world who anxiously watched one of the largest social movements of all time unfold before their eyes. For millions of activists across the globe, the Egyptian revolution inspired hope that the old social order could be swept away by popular power.

In both the Arab and non-Arab world, Mubarak's fall was celebrated by ordinary people identifying with the struggles of Egyptians.[15] Less than a week after the downfall of Mubarak, workers in Wisconsin staged a 10,000 strong demonstration against the new Republican governor who was attempting to gut the pay of public employees and revoke their right to collective bargaining. They protested by calling the governor "Hosni Walker," taking up slogans such as "Protest Like an Egyptian" and "If Egypt Can Have Democracy, Why Can't Wisconsin?"[16] In contrast, conservative commentators in the United States like Michael Scheuer even went so far as to complain that many "Americans seem to be increasingly Marxist in their absolute faith in democracy for people who have never had any experience with the process."[17] Perhaps Scheuer was on to something, as real democracy entails dismantling the oppressive structures and social relations inherent to capitalism as an economic system.

In Egypt, one of the most significant developments was the manifestation of popular power as regular people took up the duty of running society once the security forces withdrew from the streets. In nearly every modern revolution, people have formed committees or councils of some sort to carry out this function. French workers in 1968 formed and utilized workers' councils to organize what was at the time the largest general strike to ever shut down a modern industrial country. During 1972 and 1973, Chilean workers set up *cordones* to defend the Popular Unity government of Salvador Allende and demand workers' control over production. In 1979, workers in Iran created independent councils which they called the *shoras*, fundamental in overthrowing the ruthless Shah.[18]

It was in this spirit that the Egyptian people formed their "popular committees" or "neighborhood councils,"[19] not only to organize protests, but to keep society functioning at some level as the state apparatus, especially the police, collapsed around them. These committees were vital in organizing demonstrations, dealing with logistical issues and maintaining vital social services. Another important function the popular committees served was evident during February 1st as activists set up checkpoints at the entrance of Tahrir square. Organizers confirmed the identity of people entering to ensure that none of the state security forces or pro-Mubarak thugs could make their way in. The popular committees were also used to set up defense brigades and citizen checkpoints that protected homes, hospitals, museums, and other important social institutions from looters. These committees were a vital aspect of the uprising, perhaps as important as the demonstrations themselves.

Alongside the popular councils new forms of direct democracy developed as demonstrators organized into small groups, heatedly debating issues, proposing ways forward, and electing delegates to articulate the movement's demands. This process allowed for the massive crowds in Tahrir Square to participate in the decision making process directly. "Delegates from these mini-gatherings then come together to discuss the prevailing mood, before potential demands are read out over the square's makeshift speaker system," a journalist explained, "The adoption of each proposal is based on the proportion of boos or cheers it receives from the crowd at large."[20] This process was repeated in Alexandria, Suez, and various other small cities where direct democracy became an integral part of the revolutionary process.

All of these developments point to the accuracy of Marx's claim, made over a century and a half ago in *The German Ideology*, that an essential change in the consciousness of the masses occurs during the process of a revolution. He maintained that this prodigious shift in mass consciousness is both a necessity and a result of struggle. Such a development is:

> ...an alteration which can only take place in a practical movement, a revolution; this revolution is necessary, therefore, not only because the ruling class cannot be overthrown in any other way, but also because the class overthrowing it can only in a revolution succeed in ridding itself of all the muck of ages and become fitted to found society anew.[21]

The washing away of the "muck of ages" was evident with the initiation of religious solidarity and the newly accepted leadership roles for women. For a brief period of time, Egyptians were becoming "fitted to found society anew" as they developed popular councils composed of not only of a thin layer of technocrats but also workers, students, footballers, and others to protect their homes and prized social institutions, distribute water, food, and medical supplies, clean up streets and maintain Tahrir Square, carry out the day-to-day activities like traffic control, plan and orchestrate marches, demonstrations, rallies, and protests, form their own independent trade unions, defend minorities like the Coptic Christians, formulate their own demands and act in a collective manner to achieve them.

Egyptians transformed themselves into agents of change who not only dreamed of but actively participated in an effort to build society anew. Millions of people understood that they were creating history as they marched and demonstrated, debated the future of their society, discovered their own aptitude for self-organization, and challenged the oppression of their rulers. The tacit changes Egyptians experienced as they struggled to cast off the chains of oppression were transformative. As political scientist David McNally explains:

> After all, revolutions are not just about changing institutions. Most profoundly, they are about the dramatic remaking of the downtrodden. Revolutions are schools of profound self-education. They destroy submission and

> resignation, and they release long-repressed creative energies--intelligence, solidarity, invention, self-activity. In so doing, they reweave the fabric of everyday life. The horizons of possibility expand. The unthinkable--that ordinary people might control their lives--becomes both thinkable and practical.[22]

This was a popular uprising in every sense of the phrase. Despite such inspirational developments, however, these popular forms of organization were not sustained after the downfall of the regime. They failed to transform into concrete political organizations capable of taking power.

Within the popular movement four dominant currents or elements were discernable. The first was Islamist in nature and led predominately by the Muslim Brothers (*Al-Ikhwaan al-Muslimuun*). The Brotherhood was founded in the 1928 and had historically been banned for most of its existence. A series of crackdowns and persecutions, beginning with Nasser but continuing under subsequent administrations, mitigated their capacity to garner significant political power. Although it is unclear exactly how many members the Muslim Brothers had during the outbreak of the revolution, at the height of the organization's popularity in the 1940s they claimed roughly half a million active members. While years of repression may have enervated their base, it was evident that by 2011 the organization had a substantial cadre, a strong network of activists, and millions of sympathizers. Over the years, evidenced by their late entrance into the popular movement, the organization had become conciliatory towards the Egyptian state in exchange for semi-official space to operate. They largely integrated themselves into mainstream society and consistently reaffirmed their commitment to parliamentary democracy. The organizational leadership as a whole is conservative and, due in large part to the class basis of their organization, friendly to capital. This often led to clashes with younger or more liberal elements within the organization, and schisms were frequent. The Brotherhood dominated many middle-class professional associations and maintained a vast network of religious charities that stepped in to fill the void of enervated state services and subsidies, especially in rural areas. The Brotherhood's popularity has much to do with the necessary social services it provided for years, especially as economic neoliberalism hacked away at public spending in areas like health and education and wages began their precipitous decline in the post-Nasser era. Despite their pro-business ideological leaning, they instituted a large number of social programs that helped win over significant segments of the poor. Similarly, they stood up, at least rhetorically, for the rights of the Palestinians when the Mubarak regime willfully facilitated the US-Israeli strangulation of Gaza.

The second dominant trend within the movement, and the one most highly revered by Western media, was the mainstream liberal opposition. This current was largely secular in its political ideology and reflected the interests and opinions of the well-educated middle class and elite sectors of society disillusioned with Mubarak's rule. The primary vehicles through which this bloc organized in the uprising were the *Kefaya* movement (the Egyptian Movement for Change) and the National Association for Change. Mohamed ElBaradei, the Egyptian law scholar and diplomat who served as director general of the International Atomic Energy Agency at the UN, became the personification of the Western-style, educated, liberal opposition. The demands called for by this group were political in nature and confined to relatively moderate reforms, including an end to emergency laws, international civic and domestic judicial oversight of elections, open access to the media for candidates, the limiting of the presidential office to two terms, and a lessening of restrictions on who can run for president. Those espousing this view confined their critique of Egyptian society primarily to the political superstructure.

What the reformism of the Islamists and secular liberals missed in their analysis, or stood against because of their economic interests, was increasingly apparent when juxtaposed with the next two currents. The third trend represented in the popular uprising was the labor movement. Building off years of increased labor activity, including a massive wave of strikes in the past five years, the Egyptian labor movement utilized the 2011 uprising as an opportunity to articulate their own economic demands and support the political goals of the movement as a whole. Workers from all walks of life participated in the uprising, originally as individuals and later as collective entities by joining with fellow workers to strike. The demands of workers were relatively clear, and primarily involved economic concerns like higher wages, raising the minimum wage, better working conditions, the right to form independent unions, and the right for workers to strike without stringent conditions attached. The most class-conscious workers also articulated the need for a fundamental restructuring of the Egyptian economy, and the nationalization or renationalization of their workplaces.

The fourth trend, while relatively small, was an indispensable catalyst in the emergence of social justice-oriented, radical democratic activism. Comprised of a wide variety of socialists and left-wing Arab nationalists, the radical left has been particularly vital in merging the political demands of the anti-Mubarak movement with the economic demands of the working class. They also articulated their own demands that transcended the somewhat limited demands of the other groups. The Revolutionary Socialists (*Al-Ishtiraakiyun al-Thawrun*), for instance, have called not only for the restructuring of the political sphere but also for the monumental task of collectivizing and democratizing Egypt's wealth. Prior to January 25th, it was primarily the socialist left that connected the labor movement to the democracy movement and synthesized a coherent analysis between the two. They also played a vital part in forming the Democratic Labor Party (DLP, *Al-Hizb al-'amal al-Watani al-Dimuqrati*) and the short-lived Coalition of Socialist Forces (CSF, *Tahlaaf al-Qowaa al-Ishtiraakiyah*), among other ephemeral attempts at revolutionary coalitions and party-building efforts. The analysis of the Revolutionary Socialists has, in large part, informed the ideological underpinning with which this study takes place.

This broad-based, popular uprising came on the heels of thirty years not only of undemocratic rule by Mubarak, but over four decades of neoliberal economic policies that continuously deteriorated Egyptian living standards. Furthermore, criticism of the regime also revolved around Mubarak's role as puppet for Western powers, particularly the United States and, reflexively, Israel. Hossam El-Hamalawy outlined the historical context and dynamics of the Egyptian uprising:

> Revolutions don't happen out of the blue. It's not because of Tunisia yesterday that we have one in Egypt mechanically the next day. You can't isolate these protests from the last four years of labour strikes in Egypt, or from international events such as the al-Aqsa intifada and the US invasion of Iraq. The outbreak of the al-Aqsa intifada was especially important because in the 1980s-90s, street activism had been effectively shut down by the government as part of the fight against Islamist insurgents. It only continued to exist inside university campuses or party headquarters. But when the 2000 intifada erupted and Al Jazeera started airing images of it, it inspired our youth to take to the streets, in the same way we've been inspired by Tunisia today.[23]

This popular movement was undeniably political, as commentators universally observe. However, even more pertinent are the economic and social context, both inside Egypt and within the geopolitical sphere.

A multiplicity of factors galvanized the uprising. Of these, the four most pressing were: (1) the undemocratic political institutions; (2) the increasing misery vis-à-vis declining economic conditions; (3) the capitulation and then client-relationship towards the US and Israel; (4) and the revival of popular social and labor movements in recent years. The first part of this book will address each one of these issues in sequence.

In the following chapters the economic conditions and the political institutions have been separated into thematic chapters. In no way does this imply that the two are separate phenomena. The distinction is merely useful in identifying and analyzing the intricacies of the respective institutions and conditions. Both the domestic political and economic realms, as well as their functioning within a larger geopolitical context, are substantively and methodologically inseparable from one another. While a conceptual distinction has been made in order to more fully and critically analyze the details of the political institutions and the economic indicators, politics and economics are inextricably linked and cannot be isolated or examined without grasping the corollary. Similarly, I do not take the position that the political superstructure is purely a mechanical reflection of the economic base. While the base delimits and has a determining influence on the superstructure, the relationship is primarily reciprocal in nature. Therefore, in the first part of the book there will be some overlap and an attempt to fuse the economic and the political question into a cohesive analysis, despite the emphasis being on one or the other. The fusion of economic and political demands during the uprising by the Egyptian working class has only confirmed that this synthesis of the political and the economic is both a reality and an integral aspect of understanding the movement for social change in Egypt.

The second part of the book will specifically address the role of the working class in the revolution. It will not attempt to summarize every political occurrence following Mubarak's ouster. Instead, the emphasis will be to analyze the nature of working class organization and agitation during the revolution, as well as the reaction of the state as it attempted to manage and negate working class militancy. The mass nature of Egypt's democratic uprising puts to rest the idea that the Egyptian uprising can be characterized solely, or even primarily, as a "Twitter revolution" or "Facebook revolt" led by "non-violent youth." Surely these were tools in the hands of organizers, but they did not make the revolution. Nor did the "youth," itself an ambiguous term that downplays and conceals the economic underpinnings of the revolution. Instead, as they often do, young people played the role of galvanizing the revolutionary process. From the outset, however, this revolution transcended the well-to-do, western educated, English speaking, tech-savvy prototype so commonly crafted in the Western media.

Furthermore, the "non-violent" Western-friendly narrative constructed by much of the media, state officials, and representatives of prominent non-governmental organizations (NGOs) tends to conceal the class nature of the revolution. Undoubtedly, a prodigious amount of violence was due to the repressive state apparatus. According to official statistics, nearly 850 people were killed in the course of the 18-day uprising in 2011, with more being killed in the subsequent years.[24] The deaths were overwhelmingly civilians murdered by state security forces. By mid-February alone another 6,500 had been wounded[25] and 12,000 had been arrested and tried by military courts.[26] This does not, however, mean that historians ought to whitewash the strategies and tactics that revolutionaries must sometimes use when confronting violent states. As Rabab El-Madhi of *Jadaliyya* points out, the logic of the corporate media dictates that downplaying violence directed against the state masks the class conflict which it represents, and subsequently requires the "subaltern" classes be painted out of the picture:

> [By] the 28th of January all NDP (National Democratic Party) headquarters and most police stations were set on fire. This was a clear reaction to the state's systematic violence against subaltern classes, those who bore the brunt of the regime's daily torture and humiliation precisely because of their position within the neoliberal class matrix in Egypt. Unlike, the middle-class "facebook" youth, they were not immune to state violence outside the realm of political activism... Such narration is also based on the Orientalist binary of "traditional" versus "modern," and "East" versus "West," with the latter categories seen as supreme. Hence, it cannot include the use of moltov hand-bombs, which is "violent-traditional" (read: Oriental) alongside with facebook, which is "peaceful-modern" (read Western). The "educated," "Western," and "exposed" cosmopolitan Egyptians who are portrayed as the sole agents of this "revolution" cannot torch police-stations, and those who did –the subaltern- should be and are excluded from the picture.[27]

Historians would do well to delve beyond the superficial, Samuel Huntington "clash of civilizations" narrative that pits "East" and "West," negating class antagonism. Just as the Egyptian experience eclipses the narrow concept of a de-classed internet revolution led by an ambiguous "youth," so too should it dismantle the notion of a "cultural" revolution where the backwards "East," through technological diffusion, adopts the purportedly progressive model of the "West." Far from being a purely political revolution, "post-Marxist" and devoid of class contradiction, one must view the Egyptian revolution through a class lens to understand the interrelationship between class oppression, political subjugation, and the neoliberal economic order. This popular uprising did not exist in a vacuum, to be analyzed through a sort of trite technological determinism. Instead, it was birthed in a world where politics and economics were intricately bound and where political repression and imperial hegemony buttressed class division. The intersection of these various phenomena must be addressed to adequately understand Egypt's past and its potential.

[1] *Fellaheen* is the Arabic term for the peasantry.
[2] Omar Mostafa, "Egypt's Unfinished Revolution," *International Socialist Review*, no. 77 (2011), http://isreview.org/issues/77/feat-Egyptunfinished.shtml (accessed July 11, 2013).
[3] Noam Chomsky, "Is the World Too Big to Fail? The Contours of Global Order," *Huffington Post*, April 21, 2011. http://www.huffingtonpost.com/noam-chomsky/us-global-power_b_851992.html (accessed July 8, 2013). It must be noted here that as developments spread to Libya and Syria, with NATO intervention in Libya and US, Saudi and other Gulf States influencing events in the Syrian civil war, this thesis could be challenged.
[4] The original "Autumn of Fury" was a period of time of about three months prior to Sadat's assassination in 1981 which was characterized by an especially intense crackdown on the media, witch hunts against Egyptian activists, and the arrests of oppositional politicians.
[5] Hossam El-Hamalawy, "Something in the air," *3arabawy* (blog), October 31, 2010. http://www.arabawy.org/2010/10/31/something-in-the-air/http://www.arabawy.org/2010/10/31/something-in-the-air/ (accessed July 8, 2013).
[6] Mona El-Ghobashy, "Egypt Looks Ahead to Portentous Year," *Middle East Research and Information Project*. (2005). http://www.merip.org/mero/mero020205 (accessed July 8, 2013).
[7] El-Ghobashy, "Egypt Looks Ahead to Portentous Year."
[8] Ahmed Zaki Osman, "Egypt's police: From liberators to oppressors," *Egypt Independent*, January 24, 2011. http://www.almasryalyoum.com/en/news/egypts-police-liberators-oppressors (accessed July 8, 2013).
[9] Sameh Naguib, "Conversation with an Egyptian socialist," February 23, 2011. July 8, 2013. http://socialistworker.org/2011/02/23/interview-with-egyptian-socialist.
[10] Paul Amar, "Why Mubarak is Out," *Jadaliyya*, February 01, 2011. http://www.jadaliyya.com/pages/index/516/why-mubarak-is-out- (accessed July 8, 2013).
[11] Evan Hill, "The youth of Tahrir Square," *Al-Jazeera English*, February 10, 2011. http://www.aljazeera.com/indepth/features/2011/02/201129214957928702.html (accessed July 9, 2013).
[12] Hill, "The youth of Tahrir Square."
[13] Sharif Abdel Kouddous, "Exclusive Video: Protesters in Tahrir Square Voice Outrage After Mubarak Defiantly Refuses to Step Down," DemocracyNow! February 11 2011. Web, http://www.democracynow.org/2011/2/11/exclusive_video_protesters_in_tahrir_square.
[14] Anjali Kamat, "Egypt, A People Victorious,"*DemocracyNow!*, February 12, 2011.

http://www.democracynow.org/blog/2011/2/12/egypt_a_people_victorious_by_anjali_kamat (accessed July 9, 2013).

[15] The joy even hit the hop-hop community, as Big Boi, member of the rap duo Outkast, spoke out about the implications of the Egyptian revolution for the United States: "Egypt is a really true representation of power to the people. Imagine, in the United States right now, there's a top one percent that are the richest people in the world and there's 99% of us that are below that. The same thing that happened in Egypt can happen anywhere. I do mean, anywhere... People should be governed by the people, not by corporations." See: Andres Vasquez, "Big Boi Speaks on Revolution in Egypt, Self-Preservation," *HipHopDX*, February 15, 2011. http://www.hiphopdx.com/index/news/id.14076/title.big-boi-speaks-on-revolution-in-egypt-self-preservation (accessed July 9, 2013).

[16] Nichols, John. "Wisconsin's Governor to Destroy Public Sector Unions." *The Nation*, February 15, 2011. http://www.thenation.com/blog/158609/more-10000-protest-wisconsin-governor-hosni-walkers-move-destroy-public-sector-unions (accessed July 9, 2013).

[17] Michael Scheuer, "Scheuer: Americans Are 'Increasingly Marxist-Like In Their Absolute Faith In Democracy' For Egypt," Fox News via Media Matters for America. Web, http://mediamatters.org/video/2011/02/11/scheuer-americans-are-increasingly-marxist-like/176304.

[18] For more on this phenomenon, see: Barker, Colin. *Revolutionary Rehearsals*. London: Bookmarks, 1987.

[19] *Legan sha'beya* in Arabic.

[20] Jack Shenker, "Cairo's biggest protest yet demands Mubarak's immediate departure," *Guardian*, February 5, 2011. Quoted here: David McNally, "Transformed by the revolution," *SocialistWorker.org*, February 15, 2011. http://socialistworker.org/2011/02/15/transformed-by-revolution (accessed July 9, 2013).

[21] Karl Marx, *The German Ideology*, http://www.marxists.org/archive/marx/works/1845/german-ideology/ch01d.htm (accessed July 9, 2013).

[22] McNally, "Transformed by the revolution."

[23] Mark LeVine, "Interview with Hossam el-Hamalawy," January 27, 2011. July 9, 2013. http://www.aljazeera.com/indepth/features/2011/01/201112792728200271.html.

[24] "Government fact-finding mission shows 846 killed in Egypt uprising." *AP and Haaretz*, April 20, 2011. http://web.archive.org/web/20110423023923/http://www.haaretz.com/news/international/government-fact-finding-mission-shows-846-killed-in-egypt-uprising-1.356885 (accessed July 9, 2013).

[25] "Egypt's revolution death toll rises to 384." *Al-Masry Al-Youm*, February 22, 2011. http://web.archive.org/web/20110429130048/http://www.almasryalyoum.com/en/node/326562 (accessed July 9, 2013).

[26] Faisal Al Yafai, "Egypt's army fails to grasp the post-Mubarak realities," *The National*, November 22, 2011. http://www.thenational.ae/thenationalconversation/comment/egypts-army-fails-to-grasp-the-post-mubarak-realities (accessed July 9, 2013).

[27] Rabab, El-Mahdi, "Orientalising the Egyptian Uprising,"*Jadaliyya*, April 11, 2011. http://www.jadaliyya.com/pages/index/1214/orientalising-the-egyptian-uprising (accessed July 9, 2013).

Part I – Nationalism to Neoliberalism

1

Undemocratic Political Institutions

As late as February 1st, 2011, almost a week into the uprising that eventually removed him from his lifetime position as Egyptian president, Hosni Mubarak continued claiming to the world that he would continue his presidency until his term ended in September and "die on Egyptian soil." It was reported later that protestors were quite fond of suggesting to Mubarak that, indeed, the soil was ready for him.[1] The Egyptian people, after having mobilized in greater numbers than ever before, refused Mubarak outright, chanting instead for him to leave "Tomorrow, Tomorrow." Mubarak personified the extreme political corruption and anti-democratic nature of the Egyptian state. Yet, Egyptian political institutions were and remain larger than Mubarak. As one woman so eloquently stated, "When we say we don't want the regime, it does not mean we don't want Hosni Mubarak as a person and be stuck with someone else who is imposed on us. We want to choose our president because we want to take this country into the future."[2] Mubarak's shuffling around of his cabinet or replacing himself with his hand-picked vice-president would never be sufficient for the people. As Egyptians were well aware, there was nothing stopping Mubarak from falling back on the decades-long practice of using the "state of emergency" clause that would demand his firm hand in stabilizing the country, a tactic even his elected successor Mohamed Morsi would not fail to use liberally. Egyptians fought for a political and social revolution, an institutional transformation that transcended Mubarak.

Political Repression and Colonialism

Political repression follows a long line of continuity in Egypt. This hallmark of the Egyptian state has its roots in the repressive state apparatus instituted by the colonial powers of the British, followed by a Western-backed puppet monarchy that was eventually overthrown by the populist, Arab nationalist government of Gamal Abd al-Nasser. After Nasser, Egypt degenerated into the neoliberal US client state headed first by Anwar al-Sadat and then Hosni Mubarak. The country was forcefully occupied and held as a colonial possession by the British from 1882 to 1919. Timothy

Mitchell adumbrates the process by which the nascent working class was organized and supervised under colonial auspices:

> Supervision and control were required at a local level for the new methods of capitalist production, in particular the cultivation and processing of cotton. Private ownership of large estates and the investment of European capital were creating a class of landless workers, whose bodies needed to be taught the disciplined habits of wage-labour… [The overseer installed by the British] 'carried with him a sort of kourbash or long whip, with which he encouraged industry among the men and boys'… Capitalist production also required the creation and management of large bodies of migrant workers, to build and maintain the new structures being laid in place across the Egyptian countryside – roads, railways, canals, dams, bridges, telegraphs and ports. Larger projects such as the digging of the Suez Canal required the movement and supervision of tens of thousands of men. Smaller gangs of labourers were brought from southern Egypt for seasonal employment in constructing and maintain the new network of perennial irrigation canals in the north, on which the cultivation of cotton depended. The British placed such gangs under continuous police control.[3]

As the Egyptian working class became more permanent this acquiescence to British colonialism lessened. The nationalist independence movement of 1919, involving both rural peasants and the urban masses, won nominal independence from the British despite continued British military "presence" to ensure control over the Suez canal. After 1919 the Egyptian people lived under a façade of self-determination and were ruled over by a British-backed monarch, first King Fu'ad and later King Farouk.

In conjunction with the anti-British uprisings a nascent form of working class activism took hold in Egypt late in the 19th and early 20th centuries. The notion of developing official organizations representing workers was first explored by foreign immigrants and those who worked with them as skilled and semi-skilled laborers. As industrialization increased across the country, the space for Egyptian labor to express its own interests grew. Workers become concentrated in urban centers, providing them with the geographical means to unite and defend their economic interests. Labor activism exploded in 1919, with a massive wave of strikes accompanying the anti-British occupation uprising across the country. During the 1920s the Wafd, Egypt's most popular nationalist political party, utilized labor unions and class conflict as political pressure points against the British but remained ambivalent and sometimes hostile towards workers struggles which were independent of or not directly under their control. In the 1930s and 1940s, with the advent of large, mechanized industrial centers, Egyptian labor for the first time attempted to organize itself both collectively and independently of the Wafd. This effort manifested in exciting new experiments such as the Committee to Organize the Workers' Movement (*Lajnat Tanzim al-Haraka al-'Ummaliyya*). Right-nationalists, left-nationalists, and Communists battled for control of the labor movement throughout the 1940s, with the leadership of the Muslim Brotherhood also making tepid efforts at reeling in workers for its own purposes. Communists organized under a variety of competing factions, with an organization known as New Dawn first establishing roots in the Egyptian working class. However, the most prominent Communist labor organization of the 1940s and early 1950s was the Democratic Movement for National Liberation (*al-Haraka al-Dimuqratiyya li'l-Tahrir al-Watani*).[4]

The one key trend throughout all these periods was the severe political repression wrought upon workers who engaged in any sort of class conflict. Arrests, attacks, shutting down labor newspapers, and a variety of other means were used to try and suppress labor's organizational capabilities. To provide just one example of this, in 1931 during a resurgence of labor struggle, the Egyptian Prime Minister Isma'il Sidqi had police organize a general campaign of harassment by closing down the office of the National Federation of Egyptian Trade Unions, issuing violations for union activity, turning in the names of union organizers to company bosses, and clashing with workers on strike or protesting the regime. On May 14th, in response to both labor unrest and a fraudulent election, Sidqi launched an all-out offensive with police killing over one hundred people, arresting over one hundred more, and preventing over 450 workers from returning to work by blacklisting them.[5] Thus, the colonial apparatus molded by the British was adopted and used by the monarchy to maintain its own position of power and facilitate British interests, even after so-called "independence" was achieved.

The Role of the Military

At the outset of the revolution in 2011 Egypt was technically a semi-presidential republic with purportedly representative institutions. Yet, since 1952 the state has been under some form of military control. In July of 1952, a military coup overthrew the monarch Farouk and brought to power a group of young military officers, most famously Gamal Abd al-Nasser. They called themselves the "Free Officers" and were organized on the basis of abolishing the monarchy, but beyond that held wide and differing ideological and geopolitical alignments. The officers, who frequently came from lower-middle class backgrounds, stood at odds with the large landowning class which dominated Wafdist politics, the British capitalists who owned and controlled large sections of the emerging capitalist system in Egypt, and the wealth of the monarch which attempted to both represent and protect these two social forces to secure its grasp on power. The similar class background of the Free Officers did not ensure homogenous ideological dispositions, however. The ideological composition of the group ran the gamut: Brotherhood sympathizers, ardent Egyptian nationalists, pan-Arabists, Communists, and even officers who simply wanted to shift from British to US purveyance.

After a brief period of internal power struggles, Nasser came to the forefront of the Free Officer movement and secured his place as Egypt's national leader. Even though Nasser's nearly two decades in power did lead to an increased standard of living for Egyptians, it did not bring any concurrent democratization, either in the form of indirect political representation or the direct democratic control of the economy called for by socialists. The political repression witnessed under both British colonialism and the monarchy continued, albeit in an altered form and with a new ideology articulated under the Nasser regime which rapidly attained a position of hegemony. Since Nasser's time, the political institutions have remained far from democratic. Indeed, their representative and redistributive capacities have deteriorated while the repressive capacity of the state has increased.

Despite the wishful thinking within segments of the revolutionary movement in 2011 claiming that the military was a neutral force, it is clear that without the Egyptian military the Mubarak regime would have crumbled long before it did. For decades the government was stacked with current and ex-military officials, and Mubarak's power rested upon military strength coupled with his domestic police state. After all, the military was and continues to be the strongest institution in Egyptian society. The *New York Times* referred to the Egyptian military as a "behemoth that controls not only security and a burgeoning defense industry, but has also branched into civilian businesses like road and housing construction, consumer goods and resort management." To this day it builds roads, manufactures exports like stoves and refrigerators, and produces various food items. In the 1990s it was Egypt's single largest builder of suburban enclaves around Cairo, constructing thousands of acres of apartments along city's eastern perimeter for use by the officer elite.[6] Estimates put its control of the economy at around 25%.[7] In fact, it was so powerful that when the international food shortages in 2008 hit Egypt, the army was able to placate popular unrest by handing out bread from its own bakeries.[8] Ironically, as Paul Amar explains, the military plays a contradictory role in relation to the uprising:

> [T]he more protective, populist branch of the military is very powerful and is counter-balancing the police, in a good way. But of course, these military leaders are businessmen. The military run most of the shopping malls in Egypt. They run many of the beach resorts in Egypt. They make a lot of money through economic ventures, because they develop their military bases into tourism resorts and shopping malls and things, which is an interesting development. So that's why we have the military basically split between the question of its popular legitimacy and its economic interests. They want the protesters to love them...but they want to get the protesters off the streets so tourists will come back and their businesses will flourish.[9]

Subsequently, the military elites, while maintaining a sort of populist façade, are not in a position to see through fundamental political and economic change that true democracy would entail. The development of democratic institutions, especially any such institutions intended to redistribute wealth, would certainly threaten their own economic interests. The military elites are weary of democracy, operating in complete secrecy and as opaquely as possible.

The military as an institution is not simply a neutral force in Egyptian society. It is the primary component of the state apparatus, the single largest economic actor, and its leaders are intricately bound up in the political and economic system as it currently exists. By extension, the military both helps define and, importantly, enforces the sort of social relationships that exist between capital and labor, the rulers and the ruled, the oppressors and the oppressed. The military's fortification of these social relationships is in large part a manifestation of its own direct economic interests but, more importantly, its interest in maintaining the larger socioeconomic status quo. Which presidential face that symbolizes these social relations is not nearly as important as the fact that they remain in place. This was evidenced clearly in Morsi's inability to fully grasp the levers of state power.[10]

Despite this reality, there is a dichotomy that must be drawn between the military elites and the rank-and-file soldiers. This nearly half-a-million-strong service is composed of largely underpaid conscripts:

> Pro-democracy demonstrators and their sympathisers often repeated the slogans "the army and the people are one hand," and "the army is from us." They had the conscripts in mind, and many were unaware of how stark

differences were between the interests of the soldiers and the generals. Between the conscripts and the generals is a middle-level professional officer corps whose loyalties have been the subject of much speculation. The generals, for their part, want to maintain their privileges, but not to rule directly... direct rule would make it impossible to hide that the elite officers are not in fact part of the "single hand" composed of the people and the (conscript) army. They are instead logically in the same camp as Ahmad Ezz, Safwat al-Sharif, Gamal Mubarak, and Habib al-Adly — precisely the names on those lists making the rounds of regime members and cronies who should face judgment.[11]

This distinction could not be clearer than when, after Mubarak was deposed, the military council, comprised of elite military officials, took power and thanked Mubarak for his service and sacrifices to Egypt. In contrast, many soldiers, who for days had been surrounded and engaged by protesters urging them not to side with Mubarak but to take the side of the people, rejoiced at his departure.

A Permanent "State of Emergency"

Complementing this strong military state, Egypt was under a permanent emergency law since the 1967 war with Israel. This highly repressive law was used primarily to target political and labor activists. The Emergency Law allowed arrest for such trivial actions as insulting the president, blocking traffic, or distributing leaflets and posters. It also impeded many basic rights to privacy and freedom by allowing the state to indefinitely detain suspects without charge on grounds of "national security," search people and places without warrants, intercept mail, and tap telephones. The law also allowed for political activists to be tried as special "security" cases under control of the executive branch. These "security" cases were overseen by judges frequently appointed directly by the president, where defendants were denied guaranteed constitutional protections. To top it off, the verdicts were subject to the President's approval. In other words, in such cases the president took on both the executive and judicial role. The Egyptian Organization for Human Rights estimates that as late as 2010 over 16,000 people were detained without charge for security-related reasons and thousands had been sentenced in these special "security" cases, [12] with dozens arbitrarily sentenced to death.[13]

Although the emergency law had been lifted for a brief period in 1980, Mubarak declared the law in affect once again following President Sadat's 1981 assassination by an Islamist organization called Egyptian Islamic Jihad

(*Al-Jihaad al-Islaami al-Masri*). Mubarak, a military man himself, slid his way into power after Sadat's assassination. This assassination was, in large part, retribution by Islamist opponents who rejected Sadat's authoritarian repression of their organizations and his capitulation to Israel. Decades of political repression followed these events. Activists from various political parties, especially secular leftists and Islamists, were ubiquitously unable to exercise basic political rights regardless of a lack of evidence linking them to terrorist activity.

The 1990s saw a particularly vicious attack on the Egyptian public and their civil liberties. This attack on political freedoms was justified by the increasingly violent exchanges between Islamist militants and state security forces in the early 1990s. A wide network of Islamists called the Islamic Group (*Al-Jamaa'ah Al-Islaamiyah*) engaged in a series of attacks on state security forces and, in some instances, civilians with the stated goals of overthrowing the currently existing Egyptian state. The regime responded with severe repression on all segments of society and utilized the conflict with the Islamic Group as a pretext to smash any dissent criticizing neoliberal economic reform or the undemocratic political structures.

Changes to the penal code in 1992 meant severely increased repression, as "prison terms were replaced with forced labor, temporary sentences with life sentences, and life sentences with the death penalty."[14] These sentences, handed down by Supreme State Security Courts, could not be appealed except on procedural grounds. As Eberhard Kienle explains, the arbitrary nature and loose definition of "terrorism" meant that the Egyptian state could now sentence someone even for the "the threat of force…used to disrupt public order, any act which actually or potentially harmed individuals, or damaged the environment, financial assets, transport or communications, or which involved the physical occupation of sites and places, or obstructed the application of the law."[15] In this way, political activists, tenant-farmers protesting neoliberal restructuring, and even workers engaging in strikes or occupations could be tried under these special security tribunals. This was the case in 1997, when leftists defending farmers being forced off their land under the new land laws were accused of "obstructing the application of the law." Yet, for the state even the aforementioned security tribunals were not enough, and many civilians were simply tried in military courts where "judges" with little or no legal training and subject to orders from their superiors dished out sentences the regime desired. From 1993 to 1996 some 10,000 to 16,000 political detainees were held under emergency powers by state security forces.[16] Such direct repression worked in tandem with restrictions on a variety of political liberties.

Repressing Political Liberties

So-called "positive" political liberties were highly restrained in Egypt as well. Founders of any new political party were banned from engaging in all political activity prior to being approved by a government commission. This lengthy process involved both meeting the strict guidelines set forth by the government and acceptance by the commission that the party platform was significantly different from any other existing party. A major blow was dealt to freedom of speech when in 1995 the government passed the press laws which imposed heavy sentences, including excessive fines and up to five years imprisonment, for "publication crimes" such as "the printing of 'mendacious information,' 'false rumors,' or 'defamations,' in particular if these were directed against the state, its representatives and its economic interests, or if they endangered public order."[17] However, after enormous outcry and sustained protest the law was rescinded in 1996, a testament to the strength of the Egyptian public.

A litany of laws also consolidated National Democratic Party (NDP) control of the official trade union federation and professional syndicates. Since 1976, Law 35 had ensured that the Egyptian Trade Union Federation (ETUF, or *Al-Ittihad al-'aam li-Niqaabaat 'ummal Masr*) held a legal monopoly on all trade union organization in the country. In the 1990s a law was passed that granted NDP appointment of leadership positions in professional syndicates if election turnouts were too low, while another law allowed high-level managers to vote in union elections and barred fixed-term workers from voting in them. This was at a time when the number of temporary workers was dramatically increasing due to economic restructuring. The 2003 Unified Labor Law formalized that any strike not officially sanctioned by the ETUF was illegal. In 1994 a law also extended more power over the countryside as it proscribed *'umdas*, or village chiefs, from being elected to instead be chosen by the minister of the interior. Even more presidential power was concentrated in the academic field, as another 1994 law removed faculty participation in the election of their own deans. Instead, the president of the university, who was chosen by the president of the country, would appoint the deans.[18] These laws implied a higher concentration of executive power over all segments of life.

One of the ways that the regime maintained this undemocratic political structure was repressing independent judges who challenged the authoritarian state or the undemocratic election results. This was abundantly clear in 2006 when some judges questioned electoral corruption after parliamentary elections. As a 2006 US State Department memo points out, this resulted in "judicial disciplinary action against two senior judges," "suppression of activists and demonstrators supporting the judges," "state-influenced media attacks on reform advocates," "extension of the Emergency Law for two more years," "postponement by two years of local council elections," "continuing arrests and harassment of opposition activists," and "the conviction of opposition leader Ayman Nour."[19] Political activism, even attempts to participate in elections, was often met with arrest and police violence. For instance, prior to the 2008 municipal elections authorities arrested hundreds of potential candidates and prevented thousands more from registering.[20] Meanwhile, the state-owned media outlets functioned primarily as the propaganda arm of the state and independent journalists faced severe repression and prison-time.

A Massive "Omnipresent Security Apparatus"

This emergency law could be carried out for so long because, according to a leaked document from the US embassy in Cairo, the regime maintained an "omnipresent security apparatus" that acted as "a strong counter-balance to riots and demonstrations."[21] This "ramified police state" had an "internal security apparatus that numbers somewhere over one-and-a-half million people" and was meant to act as a buffer against popular protest.[22] In the 1960s Hassan Talaat, head of the General Investigations department, described the nascent state security machinery as a "patriotic apparatus" that defended the "nation's interests" and solved conflicts between "workers and entrepreneurs."[23] This "desire to solve conflicts" manifested itself as a consistent and percussive smashing of working class autonomy. In fact, the entire General Investigations department, which would later develop into State Security within the Ministry of Interior, came into existence in large part to derail independent labor activists and organizations. Its repressive scope simply broadened over the years, leading it to be direly hated by the Egyptian people as its responsibility for some of the worst cases of violence, abuse, and torture in the country became apparent. Paul Amar outlines the complex barbarity of this "omni-present" and "extremely well-entrenched" police state:

> In Egypt the police forces (*al-shurta*) are run by the Interior Ministry which was very close to Mubarak and the Presidency and had become politically co-dependent on him. But police stations gained relative autonomy during the past decades. In certain police stations this autonomy took the form of the adoption of a militant ideology or moral mission; or some Vice Police stations have taken up drug running; or some ran protection rackets that squeezed local small businesses. The political dependability of the police, from a bottom-up perspective, is not high.

> Police grew to be quite self-interested and entrepreneurial on a station-by-station level... Autonomous from the Interior Ministry we have the Central Security Services (*Amn al-Markazi*). These are the black uniformed, helmeted men that the media refer to as "the police." Central Security was supposed to act as the private army of Mubarak... The Interior Ministry and the Central Security Services started outsourcing coercion to these *baltagiya* [Egyptian street gangs], paying them well and training them to use sexualized brutality (from groping to rape) in order to punish and deter female protesters and male detainees, alike. During this period the Interior Ministry also turned the State Security Investigations (SSI) (*mabahith amn al-dawla*) into a monstrous threat, detaining and torturing masses of domestic political dissidents.[24]

Democracy cannot exist under the auspices of military and police states. Yet, the undemocratic nature of the Egyptian state extends even beyond this enormous police state.

Absence of a Democratic Political Structure

The very political institutions in which representation is supposed to take place were purposefully designed to be rebarbative and sclerotic. While the one-party system in Egypt was ostensibly dissolved in 1976, the political structure essentially guaranteed the continuance of one-party rule. Freedom House's report on Egypt stressed its highly undemocratic nature:

> Egypt is not an electoral democracy. The political system is designed to ensure solid majorities for the ruling NDP at all levels of government. Constitutional amendments passed in 2007 banned religion-based political parties, ensuring the continued suppression of the Muslim Brotherhood, a nonviolent Islamist group that represents the most organized opposition to the government. President Hosni Mubarak, who has been in power since 1981, serves six-year terms and appoints the cabinet and all 26 provincial governors. The first multicandidate popular election for the presidency was held in 2005, and Mubarak's main challenger, Ayman Nour, was jailed on dubious charges soon after the vote.[25]

Thus, Mubarak and the National Democratic Party had essentially ruled unelected and unopposed for 24 years, not even put into the position of being ostensibly elected until 2005. This election, however, was a farce. On top of banning the most popular political party, the electoral process itself was marred by fraud, vote-rigging, police brutality, and violence from paid Mubarak supporters. Aside from those problems, the election was completely illegitimate based purely on the results. In what was the first and only Presidential election in Egyptian history, only 16.4% of the population actually took the time to go to the polls, of whom an embarrassing 88.6% supposedly voted for Mubarak. In other words, out of a voting age population of 44.5 million people, Mubarak commanded the allegiance of, at most, a paltry 6.3 million.[26] Prior to this illegitimate election, equally illegitimate "referendums" were held to try and ideologically cement Mubarak's regime.

The 2005 presidential election is not an anomaly. The parliamentary elections of the 1990s provide clear examples of the undemocratic nature of the Egyptian electoral system. While an absurdly high 79% of seats went to the National Democratic Party in 1990, the results in 1995 were even more unbelievable; after "unprecedented violence and interference, the largest number ever of candidates belonging to the regime party were declared victorious," with 94% of seats going to the NDP.[27] The only time the NDP dipped below 70% was in 1987, during a time of relative political openness, when the party garnered a historic low with 68% of the total seats. It took 88% of seats in 1979, 87% in 1984, 79% in 1990, 94% in 1995,[28] and 85% in 2000.[29] The results were largely predetermined, with the elections acting primary as a façade of democracy, a spectacle for the public.

The election campaigns themselves were inundated with anti-democratic activity, assuring no real contest for the NDP. As one observer explains of the 1995 parliamentary elections:

> ...candidates officially belonging to the NDP could ignore the many legal restrictions and harassments to which their competitors were subjected. Instead, they could rely on official support, ranging from the use of public sector vehicles to the collusion of state officials appointed to run the polling stations. Unlike their competitors, they could put up posters and banderoles before the official beginning of the election campaign. And unlike opposition candidates, they did not have their campaign furniture removed at night... News bulletins on state-controlled television left Egyptians with the impression that the NDP was the only party running. Opposition parties were only granted a few short slots for campaign statements, which

> were also granted to the NDP. Even the judges who were supposed to supervise the elections were chosen by the minister of the interior…[30]

The absurdity of the spectacle was so prodigious that any respectable authoritarian would be ashamed to witness it. In one precinct, the NDP received more than 10,000 non-existent or non-registered names added to the voters' register. Directly preceding the first round of voting, 1,000 members or sympathizers of the Muslim Brotherhood were arrested, most of them campaign workers or representatives of candidates.[31] Even through the Muslim Brotherhood was officially banned, some candidates from the party ran as independents. However, those who did were hampered with harassment and repression, making it impossible to run any real election campaign.

This political context meant that all elections in Egypt were widely recognized as shams by the population, with usually less than one quarter of the voting age population even bothering to participate. As Tarek Osman explains:

> …despite huge campaigning on the government's and opposition's sides for the package of constitutional changes, fewer than 22% of registered voters (who themselves are a minority) turned out to vote in the March 2007 referendum (and that figure includes swathes of government employees who are virtually shipped to the polling booths). Moreover, in June 2007 only 7% of Egyptians bothered to vote in the election to the *shura* (the Egyptian parliament's upper house).[32]

The 2007 constitutional amendments mentioned above imposed even more restrictions on political parties and candidates. Although it changed the law requiring that new parties get approval from an NDP-controlled body linked to the Consultative Council, it banned all religious, gender, and ethnically-based parties. Furthermore, it stated that a party must have been continuously operating for at least five years and must occupy at least 5 percent of the seats in the parliament before it could nominate a presidential candidate. This removed any possibility that an opposition candidate could run in the scheduled 2011 presidential election. The outcome was predetermined. As a leaked 2009 US State Department document explained "the next presidential elections are scheduled for 2011, and if Mubarak is still alive it is likely he will run again, and, inevitably, win."[33]

Elections aside, the political institutions themselves are systematically rife with undemocratic characteristics. For instance, Egypt's lower house in parliament, the 518-seat People's Assembly, or *Majlis al-Sha'b*, has ten of the members simply chosen at the President's discretion. The rest of the members, theoretically chosen through elections, with a few exceptions largely failed to represent the interests of the majority of Egyptians. Furthermore, the assembly has only limited influence on government policy because the executive branch initiates nearly all legislation. Some of the electoral procedures established during the Sadat-Mubarak era limited workers' access to the first post-Mubarak parliament, even while symbolically including them in the law. As Joel Beinin points out:

> Law 38 of 1972 requires that 50 percent of the People's Assembly be comprised of "workers and peasants." But it effectively excludes most workers and pro-labor candidates from running in that category because it defines a worker as, "a person who depends mainly on his income from his manual or mental work in agriculture, industry, or services. He shall not be a member [an office holder] of a trade union, or recorded in the commercial register, or a holder of a high academic qualification." Consequently, many people who are not commonly considered workers, as long as they do not have advanced degrees and are not professionals, such as small or medium business owners, may run as "workers" for the People's Assembly.[34]

Thus, while lip service is paid to "workers and peasants," they are effectively forbid any real form of representation. Prior to 2010, when 64 seats were set aside specifically for women, there were just eight women serving in the assembly. The upper house, called the Consultative Council, or *Majlis al-Shura*, has even less power and acts purely in an advisory role. Of the 264 members, the president appoints 88, and the rest are elected. Power remained highly concentrated in the unaccountable and essentially unelected executive branch.

Egypt's political institutions were simply illegitimate structures of power. According to Khaled Fahmy, professor of history at the American University in Cairo, the NDP was "far from being a political party in the official sense of the word." Instead, it was "a huge patron-client network that [had] nothing to do with ideology, principles, rule of law or legality" and instead served to give corrupt politicians "access to the presidency and to the resources of the state."[35] The Egyptian political system was rotten from the inside and, subsequently, changing political faces would do very little to cement real change.[36] The decrepit nature of Egypt's political infrastructure contributed to the struggle Mohamed Morsi had in trying to maintain legitimacy after securing a narrow electoral victory in 2012. For the past four decades there had been no popular sovereignty, no accountability, and no serious democratic characteristics to speak of in Egyptian political institutions. This repressive political infrastructure existed in a symbiotic relationship with the growing wealth inequality and exploitative nature of the Egyptian ruling class.

[1] Ahmed Shawki, "The struggle surges ahead,"*SocialistWorker.org*, February 04, 2011. http://socialistworker.org/2011/02/04/the-struggle-surges-ahead (accessed July 9, 2013). Ahmed Shawki's anecdote is telling: "When Mubarak spoke on television on Tuesday night and said that he wouldn't run for re-election, he vowed that he was going to die on Egypt's soil. One *Socialist Worker* reporter quipped at the time, 'We should tell him that the soil is ready for him.' I translated that today at Tahrir Square, and I can report that it was greeted with wild applause and cheers--it's another part of the ongoing Egyptian revolution."

[2] "Interview With Pro-Democracy Activist At Tahrir Square" January 31 2011. Web, http://lybio.net/interview-with-pro-democracy-activist-at-tahrir-square/people/.

[3] Timothy Mitchell, *Colonising Egypt*, (London: Cambridge University Press, 1988), pg. 96.

[4] For more on working class activity in the first half of the 20th century, see: Joel Beinin and Zachary Lockman, *Workers on the Nile: Nationalism, Communism, Islam, and the Egyptian Working Class, 1882-1954.* Cairo: The American University in Cairo Press, 1998.

[5] Beinin, and Lockman, *Workers on the Nile*, pg 199-206.

[6] Timothy Mitchell, "Dreamland: The Neoliberalism of Your Desires," *Middle East Research and Information Project.* no. 210. http://www.merip.org/mer/mer210/dreamland-neoliberalism-your-desires (accessed July 9, 2013).

[7] Naguib, "Conversation with an Egyptian socialist."

[8] Cambanis Thanassis, "Succession Gives Army a Stiff Test in Egypt," *New York Times*, September 11, 2010. http://www.nytimes.com/2010/09/12/world/middleeast/12egypt.html?_r=2&ref=global-home&pagewanted=all (accessed July 9, 2013).

[9] Paul Amar, "Uprising in Egypt: A Two-Hour Special on the Revolt Against the U.S.-Backed Mubarak Regime," Recorded February 05 2011. DemocracyNow!. Web, http://www.democracynow.org/2011/2/5/uprising_in_egypt_a_two_hour.

[10] The classic example of this schism between an elected civilian government and state power can be seen in 1973 with Salvador Allende's Chile. As Allende moved down a more democratic, participatory path, he could never take control of the military and was eventually overthrown in a military coup when his threats to capital became too severe. Interestingly, while Morsi represented no such threat to capital, it was expedient for the military to throw him under the bus when mass protests across Egypt threatened to stop the "wheel of production from turning," a ubiquitous phrase utilized by the military.

[11] Walter Armbrust, "Egypt: A revolution against neoliberalism?" *Al-Jazeera*, February 24, 2011. http://www.aljazeera.com/indepth/opinion/2011/02/201122414315249621.html (accessed July 9, 2013).

[12] Freedom House, "Freedom in the World, 2010 - Egypt." Accessed July 10, 2013. http://www.freedomhouse.org/report/freedom-world/2010/egypt.
[13] Eberhard Kienle,"More than a Response to Islamism: The Political Deliberalization of Egypt in the 1990s." *The Middle East Journal*. no. 2 (1998): 219-235. http://chenry.webhost.utexas.edu/pmena/coursemats/2009/kienle-4329187.pdf (accessed July 10, 2013).
[14] Kienle, "More than a Response to Islamism," pg. 221.
[15] Ibid., pg. 222.
[16] Ibid., pg. 222.
[17] Ibid., pg. 223.
[18] Ibid., pg. 228.
[19] U.S. Embassy in Cairo. New York Times, "A Selection From the Cache of Diplomatic Dispatches - Domestic Troubles (CAIRO 002933)," Dated May 16, 2006. Accessed July 10, 2013. http://www.nytimes.com/interactive/2010/11/28/world/20101128-cables-viewer.html?_r=1&
[20] Freedom House, "Freedom in the World, 2010 - Egypt."
[21] U.S. Embassy in Cairo. WikiLeaks, "Mahalla Riots: Isolated Incident Or Tip Of An Iceberg? (CAIRO 000783)," Dated April 14, 2008. Accessed July 10, 2013. http://www.cablegatesearch.net/cable.php?id=08CAIRO783
[22] Sharif Abdel Kouddous, "Defying Regime Threats, Thousands of Workers Join Protesters in Tahrir Square," DemocracyNow! February 10 2011. Web, http://www.democracynow.org/2011/2/10/sharif_abdel_kouddous_defying_regime_threats.
[23] Ahmed Zaki Osman, "The rise and fall of Egypt's notorious State Security," *Egypt Independent*, March 09, 2011. http://www.egyptindependent.com/news/rise-and-fall-egypts-notorious-state-security?utm_source=twitterfeed&utm_medium=twitter (accessed July 10, 2013).
[24] Amar, "Why Mubarak is Out." Note: Paragraph order has been changed from the original article to present a cohesive outline of the police forces.
[25] Freedom House, "Freedom in the World, 2010 - Egypt."
[26] Institute for Democracy and Electoral Assistance, "Jump to section Parliamentary Presidential Voter turnout data for Egypt," Accessed July 10, 2013. http://www.idea.int/vt/country_view.cfm?CountryCode=EG.
[27] Kienle, "More than a Response to Islamism," pg. 220.
[28] Ibid., pg. 224.
[29] Election Guide, "Election Profile: Egypt." Accessed July 10, 2013. http://www.electionguide.org/election.php?ID=691.
[30] Kienle, "More than a Response to Islamism," pg. 226.
[31] Ibid., pg. 226.
[32] Tarek Osman, "Egypt: a diagnosis," *Open Democracy*, June 28, 2007. http://www.opendemocracy.net/democracy_power/protest/modern_egypt (accessed July 10, 2013).
[33] U.S. Embassy in Cairo. Wikileaks, "Mubarak's Visit to Washington (CAIRO

000874)." Dated May 19, 2009. Accessed July 10, 2013.
http://www.wikileaks.org/cable/2009/05/09CAIRO874.html

[34] Joel Beinin, Carnegie Endowment, "The Rise of Egypt's Workers," Last modified June 2012. Accessed July 10, 2013. http://carnegieendowment.org/files/egypt_labor.pdf.

[35] Amar, "Uprising in Egypt: A Two-Hour Special on the Revolt Against the U.S.-Backed Mubarak Regime."

[36] There was a running joke during the uprising among the Egyptians that if Mubarak had chosen to form a new political party one morning called the "National Republican Party," by the evening there would be two million new members in the party, sardonically mocking the fact that no one even knew what the NDP stood for and were members primarily to gain access to the spoils of the patronage system.

2

Declining Economic Conditions

For the majority of Egyptians the standard of living has declined over the past four decades. In contrast, officials within the National Democratic Party, with Mubarak as their crown figure, made a fortune running the Egyptian state. Military elites, alongside a burgeoning class of financiers and corporate figures, amassed enormous sums of personal wealth while the Egyptian working class became impoverished and the poor were cut off from vital social services. Despite this, to "describe blatant exploitation of the political system for personal gain as corruption misses the forest for the trees," as Abu Atris explains. The problem was not a result of aberrations from an otherwise rational and equitable system. Instead, the elites of Egypt "were enriched through a conflation of politics and business under the guise of privatization. This was less a violation of the system than business as usual. Mubarak's Egypt, in a nutshell, was a quintessential neoliberal state."[1] However, it had not always been this way.

The Struggle for Economic Autonomy under the Ottomans and the British

Egypt, as an increasingly autonomous state within the Ottoman Empire, began an industrialization process under the leadership of Muhammad Ali in the first half of the 19th century. By the 1830s some 30,000 recruits had been drawn from the *fellaheen* to work in the new textile mills. Protective tariffs and subsidies for domestic industry encouraged Egyptian capitalists and for a period of time it looked as if Egypt would successfully and independently industrialize. As Andrew Marshall explains:

> Resistance to these industrialization projects was strong on the part of Britain and other industrial Western powers, which wanted these countries to be in subservient positions to their own. The Europeans - and especially Britain - pressured these countries to "open up" their economies to "free trade" competition with the heavily-protected industrial goods of the West. The result, of

course, was that they could not compete on an even basis, and European industrial goods gained the major advantage, forcing these countries to focus on raw goods for export to the rich nations…[2]

In 1839 Muhammad Ali sent his army against the Ottomans, in an effort to win independence from Ottoman rule. A European intervention saved the Ottomans and Ali was subsequently forced to dismantle protective trade barriers. Declining throughout the 1840s, large-scale independent industrialization essentially died with Muhammad Ali in 1849. Consequentially, Egypt became a "European-dominated world market as supplier of a single raw material, cotton."[3] One contemporary writer categorized Egypt as "a gigantic cotton plantation,"[4] apt as roughly 70% of Egypt's exports in 1870 were cotton, rising to 93% in 1910. By 1870, in what has been accurately labeled the "Great Divergence," the chasm "widened significantly between the industrial powers (Western Europe, North America and Japan), which exported manufactured goods, and the rest of the world, which largely focused on exporting commodities needed for industry."[5]

Aside from Britain's cotton interests in Egypt, the Suez Canal, built in 1869 and sold to the British in 1875, ensured the emergence of a permanent working class in Egypt and alongside it a constant presence of European powers. In 1882, a peasant revolt led by the nationalist army officer Colonel Ahmad Urabi, under the banner of "Egypt for Egyptians," was violently suppressed by European powers and left some 250 Egyptians dead.[6] This event was to be a foreshadowing of the anti-colonial struggles to come. By 1907, Egypt had a modern working class of some 350,000 workers out of a population of 11 million. Of these, a total of over 70% were concentrated in commerce and transport, some 150,000 and 100,000 respectively.[7] Concurrent with the emergence of this nascent proletariat was the establishment of European domination. While the British occupation was not given an official title until 1915, the British colonial administration played a significant role in Egypt, in large part by running the banking sector and maintaining an ever-increasingly visible military presence. The Egyptian working class continued to grow during the first part of the 20th century under the auspices of the British occupation, but hegemony of the economic sphere remained split primarily between Egyptian landlords with enormous holdings and industrialists of European or foreign origin, referred to as the *mutamassirun*. Both the interwar period and the period after World War II saw a tremendous amount of labor activity as the working class grew in size and scope.

Nasser, Nationalism, and Economic Development

Within the two years following the 1952 military coup, Gamal Abd al-Nasser became the personal manifestation and international symbol of pan-Arab nationalism and the main proponent of a peculiar economic model of development ostensibly referred to as "Arab Socialism." This model could be more accurately understood as a form of state capitalism with an Arab-nationalist ideological twist. Nasser's Egypt was characterized by a large degree of state ownership, agricultural reform that enervated the power of the landed elites, and an increasing standard of living for Egyptian workers and peasants. Important industries were nationalized and subsidized by the state, which often insulated them from immediate market concerns such as short-term profit considerations. Instead, the state as a whole managed a wide array of enterprises in various industries via state planners collectively pursued capital accumulation. In the end Egypt's state was only a large island within both a domestic and international sea of private capital. Insofar as the state had to play by the rules of the market, especially within the international context, it cannot be adequately described as socialist. This is not to deny the vitally important social and economic programs advanced by the state under Nasser. As expected, these programs were the basis upon which Western antagonists derided Nasser's model as "communism" while proponents celebrated it as real-world "socialism."

Nasser attempted to juggle support from the United States and the Soviet Union in an attempt to augment Egypt's economic power as leader of the Arab world. Omnia El Shakry outlines the extremely complex material and ideological roots of Nasserism:

> Interpretations of Nasserism have centered on the state apparatus. Discussions have focused on the authoritarian-bureaucratic state structure, characterized by a highly state-centralized process of socio-economic development, a corporatist patrimonial state bourgeoisie, a single-party system bolstered by a repressive state apparatus, and a populist nationalist ideology…But such a monolithic model fails to adequately capture the complexity of Nasserism.
>
> Nasserism was equally characterized by an ideology and practice of social-welfare, premised upon the state apparatus as arbiter not only of economic development, but also of social welfare… revolutionary or democratic political change was exchanged for piecemeal social reform

and the amelioration of the conditions of the working classes. It was further based on...an interventionist policy of social planning and engineering.[8]

In other words, there was a significant dimension to Nasser's state capitalism that was predicated on human-needs, on bettering the economic conditions under which people lived.

This was done through a variety of means. Oil production, an important industry despite Egypt having significantly less than other states in the region, was nationalized. This provided a model for state control of production and the expansion of the public sector. Similarly, the Suez Canal was nationalized in 1956, prompting the imperial tripartite aggression by Britain, France, and Israel. Profits were partially redirected into social services and infrastructure development for a period of time. Furthermore, as Selma Botman explains:

> When Egyptians gained control of their country in 1952, for the first time since the Ottoman occupation of the early 1500's, an enormous symbolic and psychological victory was won. The population felt in control of all aspects of their existence. And from the fifties onward, real changes did occur: the businessmen, the money lenders, the department store owners, the bankers, the doctors, the decision makers, the technocrats, the military officers, and the administrative officials were of Egyptian, and not foreign or even ethnically European origin. At least, members of the indigenous culture were dominant.[9]

Alongside this major psychological victory stemming from the self-determination and control of native Egyptians, material living standards increased as people had access to jobs and services previously unavailable to them. A large network of social services provided employment, education, healthcare, subsidized goods and services, and a variety of other benefits which had been previously only supplied via various non-state actors such as the Muslim Brothers. From 1951 to 1960, real wages increased between 41% and 51%, depending on the calculation, while hourly real wages nearly doubled by 1964 due to a decline in length of the workweek.[10] The 50 hour work week, which had been standard throughout the 1950s, decreased to 44 hours of work per week by 1964.[11] Likewise, the number of unions grew from 568 in 1952 to 1056 in 1958, with an increase of workers represented in unions from 159,000 to 341,000 during the same period.[12] By 1964, the number of workers in the state-controlled Egyptian Trade Union Federation rose to 1.29 million members.[13] Nasser further broke the power of the old, landed aristocracy by instituting agrarian reform which, to some extent, empowered the rural peasantry. Between 1952 and 1961 the Free Officer agrarian reform program had successfully "redistributed about one seventh of the country's cultivable land from large landowners... to the landless and near landless fellahin rather" which led to an "improvement of rural incomes and agricultural production."[14] While this program may not have gone far enough, particularly in relation to some South Asian countries, it was the most effective land reform campaign in the region. Despite both Syria and Iraq seizing more land for state control, neither reform program distributed land directly to the peasantry in the way that Egypt's did.[15]

The phenomenon of Arab nationalism scared the Western ruling class, who feared they may lose control of the oil-rich Arab world if this development continued. Nasser and Egypt became hated enemies of the United States and Britain in the late 1950s and 1960s. The Sunday Herald reports that anti-Nasser mania became so thick among the Western elite that there were even absurd schemes to kill Nasser by poisoning his chocolates or inserting a poison dart in his cigarette.[16] In contrast, millions around the Arab world were drawn to Nasser's secular nationalism and he remained very popular within Egypt. Nasser, however, died rather unexpectedly in 1970 and, not long after, the economic model he championed would be dismantled by the Egyptian state planners who followed him.

The Contradictions of Arab Nationalism

Despite this emphasis on ameliorating life for working people and increasing the standard of living, Nasser-style social welfare was based primarily upon economic improvements from above and not democratic control from below. Deepa Kumar elucidates the nature of the Nasser government:

> In 1957, Nasser called for the establishment of a "socialist" order in Egypt. What he meant by socialism was unclear and it varied depending on the context in which he spoke about it. In practice, Nasser, who emerged from the middle classes, led a program that curbed the power of large capital through nationalizations and concentrated economic planning in the state. Arab socialism in practice was state capitalism; it involved state planning combined with authoritarian control and the use of repression to quell opposition. Politically, Nasserism sought to unify and regroup Arab territories into one nation and overturn the

arbitrary divisions imposed by the allied powers after the First World War. The principal enemy was imperialism, particularly U.S. imperialism, which emerged as the dominant power in the Middle East after the war. While Nasser sought military and financial support from the Soviet Union, he was by no means a stooge of Soviet interests... However, postwar secular nationalism, despite its radical promises, was ultimately a middle-class ideology that served the interests of this class. State capitalist measures, while moderately successful for a period, were unable to seriously address class inequalities and produce real economic change.[17]

There was no faith in the working class and its ability to act on its own in a collective, democratic manner to fundamentally restructure society. "Social welfare, of course, should not be understood as a benevolent process whereby the state shepherds citizens in their own welfare," Omnia El Shakry maintains, "Rather, it entails the social and political process of reproducing particular social relations, often based on violence and coercion, at least partly to minimize class antagonisms."[18] The aspect of state coercion was apparent almost immediately under the Nasser regime.

Workers, buying into Nasser's populism, had welcomed the coup in large part due to the illusory blend of anti-imperialist and working class rhetoric. Within weeks, however, workers who thought they were getting a revolutionary leader with their interests at heart were sorely mistaken. Thousands of textile workers in Kafr al-Dawwar went on strike in August 1952, one month after the coup. Oppressed workers who truly believed Nasser's rhetoric about combating injustice assumed that the state apparatus, now in the hands of a progressive leader, would no longer take the side of capital over labor. Instead, the army brutally repressed the strike and convicted two of the strike leaders, Mustafa Khamis and Ahmad al-Bakri, to death. They were hung in September of the same year. While Nasser personally voted against the death penalty for the two organizers, at a time when the Revolution Command Council (RCC) still made such decisions collectively, this example highlights the chasm that existed between the illusion of democratic control and the reality. Despite the vast social programs and increased standard of living Nasser's policies brought to Egyptians, he articulated the relationship between workers and the state rather under Arab Socialism succinctly: "The workers don't demand, we give."[19]

Nasser's elitism and disdain for the autonomy of popular forces was exhibited years earlier. In the 1940s he was introduced by Khaled Mohi al-Din, another Free Officer and member of the Democratic Movement for

National Liberation (DMNL), to the Communist activist and secretary general of the DMNL, "Comrade Badr." Badr revealed himself as a mechanic by trade and later, during internal Free Officer debates, Nasser disparaged Mohi al-Din by contemptuously emphasizing that "his leader is a mechanic." By using Badr's trade as an invective against Mohi al-Din, implying that a mechanic was incapable and inadequate for a leadership position in society, Nasser had already exhibited the elitism that would characterize his presidency after the coup.[20] Once in power, Muhammad Sid Ahmad recalls that Nasser used to say Marxism was a "factor to enrich us and to correct our mistakes… we deal with Marxists as consultants, for enriching and consulting."[21] Other Marxist notions, such as class struggle or workers' control, were out of the question. Throughout his rule, no independent forms of working class organization were permitted, and those who challenged the regime to articulate demands for autonomy were severely repressed.

The internal contradictions inherent in Nasser-style state capitalism meant that the model could not last forever. As Eric Ruder explains, Nasser's "attempts to win support from the US and the Soviet Union demonstrated" that the Arab leader "elevated pragmatism and realpolitik over a commitment to any particular economic or political program" and would pursue any policy which "served Egypt's bid to become the undisputed leader of the Arab world."[22] Indeed, by 1964 Egypt's GDP growth fell "precipitously" and by 1966 Nasser had already looked to the International Monetary Fund (IMF) for relief, one year before the devastating 1967 Arab-Israeli war which significantly exacerbated Egypt's problems. While some accounts claim real wages continued to increase during the last half of the 1960s,[23] most accounts show a slow leveling by 1966 and a slight decline after the 1967 war.[24] Mark Cooper argues that "these changes in wages represent a redistribution of wealth from the working classes towards the state and private sector capitalists."[25] Despite eventually rejecting the proposed IMF deal, due to the stringent "stabilization program" which included cuts to subsidies for basic commodities, the crisis of Arab nationalism was becoming apparent.[26]

The nationalist model of state development aimed at social welfare fell short of socialism in any fundamental sense. Democratic control over the means of production remained an elusive ideal for workers and socialists. The political structures, likewise, reflected the centralized control by a bureaucratic elite and not the democratic control by the masses of Egyptian citizens. As Marie-Christine Aulas argues, the state capitalist model eventually became its own inhibitor:

> …the transformation of economic structures proceeded on the basis of a state capitalism which in no way altered

> the capitalist relations of production… Once the initial stage was over, the concentration of responsibilities in the expanding bureaucratic order gave birth to a new form of economic statism and internal political rivalries. These rigid tensions had all the more paralyzing effect in that the national momentum never structured a broad social base or a will to sweep away the old social order. However great the aspirations and initial steps towards equality, any further progress was rendered highly problematic by the essential incapacity of this social class to formulate a coherent project. Its very nationalism, which had been intended as a revolutionary force, later served to mystify the crucial socio-economic differentiation of the traditional classes and of the privileged layer emerging from the new state-capitalist class.[27]

In other words, Nasser established the rule of a new elite that successfully utilized nationalist rhetoric to blunt the demands of the Egyptian working class. Nasser capitalized on this hegemonic discourse of nationalism to marginalize potential political alternatives, as with his repression and cooptation of the communist movement.[28] This elite was made up primarily of military men and old industrialists who had been drawn into the regime's grand goals of Arab nationalism:

> The Nasser regime concentrated its efforts on…co-opting the old industrial bourgeoisie to further its own aims of large-scale national industrialization. The new class that emerged and characterized the state public sector, however, was a "state bourgeoisie," made up of the new class of technocrats together with older elements of the industrial, financial, and commercial bourgeoisie who worked their way into the public sector.[29]

It was from this group that Sadat and Mubarak emerged. Both would ossify the state apparatus of repression in an attempt to further solidify their own authoritarian rule. This process was facilitated by the ideological weakness of Nasserism without Nasser. As Tareq Ismael explains, "Appealing to broad masses whose class origin and intellectual beliefs differ and are even, at times, contradictory, the Nasserites have fragmented, after Nasser, into a multiplicity of groups, collectivities, and organizations. These units often work at odds with each other under the wide banner of Nasserism."[30] Both the contradictions within the state capitalist model and Nasser's death spurred the dissolution of the forces which had rallied around him.

Subsequently, the political vacuum allowed for the possibility of economic restructuring and geopolitical realignment, an opportunity Nasser's successor would capitalize on.

Sadat's *Infitah* as the Quintessential Neoliberal Model

After Nasser's death, Anwar al-Sadat came to power and was confronted with the internal contradictions of the state-capitalist model and the legacy of defeat in the 1967 war with Israel. Faced with these two developments, and unable to make any gains in the 1973 war, Sadat took the unprecedented step in Egypt of opening up to the West and instituting neoliberal reforms. Egypt would be the testing grounds for this new phenomenon which would soon assault an array of third world states. Almost immediately upon taking power Sadat began to pioneer neoliberalism by introducing "*Infitah*," or open-door policy. Ostensibly *Infitah* was meant to deal with the debt, inflation, and high oil prices that came to represent the later stages of the Nasserite model. The primary motivation for the new economic policies, however, was a strategic political realignment with the West. Sadat's reforms were an all-out embrace of the neoliberal model and included "the loosening of currency controls, the creation of tax-free enterprise investment zones, and the return of various public sector industries to private control (or at the minimum subjecting them to market pressures)."[31] The implementation of this neoliberal model resulted in two concurrent phenomena: the concentration and centralization of wealth,[32] and the increased immiseration of the Egyptian masses.

Neoliberalism as an economic model also parades under euphemistic terms like "free trade," "free market," "laissez-faire," and more broadly, as "globalization." However, it is perhaps more accurately associated with concepts such as "unfettered capitalism," "corporatism," and "corporate globalization." Neoliberalism, first articulated by the Chicago school of economists, found its theoretical base in the works of Milton Friedman, who championed a "political trinity" consisting of "the elimination of the public sphere, total liberation for corporations, and skeletal social spending."[33] Added to this "political trinity" is the extreme ideological sanctification of the concept of private property, where the means of production are to be held in the hands of private investors and capitalists, not the public; and are certainly not to be accountable to the democratic and collective demands or interests of the people. Often, the outcome is the growth of macroeconomic indicators like gross domestic product alongside a widening of inequality and wealth disparity, a declining standard of living in terms of real wages, a lack of access to social services and employment, and a subversion of the representative capacity of government with a converse increase in corporate power.

The first characteristic, the "elimination of the public sphere," includes the privatization of state-run enterprises, communal lands, and democratically run economic institutions. The public sphere is also stripped of the authority to monitor and punish corporate abuse or malfeasance. The second aspect, "total liberation for corporations," translates into the dismantling of protective tariffs and the "liberalization" of trade. This means that capital is free to move across borders, often resulting in corporate outsourcing of jobs, whereby corporations seek to exploit cheaper sources of labor away from their country of origin. This aspect also includes the removal of regulations that may impinge upon the maximization of profits. The last aspect in the trinity, "skeletal social spending," is achieved through increasing the tax-base using regressive taxation, restricting or eliminating taxes for the rich, focusing on decreasing the deficit, redirecting remaining spending away from social services and towards financial institutions and, immensely important in the Egyptian context, towards state security apparatuses available to defend the sanctity of the privately owned means of production.

This trend characterized the trajectories of a wide range of third world countries in Asia, South America, and Africa during and after the 1970s. Nazih Ayubi articulates how this dynamic specifically played out in the Arab World:

> If the period of the 1960s and early 1970s was the era of *étatisme* [process of expanding both the size and role of the state in the economy] and bureaucratic expansion in the Arab World, the late 1970s and 1980s were to usher in a new discourse of 'opening up', liberalisation and privatisation. Privatisation programmes in the Middle East have not, however, followed from empirical evaluations of the performance of the public sector... Rather, they represent mainly a *public policy*, carried out in response to the 'fiscal crisis of the state' and under pressure/temptation from globalised capitalism and from its international institutions... It was only by the end of the 1980s that Arabic coinages for the concept [of privatisation] started to emerge: *takhsisiyya*, *khawsasa*, *khaskhasa*... [and] *tafwit* – literally 'passing on' from the public to the private sector...[34]

This process, of which Egypt is the shining star in the region, meant that after 1973 the country would move itself away from the state-capitalist model favored by the Soviet Union and towards the West. The last popular upsurge against the regime prior to 2011 was in 1977. At the time Egyptians directly contested these new economic policies. In 1977, on the heels of a major transport sector strike the year before, Sadat under pressure from the IMF reduced subsidies to several goods, bread in particular. A massive uprising followed for the next two days which left the government very cautious about abruptly implementing policies which would negatively impact the lives of the millions of Egyptians living in or near poverty. Sadat's successor Hosni Mubarak continued the trend by both decreasing the number of those eligible for subsidies and reducing the number of edibles covered. Government spending decreased from 14% of expenditures to 5% by the 1990s, and by 2002 only four items were even eligible for subsidies.[35] Still, this was not enough for State Department planners in the US who, as late as 2006 were lamenting the fact that the Egyptian government did not "seem prepared to reduce subsidies," particularly for energy, or "accept the job losses inevitable" from the closure of more state-owned companies.[36]

Within the neoliberal paradigm, a model became commonplace which drowned third world nations in debt via first world loans, and then leveraged that debt for a variety of ends. This is a process which Egypt did not escape. Sadat's open-door policy, its proponents claiming it would deal with external debt accumulated during the Nasser years, served only to exacerbate Egypt's indebtedness. Indeed, total public external debt steadily increased from $19 billion in 1980 to $27 billion two years later. By 1986, it had reached almost $40 billion, and by 1989 almost $46 billion. At the same time, total debt service, the amount paid on interest accumulated from the loans and the principle, increased from 13.4% of exports of goods and services in 1980 to 27% percent in 1986 as western financial organizations extended loan after loan to the Egyptian regime.[37]

The payoff, at least according to the economists, was that from roughly 1975 to 2005, Gross Domestic Product (GDP) increased anywhere from 1% to almost 15% annually, while GDP per capita increased an average of around 2% every year.[38] However, *Infitah* policies significantly decreased the standard of living for Egyptians. Wealth inequality increased dramatically, and the social services and public sector Egyptians had come to rely on were drastically slashed, either in the form of direct cuts or privatization. From 1961 to 1981, Egypt went from being one of the world's largest food exporters to a nation dependent upon food imports to survive. By 1990 it was clear that the Egyptian economy was stagnating, and the piecemeal neoliberal reforms that had already robbed the Egyptian masses were not augmenting macroeconomic growth as highly as expected. Purportedly, "profligate" government spending was the cause but in fact the two largest losses of revenue for the Egyptian government came from the worldwide slump of oil prices in 1985 and the loss of remittances from abroad as a result of the 1990-91 Gulf conflict.[39] Despite the slow growth of the economy and the declining living conditions of the masses of Egyptians, the Mubarak regime under the auspices of the IMF and World Bank accelerated and expanded neoliberal policies, causing untold misery through various "structural adjustment programs" and benevolent-sounding "economic reform" plans.

Mubarak as Neoliberal Poster Boy

This neoliberal nightmare was exacerbated in 1991 when Mubarak signed two agreements, one with the IMF and a Structural Adjustment Program (SAP) with the World Bank. Generally, "structural adjustment" is a euphemistic, catch-all phrase employed by economists to conceal the misery associated with neoliberal reform. The agreement led to a decrease in social spending and the mass privatization of public companies, accompanied by the unemployment concomitant with such an endeavor. By 1986, the Agriculture Minister Yusuf Wali was actively implementing agricultural liberalization policies "hand in hand with USAID and the World Bank."[40] The US invested some $1.26 billion in the agricultural reforms and when Law 96 was passed in 1992 a complete reversal of Nasser's agrarian reform took place. This law, a pillar upon which the SAP rested, encouraged the landlords of old to dispossess peasants of their land through various market mechanisms. Specifically, IMF and US tutelage allowed and encouraged Egyptian landowners to charge market rents and strip the *fellaheen* of their land tenure rights. While the goal was to boost agricultural exports through centralization and mechanization, what actually occurred was a dramatic increase in rural poverty and a concomitant reliance on food imports from outside Egypt. The obvious intended consequences of these reforms occurred and hundreds of thousands lost their ability to survive off the land. Subsequently, the former *fellaheen* flooded the informal sector in urban areas, desperately trying to survive. From 1981 to 1991, the rural poor rose from 16.1% to 28.6% percent of the total rural population. If we include those deemed "moderately poor," the percentage rose from 26.9% to 39.2% during the same period. By 1996, this last figure rose to 50%.[41]

Meanwhile, the picture in urban areas was just as severe. During the same time span, from 1981 to 1991, those deemed poor and moderately poor in urban areas increased from 33.5% to 39% of the urban population. In terms of expenditure and purchasing power during the same period, the top 20% was the only section of society which fared better, while the expenditures of the bottom 80% actually decreased. This trend continued from 1990 to 1996, signifying a sharp decline in household consumption per capita. By 1996, some 45% of urban dwellers were considered poor or moderately poor, and real wages in some sectors such as manufacturing had dropped 40% from their 1985 levels. Unemployment increased from 8.6%

in 1990 to 11.3% in 1996.[42] Some estimates claimed that around half of all consumer spending, roughly $30 billion in 1991-92, was done by 1.6% of the population.[43] The Egyptian elite augmented their economic power during this period by extracting wealth from the poor:

> While the lowest 20 percent of the population held 6.6 per cent of national income in 1960 and had improved their share to 7.0 per cent in 1965, they dropped to 5.1 per cent by the late 1970s. By comparison, the income of the highest 5 percent dipped slightly to 17.4 per cent from 17.5 per cent between 1960 and 1965 but increased markedly to 22 per cent after several years of Sadat's policies.[44]

This concentration of wealth among the elite was centralized within a small handful of families and two dozen or so major conglomerates, like the Osman, Bahgat, and Orascom Groups, whose tentacles extended widely across various private sector industries.[45] Both vertical and horizontal monopolies and oligopolies emerged. For instance, in 1999 the Orascom conglomerate, owned by the Sawiris family, controlled "eleven subsidiaries, including Egypt's largest private construction, cement making and natural gas supply companies, the country's largest tourism developments (funded in part by the World Bank), an arms trading company and exclusive local rights in cell phones, Microsoft, McDonald's and much more."[46] Many of these conglomerates produced goods and services far out of the grasp of ordinary Egyptians, reaching a thin layer of the elite, 5% to 10% of the population at most. A meal at McDonalds, for instance, costs more than the daily wage of an average worker.[47]

Not only was the neoliberal project a cutback in state support for the masses, it was a selective retargeting of the remaining state resources towards the rich. One example of this was when tax-payer money was funneled directly into a prodigious bank bailout in the 1990s:

> In response to the financial crisis, the centerpiece of the 1990-91 reforms was a gigantic effort to bail out Egypt's banks. After allowing the currency to collapse and cutting public investment projects, the government transferred to the banks funds worth 5.5 percent of GDP in the form of treasury bills.[14] To envision the scale of this subsidy, in the US during the same period the government bailed out the savings and loans industry, transferring a sum amounting to three percent of GDP over ten years. The Egyptian bailout was almost twice as large, relative to GDP, and occurred in a single year. Moreover, the government

declared the banks' income from these funds to be tax-free, a fiscal subsidy amounting to a further ten percent of GDP by 1996-97. In 1998, the government attempted to end the subsidy by reintroducing the taxing of bank profits, but the banks thwarted the implementation of the law.[15] The banks became highly profitable, enjoying rates of return on equity of 20 percent or more.[48]

"Profligate" public subsidies were simply redirected from the starving masses to the bankers and financiers. Law 203, passed in 1991, set the stage for the privatization of over 300 public firms.[49] A 2010 World Bank report celebrated the fact that Mubarak had "enhanced the business environment" and "rationalized the tax system" by slashing corporate taxes, previously ranging from 34% to 42%, to a paltry 20%. In a further display of this blatant upward redistribution of wealth the executive cabinet implemented a tax cut for the wealthy in the same year, dropping personal tax rates from 32% to 20% for the highest income earners. Mubarak was similarly praised for "improving tax administration" through the augmentation of the tax base from 1.7 million taxpayers in 2004 to 2.5 million taxpayers in 2006.[50] In other words, the tax base was widened by imposing more taxes on the poor and working class and cutting taxes for the wealthy, thereby constructing a devastatingly regressive tax structure.

These harsh economic policies were in place for three decades under Mubarak's regime. By the end, the World Bank was exuberantly hailing the regime for its "solid track record as one of the champions of economic reforms in the Middle East and North Africa region."[51] By 2005, 209 out of 314 public sector companies had been privatized, either in whole or in part. In order to prepare for the privatization process and maximize profits, the state imposed a reduction of the labor force to make public companies more appealing to private investors. In 1980 six mills in the ESCO conglomerate employed some 24,000 workers. By 2000, they had been reduced to 3,500 through a combination of attrition, hiring freezes, and buy-outs.[52] The 8,700-strong workforce at the Misr Helwan mill was forced on a three-week vacation and prior to returning management announced that only 2,800 workers would come back.[53] In preparing for this privatization process, these companies cut their work force by over half between 1994 and 2001.[54] After massive reductions in the labor force, companies were sold off at fire sale prices[55] to private investors with the result that some 12% of government proceeds came from the sale of public companies during the mid-1990s.[56] These workers, like the peasants removed from their land, were absorbed into Egypt's informal sector.

In 2006, these devastating policies were implemented in an increasingly dramatic fashion by the cabinet of then Prime Minister Ahmed Nazif.

Philip Rizk explains that Nazif "relentlessly implemented the demands of the World Bank and International Monetary Fund (IMF)" with "fast-track imposition of neo-liberal economic policies" such as "the privatisation of public factories, the liberalisation of markets, decreasing tariffs and import taxes and the introduction of subsidies for agri-businesses," displacing small farmers in an attempt to augment agricultural exports.[57] By 2010, the privatization of the public sector had led to "mass layoffs and slashing of wages and benefits," leaving some 3 million Egyptians employed as temporary and contingent workers, allowing their employers to dismiss them whenever they wanted. The framework for hiring workers under temporary and fixed-term contracts was fully and legally established in 2003 with the passage of the Unified Labor Law, a law which encouraged employers to hire workers using temporary contracts.[58] In conjunction with the privatization of public firms, this law was particularly pernicious for Egyptian workers as it provided enormous leverage to bosses by forcing labor "flexibility." One example of this "flexibility" euphemism can be seen by the common practice in which "newly hired workers are obliged to sign an undated document in which they submit their resignations, giving the employer the liberty to fire workers at any given moment."[59] Furthermore, "the absence of benefits such as health insurance in these contracts is quite alarming since temporary employment is most concentrated in fields involving high-risk physical labor, including the agriculture, construction and mining sectors."[60] Just as Sadat opened Egypt up to neoliberal restructuring, Mubarak was the neoliberal poster-boy who imposed economic decadence on Egypt with immense force. These policies ensured that any social base he could have once relied upon would be dangerously eroded by January 25, 2011.

Schisms within Elite Circles

The *Infitah* policies and the neoliberal restructuring of Egyptian society were not without consequence to ruling class cohesion. Top military leaders did not see the same benefits as the emerging private capitalists nor did an influx of new wealth line their pockets like it did for the new capitalist class. From 1995 to 2005, the number of businessmen elected to Egypt's parliament increased from 8 to 150.[61] Indeed, as the political and economic power of this new private capitalist class developed, a schism opened up within the National Democratic Party. The *New York Times* expounded upon this split between the "old" and "new" guard of the NDP:

> Much of the military's distrust of Gamal Mubarak [Hosni Mubarak's son] stems from his ties to a younger generation of ruling party cadres who have made fortunes in the

business world. The military is tied to the National Democratic Party's "old guard," a substantially less wealthy elite who made their careers as ministers, officers and apparatchiks. Military officers said they feared that Gamal Mubarak might erode the military's institutional powers.[62]

The military saw itself as the "national capitalists," in contradistinction to the neoliberal "crony capitalists" associated with Gamal Mubarak, who they felt had "privatized anything they can get their hands on and sold the country's assets off to China, the US, and Persian Gulf capital."[63] There were also splits between the elites in the Army and the Air force and between different branches of the intelligence services. In other words, while these policies undoubtedly meant misery and suffering for the Egyptian masses, they also created fissures within the Egyptian ruling class.

These schisms were primarily factional, an issue of debate between two blocs of the ruling class over how to manage the capitalist system domestically. Gamal Mubarak, for instance, was keen to point out that constitutional reform and ending the emergency laws were "not among the priorities of the National Democratic Party." After all, for Gamal, democracy was not about following "the wishes of the man on the street" and making such wishes "a reason for effecting foundational changes." Instead, social movement historian Mona El-Ghobashy captured the mood of the NDP's "self-anointed liberal spokespersons":

> Egypt's circulation of elites portends an economic transformation -- but not a political one... For them, politics is rational administration and technocratic professionalism; they have no patience with the nationalist and Islamist "populists" who clutter the landscape with bravado and infantile idealism. Politics is decidedly not the interaction of competing interests and conflicting visions to produce imperfect compromises. Democracy is not the institutionalization but the elimination of uncertainty, a glacial process of "acculturating" the vast majority of "undemocratic" Egyptians into democratic values first before allowing them any share in decision-making.[64]

For the Egyptian people, this coupling of decrepit political institutions lacking democratic pretense and the imposition of neoliberal economic policies led to an even more prodigious wealth gap, a serious decline in real wages, and millions being forced to spiral into economic misery. Despite the abstract moral distinction Egyptian military elites and some media outlets have tried to manufacture between "national" or "good" capitalists and "crony" or "bad" capitalists, the fact is that economic exploitation is an inherent aspect of the capital accumulation process. Adam Hanieh describes here the intricate interrelationship between the economic system and the oppressive state apparatus:

> The result of neoliberalism was the enrichment of a tiny elite concurrent with the immiseration of the vast majority. This is not an aberration of the system – a kind of 'crony capitalism' as some financial commentators have described it – but precisely a normal feature of capitalist accumulation replicated across the world. The repressive apparatus of the Egyptian state was aimed at ensuring that the lid was kept on any social discontent arising from these worsening conditions. In this sense, the struggle against the effects of the economic crisis would inevitably be compelled to confront the dictatorial character of the regime.[65]

After decades of neoliberalism, the nationalist discourse that proved hegemonic under Nasser proved a sham. For the mass of Egyptian workers, it mattered less whether their exploiter and oppressor had an Egyptian, American, or Chinese surname and more whether the economy worked to enhance or diminish their standard of living.

Despondent Economic Conditions at the Outset of Revolution

By 2011, Egypt was the most populous country in the region with over 80 million people officially and some estimates claiming much higher.[66] Significantly, roughly half the population was concentrated in major urban areas. Furthermore, nearly two-thirds of the population was under the age of 30. Egypt had witnessed a slow GDP increase over the course of the last three decades, but by 2004 Egypt's new "reform" cabinet began pushing the neoliberal economic agenda even further than previously imagined. From 2005 to 2008 annual GDP increased a staggering 7%. *The Economist* praised the Egyptian rulers handling of the economy in the most hagiographic manner, claiming the economy was "performing better than ever" because "the government has at last abandoned its old habits of central planning, state-managed capital allocation, high taxes and price controls." They cite the massive surge in Egypt's GDP as well as Egypt's share of world trade and foreign investment, which they claim "gushed in at record levels, notching up a cumulative total of $46 billion between 2004 and 2009."[67]

All of this is undoubtedly true. Yet, while *The Economist* maintained in 2011 that the "economy as a whole is performing better than ever," it would behoove the critical observer to ask who exactly the economy was performing for. Such "GDP-centric" models "ascribe a general assessment of a country's health on the basis of aggregate macro-statistics" which imply "an unspoken assumption that a growth trend at the aggregate level is good for the population as a whole."[68] The trend within the neoliberal model, however, has been to augment macroeconomic growth while simultaneously hiding the realities of increased wealth concentration and a decline in the standard of living for the majority of the population.

While a new faction of the ruling class may have arisen from the sort of "crony capitalism" based around the ruling NDP, for the Egyptian masses economic conditions have worsened considerably. As of 2011, infant mortality rates remained high at 26 deaths per 1,000 live births, compared with only 6 per 1,000 for the United States. Nearly one-third of all Egyptian children were malnourished.[69] Literacy remained just slightly above 71% for adults aggregately and was far lower for females at 59%.[70] The workweek remained high at 48 hours a week, and though debate aimed at curbing the work week to five eight-hour days took place during the 2000s, legislation was never passed.[71] The percentage of workers in unions declined, with almost 48% of wage and salary earners in the formal sector unionized in 1985 dropping to 38.8% ten years later.[72] By the late 1990s, the unionization rate of the non-agricultural labor force was around 25%, with union workers mostly concentrated in the public sector.[73] By 2003, the total percentage of the labor force unionized, including agricultural workers, was around 14.2%, a number that would decrease slightly to 13.9% by 2011.[74] This trend continued into the 2000s and even accelerated under Nazif's economic management. While the unionization rate remained comparatively high to other countries in the region, the top-down structure of the state-controlled Egyptian Trade Union Federation ensured that unionization did very little to improve the lives of working class Egyptians. Attempts at independent unionization continued to be met with force and repression.

In 1984, the last time the minimum wage was changed, the Egyptian pound (£E) was nearly double the worth of a US dollar. By time the revolution occurred, $1 USD was worth roughly £E 5.75. As a study from the Egyptian Centre for Economic Studies points out:

> "When minimum wage is related to per capita GNP (gross national product), it appears that this rate has decreased from nearly 60 percent in 1984 to 19.4 percent in 1991/92 and further to 13 percent in 2007," a study issued last June by the Egyptian Centre for Economic Studies (ECES)

concluded. "When the ratio of minimum wage to per capita GNP is compared to other countries, it appears amongst the lowest." Egypt's minimum wage is just 13 percent of per capita GNP, the study said. By comparison, the rate is 26 percent in Spain, 51 percent in France and 78 percent in Turkey.[75]

Demands to increase the national minimum wage from the devastatingly low $6.30 (£E 35) a month[76] to $240 (£E 1,200) a month fell on deaf ears. In opposition to workers, business leaders would grudgingly accept no more than a paltry increase to $74 (£E 400) per month.[77] This small rise in the minimum wage, setting it just slightly above the $67 poverty line, did actually take place in 2010. However, as one critic points out, this decision "was meaningless from the perspective of the 7 million Egyptians (including half the women in the work force) who work in the informal economy outside the reach of government scrutiny."[78] Women especially felt the brunt of these austere economic policies. By 2005 they earned only 23% of the income earned by men, one of the lowest rates in the Middle East and North Africa.[79]

This phenomenon is not isolated to the minimum wage. The past few decades have seen an astounding inverse correlation between GDP per capita and real wages. While the former was increasing at an average of roughly 2% per year, the latter has fallen by an average of 2.5% each year.[80] Wages did not immediately plummet when Sadat announced the *Infitah* policy in 1973. On the contrary, the late 1970s and early 1980s saw modest increases in wages, but were accompanied by an enormous increase in unemployment, from over 4% in 1976 to 11% ten years later. The modest wage increases did not last long either, as by 1996 real wages stood at roughly 83% of their 1973 level.[81] While nominal weekly wages for Egyptian workers increased from £E 38 in 1987 to £E 99 in 1996, average real wages decreased from about $54 per week to just under $41, a 25% decrease a ten year span as wages failed to keep up with inflation.[82] By 2011, the range of private sector pay for a worker was anywhere from $120 to $400 a month, the later only being achieved after a workweek consisting of six twelve-hour days, far exceeding the already taxing 48 hour workweek.[83] Estimates vary, but anywhere from 44%[84] to 52.7% of Egyptians lived on less than $2 a day prior to the revolution.[85] From 1995 to 2005, distribution of income for the lowest 10% of the population has decreased from 4.4% to 3.9% while for the wealthiest 10% it has increased from 25% to 27.6%.[86] In 1976 the official unemployment rate was 4.6%, jumping to 11% in 1986, decreasing slightly to 9% in 1996, [87] and topping off at 11.2% overall and 13% in urban areas during 2007,[88] one year before the onset of the world economic crisis. Since then, official urban unemployment has not only remained in the double digits but increased.

Meanwhile, unofficial unemployment rates were estimated at 25%.[89] Ahmad El-Naggar, Egyptian economist and director of economic studies at Al-Ahram Centre for Political and Strategic Studies, estimated that in 2009 some 7.9 million people were unemployed, putting the real unemployment rate at 26.3%.[90] This phenomenon of mass unemployment is even more pressing for youth and recent college graduates. Official unemployment figures for the age groups 15-20 and 20-25 amounted to a staggering 22.2% and 28.0%,[91] while even the World Bank admitted that this number "could be much higher."[92] It was clear that privatization has not improved conditions for Egyptian workers:

> Wages of Egyptian textile workers are among the lowest in the world: 85 percent of wages in Pakistan and 60 percent of wages in India. A weaver in a well-run private-sector enterprise makes about 1,000 pounds a month [$US 174] a spinner makes about 800 [$US 139]. The lower-paid spinners are mostly women. These wages are roughly double what workers earn in the same jobs in the public sector, but private-sector textile workers work 12 hour shifts (as opposed to eight in the public sector) and rarely receive the health insurance or other social benefits to which they are legally entitled.[93]

In spite of such miserable conditions, a leaked US State Department memo from 2006 congratulated then Prime Minister Ahmed Nazif "and his economic cabinet [for] soldiering ahead with privatization and liberalization of the economy."[94] Another document, three years later, praised Egypt's "economic reform" as a "success story" despite the fact that "Egypt still suffers from widespread and so far irremediable poverty affecting upwards of 35-40% of the population." The US official then went on to applaud "reforms in trade and tax policy, financial reform, [and] privatization," citing "7% economic growth in the last fiscal year" as the fruits of this "success story."[95] Similarly, the World Bank praised Egypt's efforts toward "economic reform" and repeatedly designated it on its top-ten "most improved reformer" list.[96]

The full picture of this "success story" can be found in the 2005 Household Income, Expenditure and Consumption Survey, which outlined the extremely appalling economic statistics Nazif's "soldiering ahead" had garnered for ordinary Egyptians. According to the report about 40.5% of the Egyptian population is in the range of extreme poor to near poor. Of this, some 21% of the Egyptian population, 14.6 million people, was classified as near poor, meaning they were on the verge of poverty. Likewise, some 13.6 million people, or around 19.6% of the Egyptian population, were considered poor, meaning they could not attain basic food and non-food needs simultaneously. Those suffering the most, the extreme poor, comprised 3.8% of the Egyptian population - roughly 2.6 million people. Those classified in this category could not obtain their basic food requirements even if they spent all their expenditure on food. World Bank estimates from 2009, one year into the economic crisis, place poverty rates, excluding those "near poverty," at 21.6%, a full 2% above the 2005 estimates. Furthermore, as the Centre for Development Policy and Research points out, reliance upon outdated 1996 figures, the misrepresentation of urban and rural slum populations, consistent underestimation of real costs, and the increase in the price of public services suggest that poverty rates are likely to be higher in reality.[97] It should be noted here that while government spending from 2002 to 2007 was reduced in the areas of social security (by 12%), health (by 25%), education (by 36%), and environmental protection (by 85%), spending did increase in two areas, national security (by 87%) and "public order" (by 51%).[98]

Egyptian Neoliberalism and the Capitalist World Order

Egyptian neoliberalism cannot be separated from the global capitalist system. In contrast to what some economists at the IMF and World Bank originally suggested, Egypt did not escape the global economic crisis beginning 2008. In fact, three variables that undoubtedly impacted the surge of unemployment and poverty in Egypt were actually global in nature: the decline of exports to Europe, the loss of remittances from Egyptian workers abroad, and sharp increase in food prices. First, exports to Europe, upon which Egypt and most of North Africa heavily rely, fell steeply due to the economic contraction of European economies. World Bank estimates show that the growth rates for Egyptian merchandise exports to the European Union fell 48% from 2008 to 2009 alone. Similarly, Suez Canal revenue declined by 7.2% in that one year span.[99] Furthermore, as Westerners felt the squeeze and tourism slowed down revenues from Egyptian tourism went from increasing 24% in 2008 to contracting by 1% in 2009. This was particularly important for Egyptian workers as the share of total employment in the service sector, within which tourism is the single largest industry, stood at 49.1% in 2000, up from 35.7% in 1980.[100]

The second mechanism through which the crisis was transmitted to Egypt is the 18% decrease in remittances sent back home from Egyptians working abroad. Remittances make up roughly 5% of the Egyptian economy and this lifeline for millions of Egyptians was shortened as Egyptians overseas were hit with mass layoffs. Lastly, as a country relying heavily upon food imports vis-à-vis neoliberal restructuring, Egypt felt the devastating impact of the 2008 global food crisis as food prices skyrocketed with grain staples like rice, wheat, and corn seeing dramatic increases across the globe. The price of rice, for instance, starting at $600 a ton in 2003 tripled to $1800 a ton by 2008.[101] Though not on the scale of 1977, Egypt saw riots from the lack of subsidized bread as the price of bread at private bakeries, shooting up fivefold during the crisis, remained out of reach for many Egyptians. From the one-month period of December 2010 to January 2011 inflation of food prices in Egypt increased from 17.2% to 18.9%.[102] A 2009 US State Department memo concisely reported what three decades of neoliberalism had done to the Egyptian population:

> Egypt's per capita GDP was on par with South Korea's 30 years ago; today it is comparable to Indonesia's. There were bread riots in 2008 for the first time since 1977. Political reforms have stalled and the GOE [Government of Egypt] has resorted to heavy-handed tactics against individuals and groups, especially the Muslim Brotherhood, whose influence continues to grow... Economic reform momentum has slowed and high GDP growth rates of recent years have failed to lift Egypt's lower classes out of poverty. High inflation, coupled with the impact of the global recession, has resulted in an increase in extreme poverty, job losses, a growing budget deficit and projected 2009 GDP growth of 3.5% - half last year's rate.[103]

These three variables, decreasing exports, loss of remittances, and increasing food prices, all international in character, were reflected directly in the decreasing standards of living for the Egyptian working class as a whole immediately prior to the uprisings.

Economic Disparity and the Paucity of Mubarak's Social Base

Wage and employment statistics alone cannot show how the crushing poverty and lack of social services enervates such a prodigious segment of Egyptian society. As Tarek Osman points out, "Egypt's lower classes are deprived not only of employment opportunities, passable education, and any luxury whatsoever; they are lacking basic human needs such as decent shelter, [clean] water, and humane transportation systems." This is exacerbated by the "gradual withdrawal of the state from its market-regulating and social-provision role."[104] This "gradual withdrawal" has meant increasing misery in terms of accessing social services like health care:

> According to economist Ahmed Al-Naggar of the Al-Ahram Strategic Studies Center, the Egyptian government spends just 1.4 per cent of its national annual budget on health care in comparison with a global average of 5.8 per cent. This translates into dramatically underpaid public sector medical staff and extremely poor conditions in public health care facilities. Consequently, the majority of Egyptians, who cannot afford private medical care, are left with practically no health care to speak of.[105]

Furthermore, the Egyptian middle classes have felt the economic decline as well. The diminishing of the public sector means that a failing education system has led to a "general low levels of skills" plaguing even Egypt's educated class. Indeed, as Hesham Sallam points out:

> The continuing decline in quality and quantity of state social services has forced many families to spend a good chunk of their paychecks on services that Egyptians used to take for granted, such as health care and education. For example, it is estimated that Egyptian families spend 10-15 billion Egyptian pounds per year on private tutoring in order to compensate for the shortcomings of formal instruction at public and private schools… Estimates show that two thirds of schoolchildren in Egypt are privately tutored and 60 percent of families that rely on these services spend at least one third of their incomes on the lessons.[106]

In terms of purchasing power, Egypt's middle class was less powerful than it had ever been by 2011. Meanwhile, the "vast prominence and influence of a small group of businessmen and financiers," along with the National Democratic Party's new guard, "left Egypt's middle class painfully aware of the hollowness and fragility of its traditional position in the society."[107]

In contrast, the Mubarak family's personal fortune is estimated conservatively at $1.3 billion,[108] while other observers have placed the number much higher.[109] Meanwhile, other major players in the National Democratic Party were worth billions.[110] This sort of blatant pilfering of the Egyptian people, alongside the increasing trend towards inequality, resulted in Mubarak dissolving any potential popular base of support. The Egyptian ruling class isolated the poor, the working class, and the middle class through a variety of measures. By the end of his regime, Mubarak's power relied internally upon the narrow layer of society composed of state security forces, party officials, strategically placed military leaders, and a small elite who relied upon government contracts. While there were some two-million civil service workers who depended upon the regime for their employment, not all of them were as loyal to Mubarak as he had probably hoped. Altogether, it is safe to estimate that elements providing reliable support for the regime constituted well under 10% of Egyptian society. While internal support was dangerously thin, a vital component in maintaining the Mubarak dictatorship was the international support and billions of dollars in external military aid from the United States funneled into the regime.

Table 2.1 – Percent of Change in Real Wages by Year (1950 baseline)[111]	
Year	Percentage of Real Wages per Week
1950	100
1951	100
1952	120
1953	116
1954	132
1956	138
1957	137
1958	139
1959	145
1960	143
1961	140
1962	141
1963	159
1964	168
1965	166
1966	167
1967	158

Table 2.2 – Percent of Change in Real Wages by Year (1973 baseline)[112]	
Year	Percentage of Real Wages per Week
1973	100
1974	94
1975	91
1976	101
1977	113
1978	111
1979	125
1980	120
1981	125
1982	128
1983	131
1984	141
1985	134
1986	120
1987	110
1990	96
1991	86
1994	81
1995	83
1996	83

[1] Armbrust, "Egypt: A revolution against neoliberalism?"
[2] Andrew Marshall, The Hampton Institute, "Egypt Under Empire, Part 1: Working Class Resistance and European Imperial Ambitions," Last modified July 11, 2013. Accessed July 14, 2013.
http://www.hamptoninstitution.org/egyptunderempire.html
[3] Zachary Lockman, "Notes on Egyptian Workers' History," *International Labor and Working Class History* (No. 18, Fall 1980), page 2. Quoted in Marshall, The Hampton Institute, "Egypt Under Empire, Part 1."
[4] Anne Alexander. *Nasser: His Life, His Times*. Cairo: American University in Cairo Press, 2005, pg. 5.
[5] Marshall, The Hampton Institute, "Egypt Under Empire, Part 1."
[6] Alexander, *Nasser: His Life, His Times*, pg. 4-5.
[7] Joel Benin, "Formation of the Egyptian Working Class," MERIP Reports (No. 94, February 1981), pg. 15. Cited in: Marshall, The Hampton Institute, "Egypt Under Empire, Part 1."
[8] Omnia El Shakry, "Egypt's Three Revolutions: The Force of History behind this Popular Uprising," *Jadaliyya*, February 06, 2011.
http://www.jadaliyya.com/pages/index/569/egypts-three-revolutions_the-force-of-history-behind-this-popular-uprising (accessed July 10, 2013).
[9] Selma Botman, *The Rise of Egyptian Communism: 1939-1970*, (New York: Syracuse University Press, 1988), pg. xix.
[10] Marsha Pripstein Posusney, *Labor and the State in Egypt: Workers, Unions, and Economic Restructuring*. New York: Columbia University Press, 1997, pg. 50. The discrepancy here, as Posusney explains, rests in the difference in estimates based in the *Survey of Wages and Working Hours* published by CAPMAS and the report released by International Labor Organization using nominal wages figures. Regardless of the exact number, there was a clear and significant trajectory upwards for real wages throughout the 1950's.
[11] Posusney, *Labor and the State in Egypt*, pg. 71.
[12] Ibid., pg. 53.
[13] Ibid., pg. 93.
[14] Ray Bush, "Coalitions for Dispossession and Networks of Resistance? Land, Politics and Agrarian Reform in Egypt," *British Journal of Middle Eastern Studies* (Vol. 38, No. 3, December 2011), page 395. Quoted in: Andrew Marshall, "Egypt Under Empire, Part 3: From Nasser to Mubarak," *The Hampton Institute*, July 24, 2013,
http://www.hamptoninstitution.org/egyptunderempireparttree.html#.UfWQEo2

1Fe9.

[15] Syria appropriated about one-fifth of agricultural land, while Iraq seized almost half. See Roger Owen, *State, Power, and Politics in the Making of the Modern Middle East* (New York: Routledge, 2004), pg. 26.

[16] Deepa Kumar cites Robert Dreyfuss, *Devil's Game: How the United States Helped Unleash Fundamentalist Islam* (New York: Henry Holt and Company, 2005). Originally found in a Sunday Herald article dated from 2000 at the following link which is now unavailable: http://findarticles.com/p/articles/mi_qn4156/is_20000319/ai_n13945412/

[17] Deepa Kumar, "Political Islam: A Marxist analysis," *International Socialist Review*, no. 78 (2011), http://isreview.org/issue/78/political-islam-marxist-analysis (accessed July 16, 2013).

[18] El Shakry, "Egypt's Three Revolutions."

[19] Posusney, *Labor and the State in Egypt*, pg. 74.

[20] Alexander. *Nasser: His Life, His Times*, pg. 29.

[21] Botman, *The Rise of Egyptian Communism: 1939-1970*, pg. 149.

[22] Eric Ruder, "From Nasserism to Collaboration: Egypt, Israel, and the United States," *International Socialist Review*. no. 70 . http://isreview.org/issue/70/nasserism-collaboration (accessed July 10, 2013).

[23] Juan Cole, "Egypt's Class Conflict," *Informed Comment*, January 30, 2011. http://www.juancole.com/2011/01/egypts-class-conflict.html (accessed July 10, 2013). Cole claims "real wages nearly doubled from 1960 to 1970," but while this may be true from 1951 to 1964, it most likely is not accurate considering the drop in real wages during the last half of the 1960's.

[24] Posusney shows a leveling in real wages from 1964 to 1966 and a slight decline in weekly real wages from 1966 to 1967. Cooper argues that while real wages are "more suspect because of the difficulty in choosing a cost-of-living deflator," trends consistently show a leveling during the mid-1960's and a "steady decline after the war."

[25] Mark N. Cooper, *The Transformation of Egypt*, (New York: Routledge, 1982).

[26] Joel Beinin, "Workers, Trade Unions and Egypt's Political Future." *Middle East Research and Information Project*. (2013). http://www.merip.org/mero/mero011813 (accessed July 10, 2013).

[27] Marie-Christine Aulas, "State and ideology in republican Egypt," in Fred Halliday and Hamza Alavi eds., State and Ideology in the Middle East and Pakistan (New York: Monthly Review Press, 1988), pg. 137-8.

[28] See Joel Beinin, "The Communist Movement and Nationalist Political Discourse in Nasirist Egypt," *Middle East Journal*, Vol. 41, no. 4 (1987): 568-584.

[29] El Shakry, "Egypt's Three Revolutions."

[30] Tareq Y. Ismael, *The Arab Left*, (New York: Syracuse University Press, 1976), pg. 82.

[31] Ruder, "From Nasserism to Collaboration."

[32] In Marxist terms, the increasing concentration of capital reflects the accumulation of more and more capital by individual capitalists, which in turn

augments the total amount of capital at their disposal. In conjunction with concentration of capital was centralization, which can be roughly defined as a redistribution of already existing capital into the hands of a smaller number of capitalists. As more capital is centralized into fewer hands, larger enterprises could produce at lower average costs than smaller enterprises, diminishing the degree of competition within the market.

[33] Naomi Klein, *The Shock Doctrine: The Rise of Disaster Capitalism*, (New York: Picador, 2007), pg. 18.

[34] Nazih N. Ayubi, *Over-stating the Arab State: Politics and Society in the Middle East*, (London: I.B. Tauris & Co Ltd., 2008), pg. 329.

[35] The four subsidies were: bread, flour, sugar, and cooking oil. Lee Sustar, "The roots of Egypt's uprising," *Socialist Worker* (US), February 3, 2011, http://socialistworker.org/2011/02/03/roots-of-egypts-uprising?quicktabs_sw-recent-articles=7-3.

[36] U.S. Embassy in Cairo. New York Times, "A Selection From the Cache of Diplomatic Dispatches - Domestic Troubles (CAIRO 002933)," Dated May 16, 2006.

[37] Kienle, "More than a Response to Islamism."

[38] *World Bank*. 1961-2011. s.v. "GDP growth (annual %) and GDP per capita (current US$)." http://data.worldbank.org/indicator/NY.GDP.MKTP.KD.ZG/countries/eg?display=graph (accessed July 11, 2013).

[39] Mitchell, "Dreamland: The Neoliberalism of Your Desires."

[40] Marshall, "Egypt Under Empire, Part 3."

[41] Kienle, "More than a Response to Islamism," pg. 232.

[42] Ibid., pg. 232.

[43] Mitchell explains that the "estimate is based on the assumption that all the missing expenditure belongs to this group. The plausibility of the assumption rests on factors such as the character of the missing expenditures and the relative proportion of incomes that different groups spend of food." Original statistics come from Ulrich Bartsch, "Interpreting Household Budget Surveys: Estimates for Poverty and Income Distribution in Egypt," *Working Papers of the Economic Research Forum for the Arab Countries, Iran and Turkey*, No. 9714. Cairo, 1997, pp. 17-19.

[44] Marvin Weinbaum, "Egypt's 'Infitah' and the politics of U.S. economic assistance," *Middle Eastern Studies*, vol. 21 no. 2 (April 1985): 217. Quoted in Ruder.

[45] Mitchell, "Dreamland: The Neoliberalism of Your Desires."

[46] Ibid.

[47] Ibid.

[48] Ibid.

[49] Beinin, "The Rise of Egypt's Workers."

[50] World Bank, "Egypt Country Brief." Last modified September 2010. Accessed July 11, 2013. http://siteresources.worldbank.org/INTEGYPT/Resources/EGYPT-Web_brief-

2010-AM.pdf.
[51] World Bank, "Egypt Country Brief."
[52] Joel Beinin, "Popular Social Movements and the Future of Egyptian Politics," *Middle East Research and Information Project* (2005), http://www.merip.org/mero/mero031005 (accessed July 11, 2013).
[53] Joel Beinin and Hossam El-Hamalawy, "Egyptian Textile Workers Confront the New Economic Order," *Middle East Research and Information Project*(2007), http://www.merip.org/mero/mero032507 (accessed July 11, 2013).
[54] Adam Hanieh, "Egypt's Uprising: Not Just a Question of Transition," *The Bullet*, February 14, 2011. http://www.socialistproject.ca/bullet/462.php (accessed July 4, 2013).
[55] To give an idea of the robbery by capitalists and party officials of the public sector, one mill, estimated at $60 million in 1999 with an additional $7 million in capital investment through tax-payer money in 2003, was sold on a three year lease of $2.5 million and a final buyout of $4 million. This means a mill worth roughly $67 million was sold for just above $11 million, slightly less than 1/6 of its actual value. See Beinin, "Popular Social Movements and the Future of Egyptian Politics."
[56] Beinin and El-Hamalawy, "Egyptian Textile Workers Confront the New Economic Order."
[57] Philip Rizk, "Egypt and the global economic order," *Al-Jazeera English*, February 15, 2011. http://www.aljazeera.com/indepth/opinion/2011/02/20112148356117884.html (accessed July 11, 2013).
[58] Beinin, "The Rise of Egypt's Workers."
[59] Nadine Abdalla, German Institute for International and Security Affairs, "Egypt's Workers – From Protest Movement to Organized Labor." Last modified October 2012. Accessed July 11, 2013. http://academia.edu/2067581/Egypts_Workers_-_From_Protest_Movement_to_Organized_Labor.
[60] Hesham Sallam, "Striking Back at Egyptian Workers,"*Middle East Research and Information Project*, no. 259 (2011), http://www.merip.org/mer/mer259/striking-back-egyptian-workers (accessed July 11, 2013).
[61] Angela Joya, "The Egyptian revolution: crisis of neoliberalism and the potential for democratic politics," *Review of African Political Economy* (Vol. 38, No. 129, September 2011), page 370. Quoted in Marshall, "Egypt Under Empire, Part 3."
[62] Thanassis, "Succession Gives Army a Stiff Test in Egypt."
[63] Amar, "Why Mubarak is Out."
[64] El-Ghobashy, "Egypt Looks Ahead to Portentous Year."
[65] Hanieh, "Egypt's Uprising."
[66] Amar, "Why Mubarak is Out." According to Amar the discrepancy is because "some parents do not register all their children to shield them from serving in the

Amn Al-Markazi or army."

[67] "A favoured spot: Egypt is making the most of its natural advantages." *The Economist*, July 15, 2010. http://www.economist.com/node/16564172 (accessed July 11, 2013).

[68] Hanieh, "Egypt's Uprising."

[69] "Nearly third of Egyptian children malnourished." *Middle East Online*, November 06, 2009. http://www.middle-east-online.com/english/?id=35538 (accessed July 11, 2013).

[70] *CIA World Fact Book*. CIA, "The World Fact Book - Africa: Egypt." https://www.cia.gov/library/publications/the-world-factbook/geos/eg.html (accessed July 11, 2013).

[71] "Economists call for 40-hour work week." *Arab News*, June 23, 2013. http://www.arabnews.com/news/455890 (accessed July 11, 2013).

[72] Internnational Labor Organization, "ILO Highlights Global Challenge to Trade Unions." Last modified November 04, 1997. Accessed July 11, 2013. http://www.ilo.org/global/about-the-ilo/newsroom/news/WCMS_008032/lang--en/index.htm.

[73] Naglaa El-Ehwany and Menal Metwally. ERF Working Paper Series, "Labor Market Competitiveness and Flexibility." Last modified August 1998. Accessed July 11, 2013. http://www.erf.org.eg/CMS/uploads/pdf/0129_ElEhwany.pdf.

[74] Figure from 2003: Michael J. Morley, Patrick Gunnigle, and David Collings, *Global Industrial Relations*, (New York: Routledge, 2006), pg. 184. Figure from 2011: Abdalla, "Egypt's Workers – From Protest Movement to Organized Labor."

[75] Cam McGrath, "EGYPT: Minimum Wage Not Enough," *Inter Press Service*, February 04, 2010. http://www.ipsnews.net/2010/02/egypt-minimum-wage-not-enough/ (accessed July 12, 2013).

[76] "Egyptians protest over minimum wage." *Al-Jazeera English*, May 03, 2010. http://www.aljazeera.com/news/middleeast/2010/05/201052161957263202.html (accessed July 12, 2013).

[77] The value of the Egyptian pound continued to depreciate, however. By 2011, 1,200 £E was approximately $216 and by 2013 it was a paltry $172.

[78] Sallam, "Striking Back at Egyptian Workers."

[79] Center for Economic and Social Rights, "Visualizing Rights - Fact Sheet Number 10: Egypt." Last modified 2009. Accessed July 12, 2013. http://www.cesr.org/downloads/egypt WEB FINAL.pdf.

[80] Gouda Abdel-Khalek, *Stabilization and Adjustment in Egypt: Reform or De-industrialization*, (Northampton: Edward Elgar Publishing, 2001).

[81] Weekly wages for 1996 calculated using wage and labor force composition data from El-Ehwany and El-Laithy, but 1973 baselines for public and private sector workers found in Posusney.

[82] Prices based on 1986 baseline. USD conversion calculated manually from LE wages provided by "Nominal Wages: CAPMAS, Employment, Wages and Hours of Work, Several Issues" cited in: Naglaa El-Ehwany, and Heba El-Laithy, International Labor Organization, "Poverty, Employment E and Policy-

Making in Egypt." Last modified 2001. Accessed July 12, 2013. http://www1.aucegypt.edu/src/wsite1/Pdfs/ILO-report.pdf.
[83] Rizk, "Egypt and the global economic order."
[84] International Labor Organization estimate cited in: Rania Al Malky, "In Egypt, a fair minimum wage is inevitable," *Daily News Egypt*, April 17, 2010. http://www.masress.com/en/dailynews/64145 (accessed July 12, 2013).
[85] World Bank Estimate: "Population living below $2/day is the percent of the population of a country living on less than $2.15 a day at 1993 international prices, (equivalent to $2 in 1985 prices, adjusted for purchasing power parity). These poverty measures are based on surveys conducted mostly between 1994 and 1999, prepared by the World Bank's Development Research Group. The international poverty lines are based on nationally representative primary household surveys conducted by national statistical offices or by private agencies under the supervision of government or international agencies and obtained from government statistical offices and World Bank country departments."
[86] Ironically, the wealth gap is smaller in Egypt than in the United States, which has one of the most unequal distributions of wealth in the world.
[87] Other estimates place this figure higher, at 11.3%. See: Kienle, "More than a Response to Islamism."
[88] Samir Radwan, International Labor Organization, "Economic and Social Impact of the Financial and Economic Crisis on Egypt." Last modified April 2009. Accessed July 12, 2013. http://www.ilo.org/public/libdoc/ilo/2009/109B09_268_engl.pdf.
[89] "Egypt Crisis Stirs Concern for World Economy." *CBS*, January 31, 2011. http://www.cbsnews.com/stories/2011/01/31/business/main7302094.shtml (accessed July 12, 2013).
[90] Ahmad El-Sayed El-Nagar, "Economic Policy: From State Control to Decay and Corruption," in Rabab El-Mahdi, and Philip Marfleet, *Egypt: the Moment of Change*, (Zed Books, 2009).
[91] Radwan, International Labor Organization, "Economic and Social Impact of the Financial and Economic Crisis on Egypt."
[92] "Research: Broad-based Youth Programs Needed." *The World Bank*, January 15, 2011. http://arabworld.worldbank.org/content/awi/en/home/featured/youth_programs.html (accessed July 12, 2013).
[93] Beinin and El-Hamalawy, "Egyptian Textile Workers Confront the New Economic Order."
[94] U.S. Embassy in Cairo. New York Times, "A Selection From the Cache of Diplomatic Dispatches - Domestic Troubles (CAIRO 002933)," Dated May 16, 2006.
[95] U.S. Embassy in Cairo. New York Times, "A Selection From the Cache of Diplomatic Dispatches - Portrait of the Intelligence Chief (CAIRO 000119)," Dated January 23, 2009. Accessed July 10, 2013. http://www.nytimes.com/interactive/2010/11/28/world/20101128-cables-

viewer.html?_r=0#report/egypt-09CAIRO119

[96] Beinin, "The Rise of Egypt's Workers."

[97] For a brief overview of this, see: Sarah Sabry, Center for Development Policy and Research, "Could Urban Poverty in Egypt Be Grossly Underestimated?." Last modified May 2010. Accessed July 12, 2013. http://www.soas.ac.uk/cdpr/publications/dv/file58993.pdf. For a more detailed analysis, see here: Sarah Sabry, International Institute for Environment and Development, "Poverty lines in Greater Cairo: Underestimating and Misrepresenting Poverty." Last modified 2009. Accessed July 12, 2013. http://pubs.iied.org/pdfs/10572IIED.pdf.

[98] Center for Economic and Social Rights, "Visualizing Rights - Fact Sheet Number 10: Egypt."

[99] Juan Kornblihtt and Bruno Magro, 2011, "El norte de África en el epicentro de la crisis mundial", *El Aromo*, 59 (March-April, 2011). Accessed July 13, 2013, www.razonyrevolucion.org/ryr/index.php?option=com_content&view=article&id=1395%3Ael-norte-de-africa-en-el-epicentro-de-la-crisis-mundial

[100] Sangheon Lee, Deirdre McCann, and John C. Messenger. International Labor Organization, "Working Time Around the World: Trends in Working Hours, Laws, and Policies in a Global Comparative Perspective ." http://www.ilo.org/wcmsp5/groups/public/@dgreports/@dcomm/@publ/documents/publication/wcms_104895.pdf.

[101] Michel Chossudovsky, "Tunisia, the IMF, and Worldwide Poverty", *Pacific Free Press* (23 January, 2011), www.pacificfreepress.com/news/1/7854-tunisia-the-imf-and-worldwide-poverty.html

[102] Hanieh, "Egypt's Uprising."

[103] U.S. Embassy in Cairo. Wikileaks, "Mubarak's Visit to Washington (CAIRO 000874)." Dated May 19, 2009.

[104] Osman, "Egypt: a diagnosis."

[105] Rizk, "Egypt and the global economic order."

[106] Sallam, "Striking Back at Egyptian Workers." Sallam cites Ahmed Zewail, "Reflections on Arab Renaissance," Cairo Review of Global Affairs (Spring 2011) and Al-Ahram, September 21, 2011, for these figures.

[107] Osman, "Egypt: a diagnosis."

[108] El-Sayed Gamal El-Din, "Egypt's Mubarak family fortune estimated at $1.3 bn," *Ahram Online*, June 21, 2011. http://english.ahram.org.eg/NewsContent/3/12/74599/Business/Economy/Egypts-Mubarak-family-fortune-estimated-at--bn.aspx (accessed July 13, 2013).

[109] Susanna Kim, "Egypt's Mubarak Likely to Retain Vast Wealth," *ACB News*, February 02, 2011. http://abcnews.go.com/Business/egypt-mubarak-family-accumulated-wealth-days-military/storynew?id=12821073

[110] Figures ranging from $8 to $18 are quoted in Armbrust, "Egypt: A revolution against neoliberalism?" Yet, these figures seem rather high. Forbes listed six Egyptian billionaires as of 2013: "Forbes list Egypt's top 6 billionaires," *Ahram Online*, March 5, 2013,

http://english.ahram.org.eg/NewsContent/3/12/66192/Business/Economy/Forbes-list-Egypts-top--billionaires.aspx.

[111] Marsha Pripstein Posusney, *Labor and the State in Egypt: Workers, Unions, and Economic Restructuring*. New York: Columbia University Press, 1997, pg. 50 and 131.

[112] Marsha Pripstein Posusney, *Labor and the State in Egypt: Workers, Unions, and Economic Restructuring*. New York: Columbia University Press, 1997, pg. 50 and 131 and Naglaa El-Ehwany, and Heba El-Laithy, International Labor Organization, "Poverty, Employment E and Policy-Making in Egypt." Last modified 2001. Accessed July 12, 2013. Weekly wages for 1996 calculated using wage and labor force composition data from El-Ehwany and El-Laithy, but 1973 baselines for public and private sector workers found in Posusney.

3

Egypt as U.S. Client State

With massive protests of millions of people erupting all across Egypt, Obama still could not utter the words that Mubarak ought to step down. Even as Hilary Clinton's "family friend"[1] and his regime orchestrated violence against demonstrators by hiring thugs and using civilian clothed state police to attack pro-democracy demonstrators, the Obama administration did not forcefully condemn Mubarak or call on him to resign. Instead, the State Department simply urged both sides to show restraint and politely suggested the Mubarak regime enact reforms in a timely manner. David Cameron's government in Britain urged "evolution...not revolution" and declared that Mubarak was "a friend of Britain" who "worked together" with him on many issues, not the least of which was to "combat Islamic extremism."[2] Tony Blair made clear to the world that there should be "no rush to elections in Egypt" and detailed how Mubarak was "immensely courageous and a force for good." After all, "where you stand on him depends on whether you've worked with him from the outside or the inside."[3] Prime Minister of Israel Benjamin Netanyahu compared the Egyptian revolution to Iran in 1979 and warned of an "autocratic, fundamentalist, Islamic organisation taking over," claiming that such a scenario is "not something we can ignore." Chief political correspondent for the Jerusalem Post Gil Hoffman emphasized this was the case since "the Israeli army has not budgeted anything over the last 30 years for dealing with a strategic threat from Egypt."[4] Apparently, for such benevolent and high-minded idealists within the US, Britain, and Israel, an autocratic, authoritarian regime is fine just so long as it aligns itself with the strategic interests of world empire. There exists no greater example of the profound hatred for democracy held by first world elites than the position they took until the midnight hour of the Mubarak regime.

Egypt's Unique Position in the Imperial Power Structure

These imperial justifications for the Mubarak regime were not the result of some commitment to non-violent change or high-minded idealism about reformist prospects. Such wishful thinking has been proven inadequate time and again, witnessed most glaringly by the Obama administration's actions in the region, including: the violent war waged against the people of Afghanistan, the continuing drone strikes that cause immense civilian suffering in the region, the promise of $30 billion in military aid over the next decade to the militaristic state of Israel, and the $60 billion arms deal with Saudi Arabia, one of the most internally repressive societies in the world. European leaders were no better, their old imperial ambitions stirring as soon as the opportunity presented itself in Libya and Syria, clamoring to provide weapons, training, and outright intervention to topple regimes they found inimical to their interests.

In this respect, as Noam Chomsky points out, Obama follows a long line of continuity with regard to US policy both in the region and the world:

> The United States, so far, is essentially following the usual playbook. There have been many times when some favored dictator has lost control or is in danger of losing control. There is kind of a standard routine: Marcos [Phillipines], Duvalier [Haiti], Ceauşescu [Romania], strongly supported by the United States and Britain, Suharto [Indonesia], keep supporting them as long as possible. Then, when it becomes unsustainable, typically say if the army shifts sides, switch 180 degrees, claim to have been on the side of the people all along, erase the past, and then make whatever moves are possible to restore the old system under new names.[5]

This is not an aberration from an otherwise democratic and principled US foreign policy. Instead, it is a direct extension of the imperial ambitions of US state planners.

For the purpose of placing Egypt within a theoretical context of imperialism, a functional definition of imperialism can be borrowed from the political scientist Michael Parenti. A scholar whose work focuses on modern empire, he defines imperialism as "the process whereby the dominant politico-economic interests of one nation expropriate for their own enrichment the land, labor, raw materials, and markets of another people." He notes that while imperialism predates capitalism, capitalist imperialism "differs from these earlier forms in the way it systematically accumulates capital through the organized exploitation of labor and the penetration of overseas markets." As the "central imperative of capitalism is expansion," it is implied that the driving feature of imperialism in the modern age is capitalist in nature. [6] He argues that "empires do not just pursue power for power's sake," as an end in and of itself, but rather there are "real interests at stake, fortunes to be made many times over."[7] Proponents of imperialism, specifically US imperialism, articulated this new imperial program as a form of "benevolent supremacy," what Deepa Kumar characterizes as an "American-dominated world" which would ostensibly "ensure liberty and democracy for all through the mechanism of free-market capitalism," with the latter being the most important element of the three.[8] Sydney Lens argues that the Washington strategy for the third world was to "establish the open door and multinational trade as the pillars of economic policy," to "weaken, isolate, and set back those political forces that arrayed themselves against this open door," especially radical nationalists and Communists, and to "gain, in Kennedy's words, 'influence and control' over pliable governments – mostly rightist – through… grants and loans with conditions attached to them, military aid, equipment and training of puppet armies, military pacts, CIA-sponsored revolts, and on occasion, when these other methods were inadequate… direct intervention by US armed forces."[9] These were the methods by which, as Parenti explains, "the dominant investor interests in one country bring to bear military and financial power upon another country in order to expropriate the land, labor, capital, natural resources, commerce, and markets of that other country."[10]

Democracy is useful only insofar as it aligns with the larger imperial project. Strategic geopolitical interests in the Middle East dictate that US foreign policy must be aimed primarily at keeping the oil-rich Gulf States, and by extension the production and distribution of oil, under US sway instead of the influence of competitive states like China. Adam Hanieh from the School of Oriental and African Studies articulates this dynamic well:

> This should not be interpreted as meaning that the U.S. wants to directly own these oil supplies (although this may be part of this process), but that the U.S. wants to ensure that the oil supplies remain outside of the democratic control of the people of the region. The nature of global capitalism and the dominant position of the U.S. state within the world market rest significantly upon its control over the Gulf region. Any move toward a broader democratic transformation of the region could potentially

threaten U.S. power at a global level. This is why the U.S. so strongly supports the dictatorships that rule the Gulf states and also why the majority of the labour in the Gulf is performed by temporary, migrant workers who lack all citizenship rights and can be deported at any sign of discontent.[11]

Obama's ambivalence towards democracy in Egypt stems from Egypt's primary role as a US client state in the Middle East. US officials tried desperately to play their cards right, balancing international public support for the Egyptian struggle with their decades-long support for military dictatorship in Egypt. Indeed, as far back as 1958, a National Security Council document argued that in any case where US-proxies could not be maintained, the US should "seek to guide the revolutionary and nationalistic pressures throughout the area into orderly channels which will not be antagonistic to the West."[12] This policy trajectory continued through the decades, culminating in the Obama administration's policy in Egypt vis-à-vis the events of 2011 and after.

Egypt, aside from Israel, was the largest recipient of US military aid in the world. Colombia, another internally repressive society, comes in as a close third. Yet, it is this prodigious sum of US military and economic aid that propped up an unpopular Mubarak regime for decades. The sheer amount of US aid provided to Egypt cannot be understated, with some $1.3 billion a year in military aid coupled with economic assistance ranging anywhere from $250 to $815 million annually since 1979. In the period from 1975, just two years after Sadat announced *Infitah*, until 1997, total US aid amounted to a staggering $44.7 billion. This ramping up of aid, particularly military aid, ran concurrent with Sadat's opening up of Egypt's economy and his acquiescence to Israel. Another $26 billion was given to Egypt from 1998 to 2011, bringing the total contribution to the Sadat-Mubarak regimes from US taxpayers to a stunning $70.7 billion since the mid-1970s. Compare this to the entirety of the 28-year period from 1946 to 1974, where less than $1 billion aid was given total, amounting to an annual average of $32 million.[13] During the same period in which US aid was heavily augmented, a narrow group of Egyptians became obscenely wealthy, especially the Mubarak family and others in the ruling National Democratic Party. In contrast, conditions for the majority of Egyptians declined precipitously into a state of complete despondence.

This support served a dual purpose, however. Not only did it cement US hegemony in the region, it also acted to subsidize large and powerful military-industrial interests. As William Hartung explains:

It's a form of corporate welfare for companies like Lockheed Martin and General Dynamics, because it goes to Egypt, then it comes back for F-16 aircraft, for M1 tanks, for aircraft engines, for all kinds of missiles, for guns, for tear gas canisters... Lockheed Martin has been the leader in deals worth $3.8 billion over that period of the last 10 years; General Dynamics, $2.5 billion for tanks; Boeing, $1.7 billion for missiles, for helicopters; Raytheon for all manner of missiles for the armed forces. So, basically, this is a key element in propping up the regime, but a lot of the money... is basically recycled. Taxpayers could just as easily be giving it directly to Lockheed Martin or General Dynamics.[14]

Throughout the uprising, numerous accounts were circulated of protesters finding tear gas canisters, used by police to disperse the popular movement, with the label "Made in the U.S.A." printed across the bottom. In January 2011, after the outbreak of the uprising, a leaked letter between the Interior and Defense ministries confirmed that the US agreed to ship 140,000 tear-gas canisters to Egypt to "deal with rioters," with the caveat that both the company and country of origin would be stripped from the labels.[15] During the height of the uprising, US supplied F-16 fighter jets flew dangerously low to protestors in an attempt to scare off the crowds, with people roaring defiantly back against sound of the jets. The United States was a principal proponent of the Mubarak regime and helped it stay in power for as long as it did through its continual contribution to the repressive military machine.

Egypt was not supported simply because it happened to be a cruel, autocratic regime. It was supported partially because Sadat and Mubarak won the bid to become the quintessential neoliberal client state in the Middle East. As such, Egypt was successfully repositioned within and as an ally of the international capitalist order. An even more vital precursor for US support has been the willingness of the Egyptian ruling class to capitulate to US military demands. Egypt, Israel, and Saudi Arabia come together to form a triangle through which the US continues to exercise hegemony over the Middle East. After Sadat incorporated Egypt into the US sphere of influence, Mubarak forcefully continued the trend in four key ways: (1) buttressing the imperial ambitions of the Bush administration, manifested most clearly in the Iraq invasion as he opened up Egyptian airspace for US use and allowed free passage for US Navy ships through the Suez Canal; (2) utilizing Egyptian state security to gather intelligence on Islamist groups; (3) engaging in the "extraordinary rendition" program that allowed US officials to carry out torture in Egyptian prisons; and (4) strengthening the crippling blockade against the Palestinians in Gaza, despite some tepid pro-Palestinian rhetorical flares. For all of this, the payoff was an annual $1.3 billion in US military aid and more in economic aid, alongside ideological support and political legitimacy in the eyes of US elites.

All of these positions were in sharp contrast to the will not only of Egyptians but to the Arab population as a whole. A comprehensive poll conducted by the University of Maryland and Zogby International concluded that Arabs were not ignorant to the aims of US foreign policy. When asked to identify the two most important US policy goals in the Middle East, 49% of respondents said it was to protect Israel, 44% to control oil resources, and 33% to preserve regional and global dominance. A phenomenal 5% of Arabs aligned with US rhetoric that spreading democracy was most important, while a whopping 6% thought US officials were concerned with human rights. When Arabs were asked which two countries were the greatest threats to their security, 88% responded Israel and 77% the United States.[16] The Pew Research Center found that in 2010 only 17% of Egyptians, as well as the same number of Pakistanis and Turks, held the US in a positive light. This was down from 30% in 2006.[17] Another Pew Research Center poll taken in 2011, two months after the downfall of Mubarak, had 54% of respondents calling for the annulment of the euphemistically-phrased "peace" treaty with Israel. Only 36% favored maintaining the treaty.[18] These staggering results show enormous Arab disdain for US policies.[19] Furthermore, this sharp divide between Arab public opinion and policy suggest that the Arab monarchs and dictators, as well as their US overlords, care little for how the majority of their citizens think or feel. After all, Arab opinion was of relatively little importance as long as dissent could be properly managed or subdued through coercion and violence. Indeed, as early as 1958, a National Security Council document noted that "In the eyes of the majority of Arabs the United States appears to be opposed to the realization of the goals of Arab nationalism... [and] is seeking to protect its interest in Near East oil by supporting the status quo and opposing political or economic progress."[20]

Egypt's Historic Role in the Colonial and Post World War II Order

Egypt has always been an important cog in the imperialist machine. The first unsuccessful attempt to colonize Egypt came from the French in 1798 and lasted until 1801. Although European influence was always present, it was contested and never absolute during most of the 19th century. It was not until 1882 that the British would become the dominant colonial power in Egypt, both to protect a source of raw materials, in this case cotton, and to maintain control over the Suez Canal. As US power grew in the interwar period and eclipsed the old Western European powers after World War II, control of the Middle East became imperative for US policy makers. In 1943, referencing the enormous oil reserves in Saudi Arabia, President Roosevelt issued an executive order declaring that "the defense of Saudi Arabia [is] vital to the defense of the United States."[21] In 1944, Roosevelt noted in a memo that "the Middle East is an area in which the United States has a vital interest."[22] In 1945 Chief of the Division of Near Eastern Affairs in the US State Department, Gordon Merriam, wrote in a memo to President Truman that Saudi oil resources "constitute a stupendous source of strategic power, and one of the greatest material prizes in world history."[23] The US, positioning itself as world superpower after World War II, recognized in a State Department document that in the immediate post-war period that while "the security of the Eastern Mediterranean and Middle East... is vital to the security of the United States," US "security" depended upon the "strong strategic, political, and economic position" of Britain in the region.[24]

While the US would eventually supersede Britain as the dominant imperial power, playing a more active role in the late 1950s and early 1960s as Soviet influence also expanded, it originally relied upon the colonial infrastructure already established by Britain during the post-war transition period. After the direct colonial power of the old European states waned, one of the primary methods for the US to maintain control was to develop strong regional proxies through which US ruling interests would be secured. While the US attempted to court Nasser and the Free Officers early on, by the mid-1950s it was evident that local social pressures and Nasser's desire to not become dependent upon US aid made the desired US-proxy relationship improbable. State Department documents dated from 1956 acknowledged that "there seems little likelihood the US will be able to work with Nasser in the foreseeable future," citing the leader's pursuance of policies "opposed to reasonable US objectives."[25] The State Department noted that while Nasser rejected US hegemony, he did not submit to Soviet rule either. The document summarized Nasser as a leader who desired "a more ambitious" role as a "third force," which would "be as inimical to the interests of the West as those of the Kremlin."[26] In other words, independence, even without a Communist pretext, could not be tolerated. It would not be until after Nasser's death that the US could secure a stable client relationship with his successors.

Israel and Egypt: Primary and Secondary Sources of Regional Hegemony

While Egypt's role is vital, corrupt Arab client states like Mubarak's only provide an ancillary source of US control in the region. The primary vehicle through which the US is able to maintain hegemony is through its relationship with Israel. Maxime Rodinson, a Jewish French Marxist, accurately characterized Israel as a "colonial settler state"[27] whose existence and perpetuation had historically been facilitated by various imperial powers. As such, one of Israel's principal geopolitical functions today is to serve US interests in the Middle East and North Africa. In turn, the US-Egypt relationship must be seen through the lens of the U.S reliance on Israel as its watchdog in the region. Both relationships, however, are predicated upon the imperial dominance of the United States:

> All other relations between the U.S. and other countries in the region are subordinated and linked to this goal of U.S. hegemony over the Gulf region. This includes the U.S.-Israel relationship (which is why any talk of an 'Israel lobby' controlling U.S. foreign policy is nonsense). The U.S. sees Israel as a key pillar of its overall Middle East policy: it is an ally that is fully dependent upon U.S. military and political support and can always be relied upon to act against the interests of the Arab masses. Precisely because Israel has its origins as a settler-colonial state founded upon the dispossession of the Palestinian people, it is seen as a more stable and steadfast pillar of U.S. power than any of the Arab dictatorships that are exposed to threat of popular revolt. This is why the interests of Israel and the Arab dictatorships are coincident, not opposed to one another – as was so clearly illustrated in the recent uprisings of both Tunisia and Egypt.[28]

The blatant disregard of Arab opinion and suppression of their interests, a phenomenon which extends back decades, exists not only as a trend among US rulers but also their Arab corollaries.

In Egypt, this trend has been particularly pertinent. Beginning with Sadat, the Egyptian ruling class tried desperately to break with Nasser-style pan-Arabism. Secular Arab nationalism was a threat because it, whatever its flaws or internal contradictions, charted a path independent of the imperial powers. Solidarity amongst all Arabs, especially support for the Palestinian liberation struggles, was to become an object of scorn:

> …as Sadat attempted to consolidate his power, he reacted by unleashing a vicious anti-Arab campaign reasserting that Egypt's primary identity is "Pharaonic." A whole period of rejecting Arabism and scapegoating the Palestinians for

Egypt's wars and poverty was led by the state-run media and permeated public culture.[29]

All of this was meant to serve as the much-needed ideological cover for Sadat's capitulation and eventual subordination to Israel and the United States, a victory garnered only through a series of military defeats laid upon Egypt by Israel.

Egyptian-Israeli wars were commonplace prior to the Camp David Accords of 1979. All but one of these were wars of aggression perpetrated by Israel against its neighbors, with the final war an attempt by Egypt and Syria to reclaim the land stolen from them in the previous wars. Egypt first became involved in the 1948 Arab-Israeli war, what the Israeli's euphemistically title "The War of Independence" and what the Palestinians refer to as *al-Nakba*, or "the Catastrophe." Some 10,000 to 20,000 thousand Egyptians soldiers fought against the Zionist colonizers in Palestine, with perhaps 2,000 being killed by forces later to become the Israeli military. At the same time, some 700,000 or more Palestinians were forcefully expelled from over 500 villages and towns to make way for the establishment of the state of Israel.[30]

In July 1956, Nasser announced to the Egyptian masses his plans to nationalize the Suez Canal, a widely popular gesture that earned him enormous respect in Egypt and the Arab world. The French compared the nationalization to Hitler's seizure of the Rhineland, and the British cabled President Eisenhower emphatically proclaiming their readiness to "use force to bring Nasser to his senses."[31] A special national intelligence document warned of the impending consequences of the Suez nationalism: "Nasser's action has strengthened anti-Western, anti-colonial, and nationalist trends throughout the area, and if successful, will encourage future moves toward early nationalization or other action against foreign-owned oil pipelines and petroleum facilities."[32] Three months later, Britain, France, and Israel attacked Egypt in a devastating show of force known as the 2nd Arab-Israeli War or, more accurately, the Tripartite Aggression. In one day they obliterated 200 planes from Egypt's air force. By the end of the tripartite invasion, thousands of Egyptian soldiers and around 1,000 civilians had been killed.

The first schism within the British-US imperial partnership occurred during this period. President Eisenhower declared in a National Security Council meeting, "How could we possibly support Britain and France if in doing so we lose the whole Arab world?"[33] Eisenhower was furious that the British would act without his blessing given the new role of the US at the vanguard of world empire. Britain and other European powers in the post-World War II era were meant to be subordinate to US leadership. That Britain attempted to act independently to enforce its imperial hegemony was not acceptable. Ironically, the interests of the two competing world powers, the US and USSR, converged as both pressured the Euro-Israeli forces to withdraw. This signified the first shift towards complete US hegemony of the region, with Britain and France turning from their historic roles as primary colonizers to ancillary imperialists. Indeed, President Eisenhower noted in December of 1956 that the US had "no intention of standing idly by" in the face of "Communist penetration and success in the Mid East." Secretary Dulles echoed this statement, explaining that the US intended "to make our presence more strongly felt in the Middle East."[34] Thus, the Eisenhower Doctrine came into existence, which stipulated the dispersal of both large scale economic assistance and the commitment of armed forces to "defend any country" against "international communism."

This "presence" mentioned by Eisenhower was buttressed by the increasingly close US-Israeli relationship. In 1958, despite the ambivalence towards the independent tripartite escapade during the Suez Crisis, a National Security Council document recommended that the US must "be prepared" to use force in order "to reconcile vital Free World interests in the area's petroleum resources with the rising tide of nationalism in the area."[35] This force was often carried out by Israel on behalf or in conjunction with the interests of the US. In 1967, Israel once again launched a surprise attack, the 3rd Arab-Israeli War, in which they raided and destroyed hundreds of Egypt's aircraft. Israeli forces killed between 10,000 and 15,000 Egyptians, as well as thousands more Jordanian and Syrian soldiers. Israel also took control of the West Bank from Jordan, the Golan Heights from Syria, and both the Gaza Strip and the Sinai Peninsula from Egypt.

One of the most prophetic quotes from Nasser came from his conversations directly after the 1967 debacle with Leonid Brezhnev, leader of the USSR from 1964 to 1982. At one point, Nasser threatened to resign, and emphatically explained to Brezhnev that "I have the courage to tell our people the unfortunate truth – that whether they like it or not, the Americans are masters of the world. I am not going to be the one who surrenders to the Americans. Someone else will come in my place who will have to do it."[36] Near the end of Nasser's rule, the economic gains made through the 1950s and early 1960s began to stagnate, the Egyptian military had been smashed by Israel, and his prized attempt at Arab Unity via the United Arab Republic, a short-lived merger of Egypt and Syria, had failed. Nasser's desire for "someone else to come" was granted when he died unexpectedly of a heart attack in 1970, right after leaving an Arab Summit conference organized to negotiate a ceasefire between Yasser Arafat's Palestine Liberation Organization and King Hussein of Jordan. Nasser foreshadowed Sadat's capitulation to the United States. It was only after the

1973 war that Sadat introduced his *Infitah* policy, welcoming private foreign capital into Egypt.

From its inception to when Nasser died in 1970, Israel had expelled hundreds of thousands of indigenous Palestinian inhabitants, stole 78% of their land, occupied the remaining 22%, and began three wars against its neighbors with European and US support. It was in this context that the 4th Arab-Israeli War of 1973 began, with Egypt and Syria leading an attack on Israeli controlled positions in the Sinai Peninsula and the Golan Heights. Both Egypt and Syria believed they could win back the land stolen from them in 1967. Although Israel suffered some crushing defeats early on, the only ones up until that point in its history, eventually Egypt and Syria proved incapable of winning back any significant territory. After only securing a partial military victory against Israel in 1973, the then-president Sadat eventually traveled to Jerusalem for the 1978 Camp David Accords, culminating in a peace treaty signed in 1979. Although the treaty granted Egypt back the Sinai Peninsula, land stolen from it in 1967, it also normalized relations with Israel, the first time an Arab country had recognized Israel's legitimacy. Thus, Egypt's first partial victory against Israel actually led to a treaty which was primarily designed to guarantee the isolation and elimination of the Palestine Liberation Organization, a goal Israel had long sought. Obviously, this was viewed as an act of betrayal by the Palestinians, and did much to codify both Sadat's and Mubarak's allegiance to the US and Israel.[37] This, alongside Sadat's repression of Islamist groups inside Egypt, was a driving factor of his assassination in 1981. While Egypt remained rhetorically committed to "peace" for the Palestinian population, this rhetoric had very little effect on its foreign policy. Sadat, who had already begun to roll back the few progressive gains of the Nasser-era, fully aligned himself with US imperialism, a calculated move to maintain power at home.

"Normalizing" Relations with Israel as a Means of Securing Hegemony

Israel's successful battering of Egypt in 1956 and 1967, coupled with Egypt's inability to win back its land in 1973, proved enough to cement Sadat fully into the US orbit. Israel exists both to help maintain the capitalist economic order, with the US at its head, and also to strengthen the system of imperialism which allows the US to maintain its hegemonic position. Therefore, one of the key facets of US-imposed neoliberalism via Arab client regimes has been to "normalize" relations between the Arab states and Israel.

One mechanism of doing this is instituting "free trade agreements" that secure Israel by forcing countries to trade with it. Within these free trade agreements, which have played an important role in Egypt and many other states in the region, the US has included as a precondition the stipulation that regimes must lift any boycott against Israel. In the case of Egypt, there is an added twist, as the agreements also include what they refer to as Qualified Industrial Zones (QIZs), which provide tariff free access to the US market for Egyptian exports. In such zones the US has included a provision that in order to qualify roughly 12% of imports brought into these zones must be Israeli. QIZ exports grew 57% annually between 2005 to 2008 and some 770 companies operated in these zones in 2009. This has served to force the integration of Israel into the Arab economic sphere and simultaneously coerce Arab states to subsidize the Israeli economy and augment their growth by providing a reliant, permanent market for Israeli exports.[38]

On top of these QIZs, the Mubarak regime extended yet another handout to the state of Israel. In 2005, Egypt agreed to a scheme whereby it would extract and sell natural gas to Israel at subsidized prices well below market rates. Israel, which relies on natural gas to generate 40-45% of its electricity, was receiving two-fifths of its natural gas supplies from Egypt. By 2014 Israel was slated to become fully dependent upon Egyptian natural gas, at which time its own natural gas resources would be depleted. As the Jerusalem Center for Public Affairs points out:

> Israel hoped that this dependence could be rendered safe by anchoring it to the vital national interests of the Egyptian economy and to the personal interests of its elites. By helping the fortunes of Egypt's business and ruling elite and providing a source of revenue to the Egyptian state – thus locking it in to a fiscal dependence – the gas trade could bring meaningful substance to the idea of "normalization"... Indeed, the Egyptian-Israeli natural gas trade was the culminating, and only now understood to be final, act in the attempt to solidify Egyptian-Israeli relations (and financially shore up the Egyptian government and its elites) through trade.[39]

Hussein Salem, the sponsor of this scheme and cohort of Gamal Mubarak, received enormous kickbacks from the natural gas sales. By the time that Mubarak was overthrown in 2011, the gas scheme had cost Egypt an estimated $500 million.[40] The level of subservience reached such an absurd high that Egypt, a few months before the 2011 uprising began, considered buying back 1.5 billion cubic meters of natural gas for $14 billion, seven times the $2 billion price tag Israel purchased it at.[41] While market prices for natural gas fluctuated anywhere from $4 per million BTUs in the United

States to $14 per million BTUs in Japan,[42] Egypt was providing Israel one million BTUs at a paltry $1.50, well below market prices. [43] The depth of the imperial influence was such that Egypt was subsidizing gas prices for a country with a gross national income fourteen times that of its own.

Despite economic links such as the QIZs and the gas-giveaway scheme, the US State Department was still tentative about praising how tightly these relations had been woven. In a May 2009 US State Department memo, officials report that Egypt's continued "peace" with Israel has "cemented its moderate role in Middle East peace efforts and provided a political basis for continued US military and economic assistance ($1.3 billion and $250 million, respectively)." Yet, it warned that "broader elements of peace with Israel, e.g. economic and cultural exchange, remain essentially undeveloped."[44] While the US and Israel could force geopolitical settlements against the will of the Egyptian population via the country's proxy status, they could not as easily force "economic and cultural exchange." However, with Mubarak having his hands on the levers of state power, including the all-important military apparatus, the imperial powers could utilize Egypt as a pliant and useful tool towards maintaining hegemony in the region.

Egypt's Imperial Functions under Mubarak

According to US State Department planners, Mubarak played an "an indispensable role on Israel/Palestine and Sudan, while helping also on Iraq, Syria, and Lebanon."[45] The primary importance of the US-Egyptian relationship, second only to the US-Israeli relationship, was its role in sustaining the US imperial project in the region. This was especially paramount with regard to Persian Gulf energy resources and the Suez Canal. The former provides an enormous segment of the base upon which both the US economy and military strength rest, while the latter serves as a singularly important international oil route and provides crucial passage for US warships.

This role goes back decades. In the 1990-91 Persian Gulf War, Mubarak played an integral role in assembling the military force deployed to protect Saudi Arabia and Kuwait. Egypt supplied 35,000 troops to the international force, almost 15% of the 250,000 deployed by the US. The Egyptian contingent was one of the largest, alongside the US, the UK, and Saudi Arabia. Mubarak enthusiastically embraced the "new world order" which President Bush Sr. promised would be the outcome of the operations. In return, the US pressured the World Bank to forgive $14 million in Egyptian loans.[46]

Since then, Mubarak attempted to play the role of imperial puppet, straddling the demands of his overlords while placating his domestic population where he could and repressing them where he could not. In 2003, while outwardly denouncing the invasion and occupation of Iraq as folly, Mubarak willingly opened up Egyptian airspace for US use and allowed free passage for US warships through the Suez Canal, despite overwhelming pressure from the Egyptian population to provide no support whatsoever. The primary reason for this reluctance to engage Iraq in the same way as 1990-91, however, can be partially attributed to the revival of popular protest during the buildup to the war. There was an additional concern on Mubarak's part, however. Namely, Egypt had maintained, both before and after the 1st Gulf War, substantial economic ties to the Gulf region, especially as Egyptian workers left to labor abroad. Egypt itself engaged in trade with Iraq worth some $2.5 billion annually as late as 2002 and any regional war would disrupt not only this trade, but tourism and Suez Canal traffic as well, both extremely important variables in the Egyptian economy.[47] In contrast, the invasion of Kuwait by Iraq in the 1st Gulf War had meant that regional war had already begun, and Mubarak was interested in looking for a way to end it as quickly as possible. Mubarak in 2003 hoped to provide as little support as it could for the US occupation without engaging in an outright refusal that would threaten its economic or military aid. This apparent change of heart from a decade earlier can be explained by both the economic pressures a war with Iraq would cause and the new forms of domestic unrest erupting from Egyptians against any potential Egyptian involvement in the war.

Egypt made use of its state security apparatus to gather intelligence on Islamist groups, moderate or radical, which in any way challenged US hegemony in the region. A series of memos detailing US officials' meetings with then chief of the Egyptian General Intelligence Service, Omar Suleiman, adumbrate Suleiman's chief concerns. The primary fear outlined is Suleiman's insistence that "radicalism was the 'backbone' of regional security threats."[48] The intelligence chief noted his anxiety regarding Hamas in Gaza, the Sudanese conflict, Somali pirates, and the threat of Iran. All of them in his view presented a threat to Egyptian security and, by extension, US control over the region. A 2009 memo explains that "Egypt's own successful campaign against radicalism in the 1990s provided a useful lesson in how to counteract extremist groups by reducing their ability to operate and raise funds" and acknowledged that only the Muslim Brotherhood remained, even though the "Egyptian government continued to 'make it difficult' for them to operate."[49] As Eberhard Kienle notes, however:

> Since the early 1990s, Egypt has experienced a substantial degree of political deliberalization which defies the notion of a blocked transition to democracy. Repressive amendments to the penal code and to legislation governing

professional syndicates and trade unions as well as unprecedented electoral fraud are only some of the indicators. Though related to the conflict between the regime and armed Islamist groups, the erosion of political participation and liberties also reflects other factors, including attempts to contain opposition to economic liberalization under the current reform program.[50]

This "backbone of regional security threats," Islamist radicalism, was used as a pretext to clamp down on political and economic dissent of any form. As Kienle argues, "political deliberalization was the immediate corollary of reforms that were meant to enhance property rights, increase private sector growth, and otherwise liberalize the economy."[51] While the regime's engagement with Islamists groups became decidedly more intense and violent, with Islamist responses echoing the state violence through their own mechanisms, the Islamist "security threat" does not fully explain the attack on political freedoms. Instead, "the restrictive measures imposed by the regime were either partly or primarily intended to prevent the losers from the crisis and the reforms from opposing the new economic policies,"[52] an economic model largely imposed on Egypt through various imperial machinations. Thus, the Islamist pretext was used in large part to clamp down on civil liberties for all Egyptians, including trade unions and political groups or organizations opposed to the neoliberal reforms.

While the Egyptian regime continued to feed information on various Islamist organizations to the US throughout the 1990s and 2000s, one of the ways the Egyptian ruling clique was most heavily involved in the imperial crimes of the US was its involvement in then President Bush's "extraordinary rendition" program. Suleiman, as chief of the intelligence agency, was one of the prime figures who facilitated the use of Egyptian prisons for the torture program implemented by Clinton in 1995 and used extensively by Bush during the "War on Terror." Essentially, Clinton's presidential decree allowed the Central Intelligence Agency (CIA) to transfer suspected terrorists to foreign countries, places especially known for their lackadaisical approach to prisoner and human rights, for interrogation. Although they officially requested the prisoners to be treated humanely, it was an unspoken rule that torture would be used extensively to retrieve information. Egypt was a prime choice for those carrying out the "extraordinary rendition" program, and Suleiman was a willing torturer. As Michael Scheuer, CIA veteran and participant in the torture program, recalls:

> When we were searching for Third World countries to interrogate suspects, in order to avoid the complications

associated with the American system, Egypt was the best choice. Egypt is the foremost recipient of foreign aid from the United States, after Israel, and is a strategic ally of the US. In addition, its intelligence apparatus is famed for its proficiency and ferocity, as well as the determination of the Egyptian regime to annihilate radical Islamists, and hundreds of the detainees were Egyptian.[53]

Egyptian intelligence agents would receive questions from their US counterparts, refuse to allow any US agent inside the interrogation, utilize whatever methods they saw fit to retrieve the information, and return whatever answers they received to the US officials. Egypt's English weekly Al-Ahram, counterpart to the Egyptian daily in Arabic, cites a US-based organization called Open Society Justice Initiative which laid out the extent of this program in one report. Their report explains that 54 governments participated in the secret program, using "different methods, including inaugurating secret prisons on their land and the contribution in seizing suspects, transporting them, interrogating them and torturing them as well as providing intelligence information and opening airways to clandestine flights."[54]

Of all the participating governments, Egypt's was one of the most vital to the program. Al-Ahram also cites a Human Rights Watch report which states that, "the American war on terror has rendered Egypt the principal destination for detainees who are transported in secret and without adherence to legal procedures." The report estimated that between 150 and 200 detainees, some from the US itself, were transported to Egypt since the September 11th attack.[55]

Proof of this immense torture system, both for the US rendition program and domestic use by state security, was brought forth in early March when sections of the state security apparatus crumbled. On the same night that celebrations were occurring in Tahrir, hundreds of people gathered around the hated State Security (SS) headquarters in Alexandria. Protesters were demonstrating against the rumor that officers were destroying documents that could have implicated them in acts of torture, brutality, and illegal detention. Not long after the crowd gathered, police attacked the crowd by shooting at them and throwing Molotov cocktails from the balconies. Immediately, in a valiant display of fearlessness, hundreds rushed the building, forcing the military to intervene and detain the state security officers, safely removing them from the building. Word of protestors storming the state security headquarters spread quickly to other cities.

Protesters ran through the building from office to office, securing evidence of state security torture, saving whatever material they could, and even freeing some political prisoners along the way. Within hours photocopies of all sorts of documents appeared online for public dissemination and use. Hossam El-Hamalawy, who had been held and tortured by state security in 2002, posted this powerful minute-by-minute, first-hand account of raids on Cairo state security offices on twitter:

> ...chants continue. We r not leaving till detainees in the torture chambers r released... the army looks helpless. They dont know what to do. But the keep assuring us no documents were burnt... the army is trying to convince us the building is empty of officers and detainees. We r now blocking the road... we now attempting to enter the compound via side gate... there is a group of Zamalek Ultras White Knights[56] too taking part in the protest... a garbage truck was seized with shredded documents... we r in!... we r finding tons of documents but still we can't reach the detention cells... the army is trying to evict us from the compound... we r still running across the compound storming buildings and offices but we cant find the entrance 2 underground cells... we are now in front of a metal gate in the underground garage. We think - we might have found the entrance... we cant find the entrance to cells. Army is now chasing us from building to building... the military police is getting aggressive... many r literally crying. We can't find the interrogation rooms. This is a citadel... military police fired in the air... leaving the compound, heading to the other SS office in Mostafa el Nahass st where i was held in 2002... the SS company still has hundreds of protesters inside, but i am dying to c the other smaller compound where i was held... fuck yeah i still can't believe it... entered the small compound where i was locked. Man, i can't believe it still... I'm back home. AMAZING DAY! I'm still speechless. I've been crying hysterically today. Fuck SS! We made it shabab! Long live the revolution...[57]

One protestor who participated in the Alexandria raid recalled that inside the building was a lavish, tax-funded gym with workout equipment, as well as an enormous amount of shredded documents, destroyed computers and hard-drives, hand cuffs with pins that could be inserted into the flesh, hooks in the ceiling where people were hung, and shock devices.[58] One unnamed police officer explained "There were many methods of torture... Beating and whipping, hanging in the air for long periods of time, cuffing up their hands and legs, using electric sticks and burning their bodies with cigarettes and depriving them of sleep or food."⁵⁹ Haytham Hassan, one of the protestors, explained "We are getting inside, and we are finding the secrets that have haunted us for so many years. This feeling is better than anything that has happened so far."⁶⁰ By the next day thousands of protesters mobilized all over the country to storm other state security "citadels" in a multitude of cities in what became known as Egypt's "Bastille Day." In Nasr City, a neighborhood in Cairo, some 2,500 people stormed the state security headquarters.⁶¹ Not only Alexandria and Cairo, but Giza, Shubra, Zakazeek, Sohag, Aswan, Domyat, Matrouh, and The Sixth of October City all saw similar protests, with some state security officials being removed preemptively by the army.⁶²

Documents containing lists of candidates with the number of votes each candidate would receive provided proof of vote-rigging in recent elections.⁶³ Evidence detailing Egypt's partnership in the rendition program was found as well. The fallout was so prodigious from these leaked documents that immediately the Obama administration phoned Supreme Council governing Egypt to deal with the documents detailing the Egyptian secret police links to the US torture program. Egypt's uniquely important position in this program reflects its importance in the larger US geopolitical sphere of power and influence. This importance was similarly reflected in Egypt's role on the Israel-Palestine front after the Camp David Accords, manifest most importantly in Egypt's role enforcing the Israeli blockade of the Gaza strip.

Mubarak Doing Israel's Bidding

Mubarak played a key geopolitical role for the US throughout his time in office, generally helping to manage public for Israel and the US. This was done through his mediation of various ceasefires after Israel slaughtered civilians, such as in 2008, his very open and public criticisms of Iran, his disruption of the flow of weapons and aid to organizations or governments the US views in contrast to its interests, and a myriad of other issues in the region which he engaged on behalf of his imperial overlords. Still, nothing was quite as striking as Egypt's vicious enforcement of the Israeli blockade on Gaza instituted in 2006. Although Gaza had been under some form of "closure" since the 2000 Intifada, this economic blockade of land, air, and sea was ostensibly meant to rid Hamas of their access to outside weapons, but in reality was used to starve and enervate the 1.5 million resident-prisoners there to a degree previously unknown. Although the blockade was eased slightly after June 2010, for four years the blockade included barring or restricting foods such as lentils and chocolate, household goods and recreational goods such as soccer balls, desperately needed reconstruction materials such as steel, glass, and cement, fuel, fishing and agricultural equipment, and various medical materials. The conditions of the blockade were so severe that at one point Israeli's daily *Haartz* reported that around only 100 items were granted access in Gaza as of May 2010.[64]

The Egyptian government actively curtailed efforts to provide aid through a variety of means. Egypt maintained a singularly important role in maintaining the blockade, as it is the only country aside from Israel that has land access to the Gaza Strip. By maintaining the blockade at the Rafah border, Egypt assisted and facilitated Israel's blockade while enforcing collective punishment on the people of Gaza for voting the wrong way in their own elections. In 2009, activists from 43 countries came to Egypt with the intent to cross the Rafah border and were stopped by Egyptian state security. Not long after, the Viva Palestina convoy, meant to deliver direly needed humanitarian aid to Gaza, was violently attacked by police at Al-Arish, with 50 aid volunteers left injured.[65] Gaza, which according to the United Nations Relief Works Agency relies upon a network of underground tunnels for 60 percent of its economy,[66] faced a consistent and threatening campaign by the Egyptian state to close the tunnels and seal Gaza off completely. In 2008, citizens of Gaza flooded Rafah for 11 days when Hamas destroyed a section of the border wall used to keep them prisoner. In response, Egypt immediately began construction of a wall that would not only obstruct movement aboveground, but was intended to limit or destroy the underground tunnel system completely:

> The new wall Egypt is building is intended to cut off these underground lifelines. Construction was first reported by the highbrow Israeli daily Ha'aretz, in an article stating that the wall will be more than five miles long, driving steel panels down to 100 feet below the surface. Some claim the barrier will be connected to pipes that will saturate the ground along the border with pumped-in seawater, thus rendering the tunnels liable to collapse. It has also been widely reported that the wall is being built with American assistance; a US Embassy official in Cairo confirmed to a delegate from the Gaza Freedom March that the US Army Corps of Engineers has provided technical support.[67]

For being such a loyal catspaw of the US-Israeli agenda in Palestine, Egypt was not want of payment. As a February 2010 article from the Middle East Research and Information Project pointed out, in exchange for Egypt's role in securing the siege on Gaza, "part of the aid it receives will now be put into an endowment (which makes it harder for Congress to make the aid conditional on particular reforms), and… it was announced that Egypt will acquire at least 20 new F-16 fighter jets from US manufacturers."[68] Of course, the Egyptian regime, which despised Hamas for its links with Egypt's on Muslim Brotherhood, also took part in the blockade for domestic considerations. Egypt's state-sponsored press, much as under Sadat, attempted to deflect criticism by appealing to narrow nationalistic sentiments and blaming the Palestinians, especially Hamas, essentially positioning them as perpetrators of the conflict and inhibitors of "peace."[69] Not to be outdone, Mubarak's successor Morsi saw it fitting to augment the campaign against the Palestinians by flooding the underground tunnels with sewage.

Israeli newspapers at the onset of the 2011 demonstrations urged that international criticism of the Mubarak regime be silenced. They feared that a popular, democratic uprising would mean more solidarity and support for the Palestinian struggle, support which had always existed but remained stifled by the regime. Egypt's ruling class understood that its position in society rested upon its imperial benefactors. Indeed, as with other corrupt Arab regimes, the Mubarak regime attempted to balance pro-Palestinian rhetoric with imperialist policies to please its real constituencies, the US and Israel, and placate its own population.

The Complex Dynamics of the Arab Uprisings and Imperial Interests

The millions of people that took to the streets to demand the overthrow of Mubarak were a direct threat to US and Israeli interests. This reality was articulated most lucidly, albeit retroactively, by commentator Ari Shavit in *Haaretz*, after the fall of Mubarak:

> The West's position reflects the adoption of Jimmy Carter's worldview: kowtowing to benighted, strong tyrants while abandoning moderate, weak ones... Carter's betrayal of the Shah [during the Iranian Revolution of 1978-9] brought us the ayatollahs, and will soon bring us ayatollahs with nuclear arms. The consequences of the West's betrayal of Mubarak will be no less severe. It's not only a betrayal of a leader who was loyal to the West, served stability and encouraged moderation. It's a betrayal of every ally of the West in the Middle East and the developing world. The message is sharp and clear: The West's word is no word at all; an alliance with the West is not an alliance. The West has lost it. The West has stopped being a leading and stabilising force around the world.[70]

What Shavit is saying in so many words is that the geopolitical strategy of the West, despite blatant corruption and increasing misery for native populations, ought to be to prop up complacent dictators in order to maintain imperial hegemony in the region. Real leftists in Israel, few as they are, saw this dynamic just as clearly decades ago through a very different lens, arguing that imperialist "domination in the region cannot be shattered without overthrowing those junior partners [such as Egypt] of imperialist exploitation, the ruling classes in the Arab world."[71]

With Tunisia and Egypt, the seeds of revolution were sown across the Arab world. The Tunisian revolution was simply the first shot in what turned out to be a much wider regional phenomenon. As John McCain proclaimed at the outset of these uprisings, "this virus is spreading throughout the Middle East. This, I would argue, is probably the most dangerous period of history in—of our entire involvement in the Middle East, at least in modern times."[72] Clearly, the Egyptian outbreak of the "virus" greatly threatened US interests. Those interests, however, were eventually secured with the acquiescence of the post-Mubarak regime.

Similarly, while the uprisings spread across the Arab world, the US and its traditionally oppressive European counterparts refused to loosen their control over the region. In Libya, the US spearheaded a NATO bombing campaign that ousted Muammar Ghaddafi and installed a group of privatizers and business men compliant with US interests. In Syria, the US, Saudi Arabia, and Qatar engaged indirectly in the civil war that broke out there between rebels and the Syrian government, this time training, providing intelligence to, and arming the rebels in an effort to dismantle the Syrian state and the truculent regime of Bashar al-Assad. Indeed, only two years later after warning the world of the Arab "virus," John McCain would be posing for pictures with members belonging to a very different strain of the "virus," composed of Sunni Syrian rebels who had just kidnapped 11 Lebanese Shia pilgrims in Syria.[73] In fact, McCain became the prime cheerleader of the "virus" in Syria. In Bahrain, the uprising was put down violently by the al-Khalifa monarchy with the help of Saudi Arabia and without a word of protest from the "liberal" West. The final tally has not been taken, and the cards are still falling as the upsurge of popular resistance to corrupt regimes in the Arab world becomes infused and tangled with the long-reaching tentacles of first world imperialism. In Egypt it seemed possible for a moment that millions of people, through their own self-activity and collective action, would finally throw off the yoke of Western hegemony. While hopes have dwindled, and the movement was temporarily stalled first by the new Muslim Brotherhood government and then by the military coup which toppled it, the battle remains incomplete, and the outcome will rest largely upon the composition of the new social movements propelling the revolution forward.

[1] Kirit Radia, "Secretary Clinton in 2009: "I really consider President and Mrs. Mubarak to be friends of my family,"" *Political Punch, ABC News* (blog), January 31, 2011, http://abcnews.go.com/blogs/politics/2011/01/secretary-clinton-in-2009-i-really-consider-president-and-mrs-mubarak-to-be-friends-of-my-family/. Full quote: "We look forward to President Mubarak coming as soon as his schedule would permit [to the United States]. I had a wonderful time with him this morning. I really consider President and Mrs. Mubarak to be friends of my family. So I hope to see him often here in Egypt and in the United States."

[2] Bob Willis, "U.K.'s Cameron Urges Peaceful Democratic Reforms in Egypt in CNN Interview," *Bloomberg*, January 30, 2011. http://www.bloomberg.com/news/2011-01-30/u-k-s-cameron-urges-peaceful-democratic-reforms-in-egypt-in-cnn-interview.html (accessed July 4, 2013).

[3] Chris McGreal, "Tony Blair: Mubarak is 'immensely courageous and a force for good'," *The Guardian*, February 01, 2011. http://www.guardian.co.uk/world/2011/feb/02/tony-blair-mubarak-courageous-force-for-good-egypt (accessed July 4, 2013). Full quote: "Where you stand on him depends on whether you've worked with him from the outside or on the inside. I've worked with him on the Middle East peace process between the Israelis and the Palestinians so this is somebody I'm constantly in contact with and working with and on that issue, I have to say, he's been immensely courageous and a force for good." British political comedian Mark Steel exposed Blair's hypocrisy, quipping in an Independent article, "I'm sure that's true. If you were tortured by him you never got to see his kindly side."

[4] Jon Donnison, "Egypt protests: Israel watches anxiously," *BBC*, February 01, 2011. http://www.bbc.co.uk/news/world-middle-east-12338222 (accessed July 4, 2013).

[5] Noam Chomsky. "Noam Chomsky: 'This is the Most Remarkable Regional Uprising that I Can Remember'." February 02, 2011. July 4, 2013. http://www.democracynow.org/2011/2/2/noam_chomsky_this_is_the_most.

[6] Michael Parenti, *Against Empire*, (San Francisco: City Lights Books, 1995), pg. 1-3.

[7] Michael Parenti, *The Face of Imperialism*, (Boulder: Paradigm Publishers, 2011), pg. 7.

[8] Deepa Kumar, *Islamophobia and the Politics of Empire*, (Chicago: Haymarket Books, 2012), pg. 37.

[9] Sydney Lens, The Forging of American Empire, (New York: Thomas Y. Crowell Company, 1971), pg. 367-8.

[10] Parenti, *The Face of Imperialism*, pg. 7.

[11] Hanieh, "Egypt's Uprising: Not Just a Question of 'Transition."

[12] Document 5, "National Security Council Report," *Foreign Relations of the United States*, 1958-1960, Vol. 12, Near East Region; Iraq; Iran; Arabian

Peninsula, 24 January 1958. Quoted in: Andrew Marshall, "Egypt Under Empire, Part 2: The "Threat" of Arab Nationalism," *The Hampton Institute*, July 23, 2013,
http://www.hamptoninstitution.org/egyptunderempireparttwo.html#.UfWQCo21Fe9.

[13] Jeremy Sharp, Congressional Research Service, "Egypt: Background and U.S. Relations." June 27, 2013. Accessed July 4, 2013.
http://www.fas.org/sgp/crs/mideast/RL33003.pdf.

[14] William Hartung, "Made in the U.S.A.: Tear Gas, Tanks, Helicopters, Rifles and Fighter Planes in Egypt Funded and Built Largely by the Pentagon and American Corporations," January 31, 2011. July 4, 2013.
http://www.democracynow.org/2011/1/31/made_in_the_usa_tear_gas.

[15] Original in Arabic found here: Muhammad Al-Khārhī, *Al-Masry Al-Youm*, February 22, 2011. http://www.almasryalyoum.com/node/1489941 (accessed July 4, 2013). Partial translation here: Andrea Germanos, "Stripped of 'Country of Origin' Label, US Agrees to Sell Tear Gas to Egypt."*CommonDreams.org*, February 22, 2011. https://www.commondreams.org/headline/2013/02/22-2 (accessed July 4, 2013).

[16] Shibley Telhami, University of Maryland with Zogby International, "2010 Annual Arab Public Opinion Survey." Last modified 2010. Accessed July 4, 2013. http://www.brookings.edu/~/media/research/files/reports/2010/8/05 arab opinion poll telhami/0805_arabic_opinion_poll_telhami.pdf.

[17] Pew Research Center, 2010. Quoted in Alex Callinicos, "The return of the Arab revolution."*International Socialism*. no. 130.
http://www.isj.org.uk/index.php4?id=717&issue=130 (accessed July 4, 2013).

[18] David Kirkpatrick, "Poll Finds Egyptians Full of Hope About the Future," *The New York Times*, April 25,
2011. http://www.nytimes.com/2011/04/26/world/middleeast/26poll.html?_r=2& (accessed July 4, 2013).

[19] Compare these results, for example, with the saber-rattling against Iran by the US officials and media. Only 10% of Arabs viewed Iran as a threat to them. Meanwhile, 57% said that Iran should have nuclear weapons, presumably to act as a deterrent to Israel which is the only state in the Middle East to have nuclear weapons. For Egyptians who thought Iran was seeking nuclear weapons, 69% said there would be a positive outcome if they had them. When asked what world leaders they most admire, 20% responded with Recep Erdogan of Turkey, presumably due to his handling of the Israeli raid on the Turkish flotilla bringing aid to Gaza. Another 13% chose Hugo Chavez of Venezeuala, which we can assume was based on his stance against US imperialism and the implementation of widespread social programs. These statistics show a great disdain for US foreign policy.

[20] Document 5, "National Security Council Report," *Foreign Relations of the United States*, 1958-1960, Vol. 12, Near East Region; Iraq; Iran; Arabian Peninsula, 24 January 1958. Quoted in: Marshall, "Egypt Under Empire, Part 2."

[21] Maurice Jr. Labelle, "'The Only Thorn': Early Saudi-American Relations and

the Question of Palestine, 1945-1949," *Diplomatic History* (Vol. 35, No. 2, April 2011), pages 259-260. Quoted in Marshall, "Egypt Under Empire, Part 2."

[22] Letter from President Roosevelt to James M. Landis, American Director of Economic Operations in the Middle East, Concerning the Vital Interest of the United States in the Middle East, Foreign Relations of the United States, The Near East, South Asia, and Africa, 6 March 1944. Quoted in: Marshall, "Egypt Under Empire, Part 2."

[23] Report by the Coordinating Committee of the Department of State, "Draft Memorandum to President Truman," *Foreign Relations of the United States*, Diplomatic Papers, The Near East and Africa, Vol. 8, 1945, page 45. Quoted in: Marshall, "Egypt Under Empire, Part 2."

[24] Peter L. Hahn, "Containment and Egyptian Nationalism: The Unsuccessful Effort to Establish the Middle East Command, 1950-53," *Diplomatic History* (Vol. 11, No. 1, January 1987), pages 24. Quoted in: Marshall, "Egypt Under Empire, Part 2."

[25] Geoffrey Warner, "The United States and the Suez Crisis," *International Affairs* (Vol. 67, No. 2, April 1991), pages 304-308. Quoted in: Marshall, "Egypt Under Empire, Part 2."

[26] Document 62, "Paper by the Secretary of State's Special Assistant (Russell)," *Foreign Relations of the United States*, 1955-1957, Vol. 16, Suez Crisis, 4 August 1956. Quoted in: Marshall, "Egypt Under Empire, Part 2."

[27] Maxime Rodinson, *Israel: A Colonial-Settler State?* (New York: Pathfinder Press, 1973).

[28] Hanieh, "Egypt's Uprising: Not Just a Question of 'Transition."

[29] Ruder, "From Nasserism to Collaboration."

[30] Ilan Pappe, *The Ethnic Cleansing of Palestine*, (Oxford: Oneworld Publications, 2007).

[31] Warner, "The United States and the Suez Crisis," pg. 308-309. Quoted in Marshall, "Egypt Under Empire, Part 2."

[32] Document 40, "Special National Intelligence Estimate," *Foreign Relations of the United States*, 1955-1957, Vol. 16, Suez Crisis, 31 July 1956. Quoted in Marshall, "Egypt Under Empire, Part 2."

[33] Document 455, "Memorandum of Discussion at the 302d Meeting of the National Security Council, Washington, November 1, 1956, 9 a.m.," *Foreign Relations of the United States*, 1955-1957, Vol. 16, Suez Crisis, 1 November 1956. Quoted in Marshall, "Egypt Under Empire, Part 2."

[34] Peter L. Hahn, "Securing the Middle East: The Eisenhower Doctrine of 1957," *Presidential Studies Quarterly*, (Vol. 36, No. 1, March 2006), pages 39-40. Quoted in Marshall, "Egypt Under Empire, Part 2."

[35] Document 5, "National Security Council Report." Quoted in Marshall, "Egypt Under Empire, Part 2."

[36] Alexander. *Nasser: His Life, His Times*, pg. 154.

[37] David North, "The Egyptian working class moves to the forefront." *World Socialist Web Site*, February 10, 2011. http://www.wsws.org/en/articles/2011/02/pers-f10.html (accessed July 13,

2013).
[38] Hanieh, "Egypt's Uprising: Not Just a Question of 'Transition."
[39] David Wurmser, Jerusalem Center for Public Affairs, "The Geopolitics of Israel's Offshore Gas Reserves," Last modified April 04, 2013. Accessed July 13, 2013. http://jcpa.org/article/the-geopolitics-of-israels-offshore-gas-reserves/.
[40] Mira Awwad, "Egyptian minister questions gas agreements with Israel," *Globes*, March 09, 2011. http://www.globes.co.il/serveen/globes/docview.asp?did=1000629035&fid=1725 (accessed July 13, 2013).
[41] "Egypt may buy back gas from Israel." *The Jerusalem Post*, September 24, 2010. http://www.jpost.com/Business/Business-News/Egypt-may-buy-back-gas-from-Israel (accessed July 13, 2013).
[42] U.S. Energy Information and Administration, "Global natural gas prices vary considerably." Last modified September 30, 2011. Accessed July 13, 2013. http://www.eia.gov/todayinenergy/detail.cfm?id=3310.
[43] John Daly, "Egyptian-Israeli Natural Gas Agreement Now Officially Over," *Oil Price*, May 05, 2012. http://oilprice.com/Energy/Natural-Gas/Egyptian-Israeli-Natural-Gas-Agreement-Now-Officially-Over.html (accessed July 13, 2013).
[44] U.S. Embassy in Cairo. Wikileaks, "Mubarak's Visit to Washington (CAIRO 000874)." Dated May 19, 2009.
[45] U.S. Embassy in Cairo. New York Times, "A Selection From the Cache of Diplomatic Dispatches - Domestic Troubles (CAIRO 002933)," Dated May 16, 2006.
[46] Lance Selfa, "The 1991 Gulf War: Establishing a New World Order," *International Socialist Review*. no. 7 (1999). http://www.isreview.org/issues/07/1991GulfWar.shtml (accessed July 13, 2013).
[47] Abdennour Benantar, "Egypt and the War on Iraq: Implications for Domestic Policy." Journal of Third World Studies 24, no. 1 (Spring 2007): 227-247. Also available here: http://www.thefreelibrary.com/Egypt+and+the+war+on+Iraq%3A+implications+for+domestic+politics.-a0164525344 (accessed July 13, 2013).
[48] U.S. Embassy in Cairo. New York Times, "A Selection From the Cache of Diplomatic Dispatches – Intelligence Chief on the Threat of Radicalism (CAIRO 000746)," Dated April 30, 2009. Accessed July 10, 2013. http://www.nytimes.com/interactive/2010/11/28/world/20101128-cables-viewer.html?_r=0#report/egypt-09CAIRO746
[49] Ibid.
[50] Kienle, "More than a Response to Islamism," pg. 219.
[51] Ibid., pg. 221.
[52] Ibid., pg. 231.
[53] Mohamed El-Menshawy, "Is Egypt still part of America's extraordinary rendition programme?" *Ahram Online*, April 02, 2013. http://english.ahram.org.eg/NewsContentP/4/68282/Opinion/Is-Egypt-still-part-of-Americas-extraordinary-rend.aspx (accessed July 13, 2013).

54 El-Menshawy, "Is Egypt still part of America's extraordinary rendition programme?"
55 Ibid.
56 The White Knights form one of the "ultras" football clubs based out of Zamalek. For more on the role of "ultras" in the Egyptian Revolution, see Dave Zirin, "Soccer clubs central to ending Egypt's 'dictatorship of fear'," *Sports Illustrated*, January 31, 2011, http://sportsillustrated.cnn.com/2011/writers/dave_zirin/01/31/egypt.soccer/.
57 Tweets separated by ellipses. Hossam El-Hamalawy, Twitter, posted March 5, 2011. Available https://twitter.com/3arabawy.
58 Zayed Salem, "State Security Downfall, Alexandria, 4-5th March 2011," *Z Space* (blog), March 05, 2011. http://zeyadsalem.wordpress.com/2011/03/05/state-security-head-quarters-alexandria-4-5th-march-2011/ (accessed July 13, 2013).
59 Alastair Leithead, "Egyptians demand secret police give up torture secrets," *BBC*, March 08, 2011. Egyptians demand secret police give up torture secrets (accessed July 13, 2013).
60 William Wan and Liz Sly, "State Security HQ overrun in Cairo," *Washington Post*, March 05, 2011. http://www.washingtonpost.com/wp-dyn/content/article/2011/03/05/AR2011030504356_2.html?hpid=artslot (accessed July 13, 2013).
61 "Egyptians raid state police offices." *Al-Jazeera English*, March 05, 2011. http://english.aljazeera.net/news/middleeast/2011/03/201135211558958675.html (accessed July 13, 2013).
62 Mostafa Ali, "Two steps forward in Egypt," *Socialist Worker*, March 09, 2011. http://socialistworker.org/2011/03/09/two-steps-forward-egypt (accessed July 13, 2013).
63 Gregg Carlstrom, "A first step towards prosecutions?" *Al-Jazeera English*, March 06, 2011. http://www.aljazeera.com/indepth/spotlight/anger-in-egypt/2011/03/2011368410372200.html (accessed July 13, 2013).
64 Amira Hass, "Gazans get halva, but not cookies," *Haaretz*, June 10, 2010. http://www.haaretz.com/print-edition/news/gazans-get-halva-but-not-cookies-1.295228 (accessed July 13, 2013).
65 Ursula Lindsey, "Egypt's Wall," *Middle East Research and Information Project*. (2010). http://www.merip.org/mero/mero020110 (accessed July 13, 2013).
66 Lindsey, "Egypt's Wall."
67 Ibid.
68 Ibid.
69 Abigail Hauslohner, "In the Siege of Gaza, Egypt Walks a Delicate Line." *TIME*, January 11, 2010. http://www.time.com/time/world/article/0,8599,1953015,00.html (accessed July 13, 2013).
70 Ari Shavit, "The Arab revolution and Western decline,"*Haaretz*, February 03, 2011. http://www.haaretz.com/print-edition/opinion/the-arab-revolution-and-

western-decline-1.340967 (accessed July 13, 2013).
[71] Moshe Machover, *Israelis and Palestinians: Conflict and Resolution*, (Chicago: Haymarket Books, 2010), pg. 17.
[72] "McCain Compares Arab Pro-Democracy Movement to a "Virus"." DemocracyNow! February 04 2011. Web, http://www.democracynow.org/2011/2/4/headlines/mccain_compares_pro_democracy_movement_to. Full quote: "This virus is spreading throughout the Middle East. The president of Yemen, as you know, just made the announcement that he wasn't running again. This, I would argue, is probably the most dangerous period of history in — of our entire involvement in the Middle East, at least in modern times."
[73] Luke Johnson, "John McCain Pushes Back Against Lebanese Report Of Photo With Syrian Rebel Kidnapper," *Huffington Post*, May 30, 2013. http://www.huffingtonpost.com/2013/05/30/john-mccain-syria_n_3359166.html (accessed July 13, 2013).

4

Revival of Popular Movements

The dual theme of working class struggle and state repression of social movements has been recurrent throughout Egyptian history. The origins of a modern industrial proletariat in Egypt date back to at least the 1870s and grew continuously until the 1919 anti-colonial uprising. Left-wing socialist thought grew slowly and steadily this period, but gained a wider audience after the First World War as the modern industrial proletariat became a distinct and important social force. Competing with the political Islamism of the Muslim Brothers and the nationalist politics of the *Wafd*, the popularity of left-wing politics culminated with the coming to power of Nasser, at which point the size and scale of the industrial working class dramatically increased in conjunction with the massive state investment in modern industry. Yet, the state domination of political and economic life also meant that independent left-wing thought was mostly extinguished during this period, only to reemerge as a dialectic force in opposition to Sadat's *Infitah* policies during the 1970s. The 1990s and 2000s witnessed an enormous increase in contentious labor action and a concomitant revival in popular politics, a vital precursor to the ousting of Mubarak in 2011.

The Growth of a Modern Working Class in Colonial Egypt

Left-wing political thought was imported to Egypt as skilled foreign workers migrated to the country primarily from Italy and Greece, but also from other European states. As these workers mingled with the nascent Egyptian proletariat, radical ideas about the role of labor and the working class in modern society gained modest ground. Their interaction with the emergent Arab working class – particularly cigarette rollers, printers, and service workers – encouraged anarchist, socialist, and anarcho-syndicalist thought to develop as a small but important political current in Egypt. The first major strike was led by Cairo cigarette rollers in 1899, with other strikes following in their wake. As most of Egypt's large industrial employers were of foreign origin, and the British had army occupied Egypt since the 1882 Urabi revolt, Egyptian working class activity largely converged with nationalist demands aimed at ending foreign dominance. This early working class activity, concentrated in transport and public utilities, laid important foundations in the pretext of the 1919 national popular uprising against British rule.

Leading up to and playing a role in the 1919 Revolution against British colonialism, the working class was a vital force in achieving the marginal form of independence won in 1922, which still kept Britain in control through an acquiescent monarchy. Despite the important role of organized labor action, the working class was granted neither the economic demands nor the political freedoms, such as the right to form unions, it sought. Indeed, as Anthony Gorman points out, the British "oversaw a policy of clamping down on all political activities, interning nationalists, surveilling or deporting foreign anarchists and closing down newspapers."[1] Aside from a brief time during World War II in which trade unions became legal, workers were never allowed any form of legal, collective organization. Indeed, although the nationalist *Wafd* (Delegation) Party won every relatively free parliamentary election during this period, the party's elite largely represented the Egyptian landed aristocracy. Of the 50 cabinets formed during the tumultuous years from 1914 to 1952, on average some 58% of cabinet members were landlords.[2] Thus, after the installation of an ostensibly independent monarchy, the high politics of the elite were oriented around the "triangle of opposing interests"[3] manifest in the monarchy, the British High Commission, and the nationalist elites, while Egyptian popular politics outside of elite control operated largely within the ideological domains of political Islam, radical nationalism, and Communism. The social base of these emerging political ideologies was largely drawn from workers, peasants, students, and the lower middle classes, including young military officers.

While leftists and Communists were important oppositional figures that provided some level of leadership to working class movements, the radical nationalists connected to the *Wafd* were arguably more influential. The radical nationalist wing of the *Wafd* remained largely marginalized by the elite leadership of the party, but it did garner some popular legitimacy among workers and peasants. Yet, the radical nationalist section was used largely as a tool to bring working class activity under the *Wafd* umbrella, to be directed against certain opponents, particularly foreign owned institutions, and not against "progressive nationalist elements" owned by ethnically Egyptian capitalists and landlords. In this sense, the radical nationalist movement inhibited the development of independent working class activity.

Egypt's First Mass Movement: the Society of the Muslim Brothers

The largest and widest popular social movement with the deepest social roots in Egyptian society was the Society of the Muslim Brothers (*Al-Jamaa'ah al-Ikhwaan al-Muslimuun*), frequently referred to in the English press as the Muslim Brotherhood. Although founded by Hasan al-Banna in 1928, the organization can trace its roots back to the late 19th century pan-Islamic and anti-colonial ideas Jamal al-Din al-Afghani. The Brotherhood gained substantial support throughout the 1930s and 1940s, but garnered its largest social base after World War II, peaking at nearly half a million members spanning some 2,000 branches. The Muslim Brotherhood drew its activist base from lower middle-class elements of Egyptian society, but appealed to poorer constituencies through its large network of social programs. The organization engaged in social, cultural, and educational affairs by setting up schools, hospitals, factories, and mosques to partially fill in the social, economic, and ideological vacuum left open by the state. These deficiencies on behalf of the state were greatly augmented in the post-Nasser era and provided space for the Muslim Brotherhood, despite its semi-legal status, to operate and regain its pre-coup status.

Ideologically, as Wael Hallaq explains, "For the Islamists, the moral…is the declared central domain… [and] the problems of all other domains, including the economic and political, 'are solved in terms of the central domain – they are considered secondary problems, whose solution follows as a matter of course only if the problems of the central [moral] domain are solved'."[4] While the organization established shaky anti-imperialist credentials, aiming to remove the British from Egyptian society but vacillating between cooperation and resistance with the British-installed monarch, "its most active efforts were directed against secularism and liberalism, which were deemed contrary to Islamic values."[5] Another primary component of the Brotherhood's ideology was the "harmonization" of class interests, a position similar to the nationalist *Wafd* despite the rancor between the two organizations. The Muslim Brotherhood attempted to control working class activity, supporting strikes when politically convenient but disparaging labor activity independent of the organization's interests.

This attempt to control working class organization and promote a "harmonization" of class interests, no matter how improbable or impossible, is a result of the class base of the organization. As Chris Harman notes, political Islam, a phenomenon which the Muslim Brotherhood is probably the largest and most widespread manifestation of, consists of four separate and often conflicting social classes in society: the old exploiters, the new exploiters, the poor, and the new middle class. The old exploiters consist of "members of the traditional privileged classes who fear losing out in the capitalist modernisation of society – particularly landowners (including clergy dependent on incomes from land belonging to religious foundations), traditional merchant capitalists, the owners of the mass of small shops and workshops" and often provide "finance for the mosques and see Islam as a way of defending their established way of life and of making those who oversee change listen to their voices." The new exploiters often emerge from this group, and are composed of "some of the capitalists who have enjoyed success despite hostility from those groups linked to the state" and who had found "their way into the economic fabric of Sadat's Egypt at a time when whole sections of it had been turned over to unregulated capitalism." Prime examples of this second group could be the "Egyptian Rockefeller" Uthman Ahmad Uthman during the Sadat era and Khairat El Shater during the Mubarak era and after.

The third group consists of "the rural poor who have suffered under the advance of capitalist farming and who have been forced into the cities as they desperately look for work." Meanwhile, these same displaced peasants "lost the certainties associated with an old way of life – certainties which they identify with traditional Muslim culture – without gaining a secure material existence or a stable way of life," and could "identify the 'non-Islamic' behaviour of [the ruling] elite as the cause of their own misery." These *fellaheen*, often converted into urban workers, were subsequently drawn to political Islam both through an ideological harkening back to an older age and through the large scale charity and social service networks put in place by the Muslim Brotherhood. These became particularly important as state social services were increasingly decrepit or non-existent while operating within the confines of neoliberal reform.

However, it is neither the exploiting classes nor the impoverished masses which, on the whole, provide the base of political activists for the Muslim Brotherhood. Instead, it is the new middle class which forms "the cadre of activists who propagate its doctrines and risk injury, imprisonment and death in confrontation with their enemies." [6] Indeed, as Richard Mitchell explains, it was the "urban, middle class, *effendi* [modern-educated professionals usually in the civil service] predominance among the activist membership" which "shaped the Society's political destiny."[7] Brynjar Lia argues that the Muslim Brotherhood represents, "to a great extent, a reflection of class interests... specifically... the class interests of the professional urban middle class." Lia cites surveys suggesting that the Brotherhood "recruited an overwhelming proportion of their members from this class, particularly those who were recent immigrants to urban areas." These activists form the "articulate and policy-making sections of the Muslim Brothers,"[8] and were and continue to be educated, lower middle class graduates such as teachers, doctors, lawyers, low-level religious clergy, and others who analyze the problems of society through Islamic rhetoric and propagate a vision of reform with Islam at its center.

The popularity of the Muslim Brotherhood can further be attributed to the fact that sometimes the positions taken by the organization were inherently correct, while the dominance of Stalinism within the Communist movement ensured an inability of the left to appropriately respond to events. For instance, while the dominant ideology of the Brotherhood was inimical to the interests of workers generally, they still maintained a level of ideological hegemony by engaging in anti-imperialist ventures, such as recruiting volunteers to fight in Palestine during the 1948 war. In contrast, the USSR, after various periods of inconsistent foreign policy regarding Zionism, officially recognized the establishment of Israel. The commitment on behalf of many Egyptian leftists to the international political maneuvering of Stalin and the USSR greatly hindered their ability to achieve hegemony or any serious inroads within the working class movement.

Workers and Brothers after the Military Coup

Just as workers played an important role in the 1919 revolution, organized working class protests played an enormous role in destabilizing the Farouk monarchy and facilitating the 1952 military coup that eventually brought Gamal Abd al-Nasser to power. Those espousing socialist ideologies, alongside the popular political Islam of the Muslim Brotherhood, played important roles enervating the legitimacy of the monarchy. It is important to note that the Egyptian communist movement was never a mass movement and never penetrated civil society in the same way that the Iraqi Communist Party did.[9] However, as Selma Botman points out, despite the fact that Marxists never held state power, they did "contribute to the tradition of dissident thought," a tradition that helped grant the military coup d'état "widespread endorsement partly because of the earlier efforts of the left to undermine the ideological support of the royalist regime."[10]

Despite their contribution to the struggle, working class organizations were quick to feel the heavy-hand of the state if they veered too far from the political and economic obedience required of them. The glimmer of hope that workers and unions would be able to function independently, manifest most lucidly in the 1952 textile workers strike at Kafr al-Dawwar, was smashed when the military brutally suppressed the strike and hung two of their leaders. While Nasser himself voted against the executions, this event set the tone for the harshness with which dissidents and movements outside of state-control would be handled in the future. Two years later, a united front of students, Wafdists, Communists, Muslim Brothers, and others protested the military dictatorship and called for a return to civilian rule. Nasser responded by consolidating his rule through a blend of cooptation and violence. Omnia El Shakry explains:

> Politically, the regime sought to contain the possibility of any broad-based popular movement, hence the attempts at cooptation and the violence perpetrated against its two main ideological contenders, the Muslim Brothers and the Marxist-Communist Left, as well as the abolition of political parties and organizations. Similarly, the regime's policy towards labor activism and trade unionism was characterized by a two-pronged policy of co-optation of labor and union leaders through their incorporation into the state apparatus and extensive revisions of labor legislation (for example, legislating job security and improved material benefits). Autonomous labor action and the political independence of the trade unions were curtailed by a legislative ban on all strikes, laws on the arbitration and conciliation of labor disputes, and a new trade-union law.[11]

The Democratic Movement for National Liberation (DMNL) was the largest Marxist organization, with links to some individuals within the Free Officer movement. On the whole, the DMNL helped provide ideological leniency for Nasserism on the radical left. The DMNL argued for a "two-stage" theory of revolution, promoting the idea that democracy must emerge from the national liberation struggle prior to the development of socialism. Despite the fact that neither democracy nor socialism was delivered, the DMNL attributed a progressive role to Nasser and his state-capitalist economic program, even if it blunted popular action favoring democratic control over the means of production.

For his part, Nasser utilized a carrot and stick approach that proved immensely effective in neutralizing the Marxists. The various communist organizations were almost never able to agree on a unified strategy or plan to deal with the Nasser regime. Instead, from 1952 to 1953 a variety of assessments, ranging from celebration to dismissiveness to outright condemnation, were circulating amongst Marxist intellectuals. Only for the brief period from 1953 to 1955 were most Communist organizations united in their opposition to Nasser, a time when he was widely considered to be aligning himself with the US. These were also years of repression. In the first half of 1955 alone some 750 communists were rounded up and imprisoned.[12] However, when Nasser engaged in his foreign policy of "positive neutralism," thereby expanding relations with the Communist bloc countries, Egyptian Marxists began to change their analysis, even while members of their own organizations were sitting in prison. From 1956, after the nationalization of the Suez Canal, until 1958 a period of relatively warm relations between Nasser and the Marxists developed. It was in the midst of this period that a united Egyptian Communist Party (ECP) was declared in 1958. By the end of 1958, however, the stick was once again in motion, with nearly one thousand communists arrested from December 31, 1958 to April 1959.[13] Youssef Darwish, a well-known Communist lawyer who had been imprisoned repeatedly by the monarchy, was again arrested by Nasser and held from 1958 to 1964. He explains how prison conditions under the military regime were even worse than imprisonment during the Farouk era: "Under the monarchy there was no torture in jails... Some things I can't even talk about. At one point I couldn't take it anymore, I stopped eating. Then a guard whispered to me: 'you have to eat, don't you know they want you to die.' These simple, humane words gave me the courage to go on."[14] Darwish was not alone. Many Marxists languished in prison from 1959 to 1965.

Following the acquiescent political tradition of the DMNL, alongside years of infighting and state repression, the ECP dissolved itself in 1965. Many of the remaining leaders took up Nasser's offer to hold positions as individuals in the Arab Socialist Union (ASU). The final communique issued by the ECP declared that a "deep-rooted social transformation" was taking place under Nasser, and that only the ASU could "carry the responsibilities of continuing the revolution in all national patriotic social, economic, and cultural spheres." In its conclusion, it celebrated that "this is the first time in history that a communist party ends its independent existence and accepts the leadership of the national socialist revolutionary forces."[15] This decision, which Darwish argued vehemently against at the time, was justified by the ECP along the lines that Nasser "alone was competent to carry out the tasks of the revolution."[16] As Tareq Ismael and Rifa'at El-Sa'id explain, not long after the party dissolved itself, "its members were totally demoralized." Instead of directing the socialist revolution from above via the ASU, the Marxists "soon discovered that they were isolated, quarantined, and contained."[17] A similar dynamic played out within the Muslim Brotherhood. Internal battles within the organization over the nature of the coup, as well as the increasingly apparent class contradictions within the organization, allowed Nasser to effectively marginalize and enervate it through various mechanisms.[18]

The role of the state in smashing collective movements was continued in the post-Nasser era after 1970. The social welfare dimension of Nasserism was emphasized less and less. "The workers don't demand, we give," had to be slightly altered during the Sadat-Mubarak years so it did not clash with the neoliberal dogma of Egypt's new Western backers. Instead, the Nasser slogan was replaced by a new ideology: "The workers don't demand, we take." Not only did they take, they repressed and beat back any attempts at formulating popular movements over the next forty years.

This process was concurrent with reform inside the Muslim Brotherhood, where the "reformist" wing defeated the more militant activists inside the party intent on armed struggle against the state. This led to an increasingly accommodating approach to the Sadat regime, which in turn provided the Brotherhood some unofficial space to organize. In 1975, a renewed Egyptian Communist Party was declared and nascent alternative left-wing formations emerged as well. As a show of loyalty, the Muslim Brotherhood spent much of the 1970s purging public spaces, especially the universities, of Nasserist and communist currents. In 1977, when working people rose up against cuts to food subsidies, they were violently put-down by Sadat's military, and the Muslim Brotherhood condemned the uprising despite its popular nature. After Sadat's engagement with Israel, however, many younger, more radical activists inside the organization turned away from the moderate Muslim Brotherhood and began articulating the need for a new armed struggle against the state. This formed the backdrop to Sadat's assassination in 1981 and the increasing hostility with which Mubarak met Islamist social movements in the 1990s, using anti-Islamist laws as a pretext for crushing any dissent, particularly economic action such as strikes.

Politics of Contention in the 2000s

In the years prior to 2011 Egypt witnessed a revival of mass struggle primarily in two areas. First, the Palestinian Intifada of 2000 and the invasion of Iraq in 2003 galvanized large-scale political action. Second, a proliferation of labor actions throughout the 1990s and 2000s reached a zenith with the contentious 2006 textile strike in al-Mahalla al-Kubra. This strike opened a new era in labor struggle and sparked the onset of an enormous strike-wave that gripped the nation and threatened the stability of the Mubarak regime. The Egyptian revolution cannot be separated from the recent history of struggle that gripped Egypt in the prior decade. A third factor was the increasingly civil relationship between leftists and the Muslim Brotherhood. This phenomenon may have influenced the ability of various political parties to come together and take a united stand against the Mubarak regime. In conjunction with one another, these three variables opened up a political space wide enough that, after witnessing the success of the Tunisian uprising, Egyptian activists were in a position to galvanize a similar uprising in their own country.

The Second Palestinian Intifada of 2000 was met with widespread support among the Egyptian people. Egyptians, despite the propaganda campaigns to the contrary, recognized and rejected the anti-Palestinian policies of their leaders. University students organized a demonstration supporting Palestinian resistance to Israeli occupation and it quickly spread to the high schools and the population at large. Activists pushed for solidarity with the Palestinian struggle and condemned the Arab regimes that were actively capitulating to the US and Israel. Likewise, and against the wishes of their pro-US dictator, some fifty thousand people took to Tahrir square in 2003 at the onset of the US invasion of Iraq. Despite the brutality of the police, protestors and demonstrators carried on. It was Mubarak's compliance and subjugation to imperial powers, combined with the corrupt political system and declining economic conditions, which pushed Egyptians over the top. One Egyptian socialist details the movement's evolution:

> In December 2004, the first public demonstration for the new movement for change happened, which we refer to as Kifaya, which means "enough." The first slogan of the movement was, "Down, down [with] Mubarak!" Other slogans appeared against Mubarak's plan to transfer power to his son, Gamal, to be the next president. The slogan of the movement was no to the continuation of the regime and no to the handing over of power to his son Gamal. This led to other demands, including an end to the emergency laws that were in place for more than twenty years, and another was to call for a free, democratic process for political parties and movements.[19]

Kefaya was vital in reforming the political culture within Egypt. While it was particularly successful in utilizing both the mainstream and alternative media outlets, it did not make deep inroads within the working class, the poor, or the peasantry, and failed to accurately articulate their demands. As Hossam El-Hamalawy explains, "Millions of Egyptians, while sitting at home, could watch those daring young activists in downtown Cairo mocking the president, raising banners with slogans that were unimaginable a decade before."[20] *Kefaya* was buttressed by the *Shayfenkom* movement, which translates roughly into "We Are Watching You." This grassroots movement arose during the 2005 elections, and pledged to monitor elections by sending members to committees and booths as election observers. The movement encouraged citizens to report election violations to their website or through their cell phones.[21]

Labor Militancy in the 1990s and 2000s

While this nascent political awakening occurred, economic conditions for Egyptians continued their descent. With this stark reality, it was not simply political issues and foreign policy that concerned Egyptians. Conditions for the Egyptian masses were dire throughout the 1980s and 1990s and moves by labor during this period to increase their economic standing in society were met brutally by police. In 1989, state police used live ammunition against strikers in the steel mills. They did the same in the textile strikes of 1994. In such cases the state machinery was blatant in its defense of capital. Furthermore, since 1957 when the Egyptian Trade Union Federation (ETUF) was established, official unions have functioned as arms of the Egyptian state. Law 35 passed in 1976 formalized the ETUF's legal monopoly on all trade union activity. This meant the role of unions under the ETUF was not to act as independent, militant entities through which workers could articulate their own demands. Instead, they were institutions through which the legitimate demands by the working class could be funneled by the regime into "safe" channels and consequentially stifled. Anne Alexander outlines the "dual role" of ETUF and its affiliated unions:

> ...as organs of social control they channeled benefits such as access to workplace-based social welfare schemes to workers and worked hand in glove with state employers to enforce "social peace" within the workplace. As organs of political control they acted as an electoral machine for the ruling party, controlling nominations for the 50 percent of seats in parliament which were reserved for "workers and peasants", and a mechanism for mobilising a stage army of apparently loyal regime supporters whenever the regime felt it needed to make a show of its "mass base".[22]

The ETUF, as the only legal trade union federation in Egypt until 2011, claimed representation of some 3.8 million workers out of a labor force of roughly 27 million.[23] It largely represented government or public sector workers, and found its strength from Nasser's expansion of the public sector from the mid-1950s until his death in 1970. By the Mubarak era, the NDP controlled the ETUF, with a majority of candidates in every level of the union's pyramid structure. Candidates who did not conform to Sadat and Mubarak's political and economic program were discarded by the so-called "socialist prosecutor," an office established to remove unwelcome critics of the regime. A 1995 law further eroded the social content of the ETUF, as high-level managers were granted the right to vote in union elections and workers on fix-termed contracts were barred from running in elections. This was quite convenient for the regime, as neoliberal reforms meant that the public sector stopped issuing permanent contracts to their employees. Another law also targeted the professional syndicates (*niqabat mihniyya*), granting NDP appointed officials control over the syndicate if election turn outs were too low.[24]

Another of the blatant ways the official unions acted as an extension of the state could be seen in how they manipulated the "legality" of strikes:

> Since the enactment of Egypt's Unified Labor Law of 2003, it has technically been legal for workers to strike, but only if approved by the leadership of the General Federation of Egyptian Trade Unions. Since the federation, along with the sectoral general unions and most enterprise-level union committees, are firmly in the grip of the ruling National Democratic Party (NDP), all actual strikes since 2003 have been "illegal."[25]

Yet, Egyptian workers in the two decades leading up to the 2011 uprising began engaging in contentious labor action, willfully disobeying the official trade union rulings. In the 1980s three high-profile strikes took place, including the 1984 textile strike in Mahalla al-Kubra, the 1986 rail workers' strike, and the 1989 Helwan steel strike. The early 1990s, coinciding with Mubarak's newest agreements with the IMF and the World Bank, saw a steady increase in labor activity. Reported strikes rose steadily every year, from 8 in 1990 to 26 in 1991, 28 in 1992, and 63 in 1993. In September 1994 a major strike occurred at Kafr al-Dawwar, the same site of the 1952 strike where the Revolutionary Command Council hung two leading organizers. This time, three people were shot and killed by the police and many others were wounded.[26] As Joel Beinin notes:

> The highest estimate of the total number of labor protests from 1988 to 1993 is 162—an average of 27 per year. From 1998 to 2003 the annual average for collective actions rose to 118. But in 2004 there were 265 collective actions; over 70 percent occurred after the Nazif government took office in July.[27]

From 1998 to 2010, two to four million Egyptians participated in some 3,400 to 4,000 strikes, sit-ins, and other forms of collective action.[28] Of this, over 1,900 of these actions involving some 1.7 million workers occurred from just 2004 to 2008,[29] as Nazif was "soldiering ahead with privatization and liberalization of the economy." Workers were radicalizing and willing to challenge the corrupt state-controlled unions. In large part, workers were forced to create their own, independent unions, even if they maintained an illegal status and were met with heavy repression by the state.

The growth in labor militancy has been an "unwelcome consequence of economic growth" seen during the last decade as foreign direct investment in Egypt has skyrocketed. This growth was fueled by an enormous inflow of international capital into the country, as Foreign Direct Investment increased from $400 million in 2000 to $13.2 billion in 2007-08, making Egypt the largest recipient of capital inflow on the African continent.[30]
Interestingly, it is not just the old players like the United States and Britain, either. So called "Free Trade Zones" have opened up all over Egypt, with capital pouring in from India, Russia, China, and even Kazakhstan. Some of this investment has been linked with military production facilities, another example of military dominance in Egypt.[31] What this increased flow of capital means is that while working conditions remained dangerous and living conditions were declining, there was simultaneously an augmentation of the labor force resulting from the new industrial and manufacturing base. These new industries have also been as a nexus through which workers have been able to organize.

The Groundbreaking Strike at Mahalla

Class struggle escalated tremendously in Egypt after the sham election of 2005 and the deepening of neoliberal economic policies in 2006. After Mubarak's spectacle of democracy, Egyptians understood the anti-worker policies of privatization and attacks on labor would continue. In late 2006, workers fought back and organized the most enormous strike wave in Egypt since the end of World War II. Al-Mahalla al-Kubra, a Nile Delta town known for its large public sector textile mill, Misr Spinning and Weaving, has a historic reputation for its contentious labor activity. As far back as 1947 workers had engaged in militant strike action at the company, which sparked strikes by other textile workers in Alexandria, oil workers in Suez, telegraphists, and teachers.[32] This historic legacy was born anew in 2006. After decades of economic battering, workers at the mill in 2006 made drastically low wages. For instance, one of the strike leaders, Muhammad al-'Attar, made a paltry sum of $75 a month, including profit-sharing and incentive bonuses. Workers in Mahalla were the spark that lit the Egyptian labor movement on fire. Starting December 7, production ground to a halt as some 3,000 female textile workers walked off the job to protest the fact that they were not given their promised end of the year bonus.³³ The female workers marched towards the male workers, who had not yet stopped their machines, reversing a popular football chant: "Where are the men? Here are the women!" The men finally joined in and quickly the spirit of resistance spread to nearly all of the workers at the state-owned textile plant, some 24,000 in total. "We had a massive demonstration, and staged mock funerals for our bosses," explained al-'Attar, "The women brought us food and cigarettes and joined the march. Security did not dare to step in. Elementary school pupils and students from the nearby high schools took to the streets in support of the strikers." Eventually, the government offered a large bonus and assurance that the company would not be privatized, a fear that many workers shared.³⁴

Taking inspiration from the Mahalla workers, the strike spread like wildfire to nearly every sector of society:

> Over the following ten months, virtually all sectors witnessed strikes or sit-ins. From December 7, 2006 to September 23, 2007, according to a report by the Giza-based Center for Socialist Studies, more than 650 workers' protests took place across the country, a large proportion of which were strikes. This period saw 198,400 workers take strike action, and an even higher number staged sit-ins and street protests, from civil servants, drivers and cashiers of metros and subways, cement factory workers, garbage collectors, fishermen, and even real estate tax collectors. The tax collectors who struck for three months, bringing tax collection down by 90 percent and winning a victory after they set up a camp in front of the ministerial cabinet headquarters in downtown Cairo.³⁵

Gaining confidence in themselves and their ability to fight back against a repressive regime, workers furthered the struggle. Organizers began to fuse economic and political demands. In February of 2008, tens of thousands of workers and fellow citizens in Mahalla took part in the largest anti-Mubarak labor protest prior to 2011. Chants against both Mubarak and his son Gamal meshed together with economic demands such as raising the national minimum wage. Then, in March, professors went on strike to protest the repressive actions against them by state security forces. Dissidents and organizers began calling for a general strike, centered in Mahalla, to raise the minimum wage. To preempt this, the government reacted with coercion and severe repression to ensure the strike would not occur. The last straw came when a police officer assaulted a woman in the city center. In response, massive protests broke out against police brutality, increasing food prices, terrible economic conditions, and the despised regime.

The ensuing battle at Mahalla is, perhaps, the single greatest event foreshadowing the 2011 rising. Hossam El-Hamalawy reported at the time:

> On the April 6 [2008], thousands of police troops occupied the town of Mahalla, and security took control of the factory, thus preempting the strike. Spontaneous demonstrations broke out in the town, however, including thousands of the urban poor, the young employed, and workers chanting against the president, corruption, and price increases. The demonstrators were met with police tear gas, rubber bullets, and live ammunition, which left at least two young men, ages 15 and 20, dead. For two days the city turned into a scene similar to the Palestinian Occupied Territories, where demonstrators hurled stones at Mubarak's police force and armored vehicles, while shouting "the revolution has arrived!" according to eyewitnesses. Posters of the dictator Mubarak were defaced and destroyed by the rioters in Mahalla's public squares.[36]

The protests "were only quelled by extreme police force, mass arrests and the use of government-hired thugs to loot and burn public institutions with the aim of sowing division among the protesters," a tactic that would be used by the regime three years later.[37] Although the strike was crushed preemptively, this surge in labor radicalism combined with the complementary mini-uprisings elucidate a strong line of continuity between the revolution of 2011 and the collective accumulation of events leading up to it. Egyptian labor historian Joel Beinin explicated upon this point:

> This was the first time in recent years that workers tried to organize something nationwide with a political component to it. Raising the minimum wage is not simply an economic demand, it's a political demand, because it is in opposition to the whole neoliberal economic restructuring project that has been proceeding very rapidly in Egypt, especially since the government that was recently deposed was installed in July 2004.[38]

Al-'Attar, who had helped lead the December 2006 strike, told a mass meeting of workers, "Politics and workers' rights are inseparable. Work is politics by itself. What we are witnessing here right now, this is as democratic as it gets."³⁹

The Significance of Mahalla and the Birth of Independent Trade Unionism

Mahalla was a significant turning point in Egypt. Not only did it break the grip of fear that the Mubarak regime had maintained for years, it actually instilled fright within the ranks of the Egyptian elite. As a leaked US cabal reads:

> Six months ago, economic cabinet ministers openly discussed phasing out food and fuel subsidies in favor of transfer payments to the very poor. That initiative now seems to be off the table. We are also hearing that unrest over prices has strengthened the security ministers in the cabinet in resisting privatization and other efforts towards liberalization… On April 15, [Egyptian] Foreign Minister Aboul Gheit, meeting with the [U.S] Ambassador, cited the Mahalla incident as a strain and added that he hoped that the United States would be supportive of Egypt during this difficult period.⁴⁰

Although not all the links are direct, one prime example of this line of continuity was manifest in the April 6 Youth Movement, a Facebook group created at this time by youth organizers in support of the Mahalla workers. A call on Facebook for a strike put forth by the April 6 group attracted 70,000 people online and garnered widespread national attention. Although US officials in Cairo falsely assumed that future "spasms of violence" would be "isolated and uncoordinated, rather than revolutionary in nature," they did suggest that the "nexus of the upper and middle-class Facebook users, and their poorer counterparts in the factories of Mahalla, created a new dynamic."⁴¹ There was no denying that the April 6 group would later play a vital role as catalyst, forum, and organizing tool for the activists who sparked the uprising in 2011.

Other developments followed on the heels of the Mahalla strike. Mustafa Bassiouny and Omar Said argue that the labor battles that followed in the wake of Mahalla were strategically important in laying the foundations for future independent labor organizations to develop. As strikes lasted longer and required sustained organizational commitment, and as the regime attempted to engage in negotiations with workers to avoid direct repression, labor leaders gained invaluable experience both representing workers and navigating the complexities of maintaining drawn out strikes.⁴² The fruits of such activity could be seen when, in the fall of 2007, the Real Estate Tax Authority workers formed a national strike committee, headed by Kamal Abu 'Aita, to demand wage parity with higher salaried tax workers employed directly by the Ministry of Finance. During the campaign, some 8,000 workers and their families occupied the street in front of the cabinet offices in downtown Cairo. In what was a major victory, the workers quickly secured a 325% wage increase. Capitalizing on this momentum, the strike committee spent a year organizing an independent union, and by 2008 over 30,000 of the 50,000 workers employed by local authorities were part of the new union. The Independent General Union of Real Estate Tax Authority Workers (IGURETA) was recognized, an ironically illegal action under Law 35, by the government in 2009. IGURETA was the first independent trade union in decades, and both health-care technicians and teachers would form their own independent counterparts by the end of 2011.[43]

These battles, especially the Mahalla strike, infused the Egyptian working class with a new spirit of resistance. Khalid 'Ali, the founding director of the Egyptian Center for Economic and Social Rights, represented Nagi Rashad, a worker at the South Cairo Grain Mill, in a lawsuit resulting in a 2010 court order requiring the government to establish a "fair" minimum wage. While the National Council on Wages proposed increasing the monthly minimum wage to a paltry EGP 400, which at the time was about $67 and represented one-third of what workers were calling for, the government never even enacted the proposal. Following this decision, hundreds of workers and supporters gathered in front of parliament calling for a minimum monthly wage of EGP 1,200. Joel Beinin cites the mood of the demonstration:

> They chanted, "A fair minimum wage, or let this government go home" and "Down with Mubarak and all those who raise prices!" Khalid 'Ali told the press, "The government represents the marriage between authority and money—and this marriage needs to be broken up... We call for the resignation of Ahmad Nazif's government because it works only for businessmen and ignores social justice."[44]

Those involved in the revolution were lucidly aware that recent years had been "marked by mass national strikes, nation-wide sit-ins, and visible labor protests often in the same locations that spawned this 2011 uprising." Even in the rural areas, uprisings against the "government's efforts to evict small farmers from their lands" had been evident prior to 2011 as rural-dwellers opposed "the regime's attempts to re-create the vast landowner fiefdoms that defined the countryside during the Ottoman and British Colonial periods."⁴⁵ Yet, even with the partial victory of these strikes, and the eventual recognition of a new union for thousands of workers, there remained serious differences between the revolution in Egypt and the union-led revolution in Tunisia:

> One major distinction between us and Tunisia is that although it was a dictatorship, Tunisia had a semi-independent trade union federation. Even if the leadership was collaborating with the regime, the rank and file were militant trade unionists. So when time came for general strikes, the unions could pull it together. But here in Egypt we have a vacuum that we hope to fill soon. Independent trade unionists have already been subjected to witch hunts since they tried to be established; there are already lawsuits filed against them by state and state-backed unions, but they are getting stronger despite the continued attempts to silence them.⁴⁶

Thus, independent trade unionism in Egypt was on an upward trajectory. However, it was not until the revolutionary process of 2011 that the labor movement would find the political space to rapidly augment its size and scope.

Socialists Reach Out to the Muslim Brothers

Within these developing political and class struggles a new and unlikely civility began to develop between two previously bitter enemies. The radical left, especially newer organizations centered around the Revolutionary Socialist tendency, began to form creative "united fronts" with younger members of the Muslim Brotherhood. Prior to this, fistfights on university campuses were commonplace between the two groups:

> Bad blood between the Egyptian left and the Brothers has a long history, from the Islamists' coordination with King Farouq in breaking strikes in the 1940s to President Anwar al-Sadat's encouragement of violent Islamist assaults on leftist university students in the 1970s. Most independent leftist organizations in the 1980s and 1990s hewed to a line on political Islam similar to that of the Egyptian Communist Party…equating Islamist organizations, reformist or radical, with fascism.⁴⁷

This was not without warrant. For instance, the Muslim Brothers had broken many strikes and opposed labor activity since the 1940s. Infamous clashes with communists in the textile center of Shubra al-Khayma, north of Cairo, were not forgotten by the left. The 1980s and 1990s saw a continuation of this anti-leftist stance but, significantly, during this period there was an amelioration of relations between sections of the labor movement and the Muslim Brotherhood. Eventually the Brotherhood adopted a less critical, more ambivalent stance towards labor, although this did not always manifest itself in pro-labor practices.[48] Standing against any united front policy, the entrenched leftist organizations, stained by the history of their interactions with the Muslim Brothers, maintained that the Brotherhood was more or less an ideological tool for the capitalist class to maintain neoliberal hegemony. Still, the opening of a dialogue between sections of the left and the Brotherhood began, a development that was to prove important later. It would be the new Egyptian left, and not the older leftist organizations, that took this opportunity seriously. The revolutionary left rejected the broad, generalized condemnation of Islamists. Instead, a new slogan emerged around the Revolutionary Socialists: "Sometimes with the Islamists, never with the state!"

Samir Naguib of the Centre for Socialist Studies (CSS) was vital in articulating this argument. He contended that the Muslim Brotherhood should be understood not simply as a reactionary force in society but, instead, a movement that at least in part involved many activists drawn from the ranks of the working class, the poor, and the oppressed. Some were leftists, or at the very least those who had been open to leftist ideas but who felt alienated by the Nasserist regime. This was especially true after the neoliberal turn in the 1970s. Splits and schisms within the organization were witnessed time again, such as in 1996 when liberal critics of the leadership left to form the Wasat Party, or in 2010 when members formed the Reform Front in an effort to democratize the internal structure of the organization. Naguib maintained that while socialists should act independently of Islamists, they should not be dismissive of them. Subsequently, socialists ought to defend them when their demands, such as the withdrawal of the emergency laws or more democratic participation, clashed with the oppressive state apparatus.

This argument was crucial with the advent of the new political movements revolving around the Palestinian intifada. Often spearheaded by leftists, this pro-Palestinian activist work drew in some of the younger Muslim Brotherhood members who in turn opened up to their socialist counterparts. Likewise, younger leftists began to reject the "fascist" label that was broadly applied to all Islamist organizers. A split began to emerge between the older, more conservative leadership and the younger, more militant Muslim Brothers willing to work side-by-side with socialists. Thus, it was not just the socialists that were developing a less sectarian approach. This was evident when the Brotherhood came under heavy criticism by Christian and socialist coalition partners for their 'Islam is the solution' slogan. In 2005 they withdrew the slogan because of the pressure from allies. Likewise, the Palestinian Intifada and the struggles surrounding it provided the Revolutionary Socialists with opportunities for growth. During this period of heightened political activity, the organization grew to a couple of hundred members from just a few activists in 1995.[49] Yet, as El-Hamalawy points out, there still existed serious divisions:

> Today, the majority of factions on the left still stand opposed to (or express caution about) joint actions with the Islamists, most notably the newly evolving Democratic Left (a reformist tendency centered around *al-Busla* magazine), the Egyptian Communist Party, the People's Socialist Party and a faction of the human rights community. But the Brothers and those comrades who will work with them remain engaged in mutual confidence building. The Muslim Brothers' leadership is staunchly gradualist, and always on the lookout for compromises with the Egyptian regime. That stance will likely impede a further rapprochement with the radical left, unless the Brotherhood's base of youth attains a greater say in when, and how, their powerful organization bestirs itself.

Despite this somewhat sectarian attitude on behalf of the older leftist groups, the potential for a broad coalition against Mubarak blossomed during the decade prior to the revolution of 2011. The anti-sectarian stance among the younger generation, especially the younger socialists and secular leftists, allowed for the cultivation of an extraordinarily diverse and multifaceted coalition in 2006.

A Loose Alliance Forms

By 2006 a loose political alliance was formed between a variety of parties and organizations representing the three main ideological groupings of Islamism, Secular Liberalism, and Left-Socialism. Within the Islamist camp was the conservative Muslim Brotherhood, with its vast social network, and the reformist Egyptian Islamic Labor Party. Notably, the ultra-conservative Salafist movement, which later developed into the *Al-Nour* Party after the revolution, refused to partake in the anti-Mubarak uprising despite the immense political benefit they garnered from his downfall. Within the secular liberal camp fell the *El-Ghad* party, a right-wing, "free-market" offshoot of the *Wafd* party, and the more moderate National Association for Change, headed up by Mohamed ElBaradei, who was to remain a key player in the political realm after Mubarak's downfall. *Al-Tagammu*, also known as the National Progressive Unionist Party, was probably the largest component of the left-wing of the broad front, and has historically been the main legal opponent of the neoliberal restructuring, despite its top-down, autocratic approach that would later alienate many members. *Al-Karama* (Dignity), founded in 1996, was a smaller but important offshoot of the Arab Democratic Nasserist Party, which lost many members when it embraced the economic restructuring programs of the 1970s. The Revolutionary Socialists, associated with the International Socialist Tendency, were perhaps the smallest of the three left parties but played a role both in reaching out to other organizations and providing an analysis that breached territory the older left-wing organizations were unable or unwilling to. These various groupings were drawn together in the nexus of *Kefaya*, a broad, non-ideological anti-Mubarak alliance.

What is clear is that such a broad alliance would have been difficult to maintain without the more advanced analysis of the Muslim Brotherhood and other Islamists put forward by the newer, younger left currents, especially the Revolutionary Socialists. These analytical developments suggest that the potential for collective political action was developing prior to 2011. Mubarak's capitulation to the US and Israel, the increasingly desperate condition of working people, and the increased political activity and civil dialogue between opposition groups were all vital components in preparing the Egyptian people for the revolutionary uprising in 2011. The non-sectarian arguments articulated by the new Egyptian left ensured that they were an integral part of and not alienated by the mass movements that developed prior to the ouster of Mubarak.

Furthermore, while it is true that *Kefaya* was largely inspired by the Egyptian youth, there was a pressing class dynamic to this as well. By 2011, roughly 52% of Egypt's population was under the age of 25. Youth unemployment officially remained in the mid to high 20 percent range, with unofficial estimates placing it significantly higher. Many more young Egyptians were working for low pay in fields unrelated to their education. This was the demographic base which provided much of the fuel for the *Kefaya* and April 6th movements and prompted the protests of 2011, eventually leading to the dismantlement of the decades-long dictatorship.

[1] Anthony Gorman, "Diverse in Race, Religion and Nationality... But United in Aspirations of Civil Progress: The Anarchist Movement in Egypt 1860-1940," in Steve Hirsch and Lucien van der Walt (eds), *Anarchism and Syndicalism in the Colonial and Postcolonial World, 1870-1940: The Praxis of National Liberation, Internationalism and Social Revolution* (Boston, Brill, 2010), pg. 26. Quoted in: Marshall, "Egypt Under Empire, Part I."
[2] Botman, *The Rise of Egyptian Communism: 1939-1970, pg. xiv.*
[3] Alexander, *Nasser: His Life, His Times*, pg. 6.
[4] Wael B. Hallaq, *The Impossible State: Islam, Politics, and Modernity's Moral Predicament*, (New York: Columbia University Press, 2013), pg. 12-13.
[5] Chris Harman, "The Prophet and the Proletariat," *International Socialism*, no. 64 (1994), http://www.marxists.org/archive/harman/1994/xx/islam.htm
[6] Harman, "The Prophet and the Proletariat."
[7] Richard P. Mitchell, *The Society of Muslim Brothers*, (Oxford: Oxford University Press, 1969), pg. 329.
[8] Brynjar Lia, *The Society of the Muslim Brothers in Egypt: The Rise of an Islamic Mass Movement, 1928-1942*, (Reading: Garnet Publishing Limited, 1998), 199-200.
[9] See Ilario Salucci, *A People's History of Iraq: The Iraqi Communist Party, Workers' Movements, and the Left, 1924-2004* (Chicago: Haymarket Books, 2005).
[10] Botman, *The Rise of Egyptian Communism: 1939-1970*, pg. xx.
[11] El Shakry, "Egypt's Three Revolutions."
[12] Beinin, Joel. "The Communist Movement and Nationalist Political Discourse in Nasirist Egypt." *Middle East Journal*, Vol. 41, no. 4 (1987), 575.
[13] Beinin, "The Communist Movement and Nationalist Political Discourse in Nasirist Egypt," 581.
[14] Faiza Rady, "Youssef Darwish: The courage to go on," Al-Ahram Weekly Online, December 2004, http://weekly.ahram.org.eg/2004/719/profile.htm.
[15] Tareq Y. Ismael and Rifa'at El-Sa'id, *The Communist Movement in Egypt, 1920-1988* (New York: Syracuse University Press, 1990), 125-6.
[16] Philip Marfleet, "Never going back: Egypt's continuing revolution," International Socialism (137), http://www.isj.org.uk/?id=866.
[17] Ismael and El-Sa'id, *The Communist Movement in Egypt, 1920-1988*, 127.
[18] There is a video clip of Nasser addressing a large audience after coming to power where he recounts a meeting he had with the leader of the Muslim Brotherhood. He claims the first thing the Brother requested was for all women to wear the *hijab/tarha* (head covering) when in public. Nasser responds, "Sir, you have a daughter in the School of Medicine, and she's not wearing the *tarha*. If you are unable to make one girl – who is your own daughter – wear the *tarha*, you want me to put the *tarha* on ten million women, myself?" The crowd received the joke with wild applause, and the anecdote exhibits the charisma and humor that Nasser utilized to help maintain his popularity in the Arab world.

[19] Unnamed Strike Leaders, "Class struggle in Egypt," *International Socialist Review*, no. 59 (2008), http://www.isreview.org/issues/59/feat-egyptstrikes.shtml (accessed July 17, 2013).
[20] Hossam El-Hamalawy, "Egypt's revolution has been 10 years in the making." *The Guardian*, March 02, 2011. http://www.guardian.co.uk/commentisfree/2011/mar/02/egypt-revolution-mubarak-wall-of-fear?CMP=twt_gu (accessed July 17, 2013).
[21] Jennifer Jones, "Virtual community: Formation and mobilization of a collective, democratic identity in Egypt." (master\., Department of Political Science - University of California, Irvine, 2011), http://www.democracy.uci.edu/files/democracy/docs/conferences/grad/2011/Virtual Egyptian Communities- J.J.Jones.pdf.
[22] Anne Alexander, "The Egyptian workers' movement and the 25 January Revolution," *International Socialism* (133), January 9, 2012, http://www.isj.org.uk/?id=778.
[23] Beinin, "The Rise of Egypt's Workers."
[24] Kienle, "More than a Response to Islamism."
[25] Beinin and El-Hamalawy, "Egyptian Textile Workers Confront the New Economic Order."
[26] Kienle, "More than a Response to Islamism."
[27] Beinin, "The Rise of Egypt's Workers."
[28] Ibid.
[29] North, "The Egyptian working class moves to the forefront."
[30] Ibid.
[31] Amar, "Uprising in Egypt: A Two-Hour Special on the Revolt Against the U.S.-Backed Mubarak Regime."
[32] Botman, *The Rise of Egyptian Communism: 1939-1970*, pg. 75.
[33] Beinin and El-Hamalawy, "Egyptian Textile Workers Confront the New Economic Order."
[34] Ibid.
[35] Hossam El-Hamalawy, "Revolt in Mahalla," *International Socialist Review*, no. 59 (2008), http://www.isreview.org/issues/59/rep-mahalla.shtml (accessed July 17, 2013).
[36] El-Hamalawy, "Revolt in Mahalla."
[37] Rizk, "Egypt and the global economic order."
[38] Joel Beinin, "Striking Egyptian Workers Fuel the Uprising After 10 Years of Labor Organizing," Web, http://www.democracynow.org/2011/2/10/egyptian_uprising_surges_as_workers_join.
[39] Beinin, "The Rise of Egypt's Workers."
[40] U.S. Embassy in Cairo. WikiLeaks, "Mahalla Riots: Isolated Incident Or Tip Of An Iceberg? (CAIRO 000783)," Dated April 14, 2008.
[41] Ibid.
[42] Mustafa Bassiouny and Omar Said, "A new workers' movement: the strike wave of 2007," *International Socialism*, March 31, 2008,

http://www.isj.org.uk/?id=429.
[43] Beinin, "The Rise of Egypt's Workers."
[44] Ibid.
[45] Amar, "Why Mubarak is Out."
[46] LeVine, "Interview with Hossam el-Hamalawy."
[47] Hossam El-Hamalawy, "Comrades and Brothers," *Middle East Research and Information Project*, no. 242, http://www.merip.org/mer/mer242/comrades-brothers (accessed July 17, 2013).
[48] Beinin, "Popular Social Movements and the Future of Egyptian Politics."
[49] "Egyptian revolutionary: 'We are changed forever'." *Socialist Worker (UK)*, February 01, 2011. http://www.socialistworker.co.uk/art.php?id=23782 (accessed July 17, 2013).

PART II – Labor and the Revolution

5

Labor Enters the Scene: "Take Tahrir to the Factories"

Much of the discourse surrounding the uprising focuses on the impact of social media and the role played by Western educated, middle-class activists on and after January 25, 2011. While it is clear that it was not the organized working class who comprised the vanguard of the revolution, this discourse, not to be ignored completely, overlooks the three-pronged role the working class played by: (1) setting the stage for the revolution of 2011; (2) responding en masse to oust Mubarak on February 8th when the regime called for normalization; and (3) helping dictate both the pace of the struggle and the reform process after the collapse of the Mubarak regime. Just as militant labor activity contested the legitimacy of the regime prior to 2011, the working class played an indubitable role dismantling the regime during the course of the revolution. This was especially true once the regime attempted to "normalize" economic life on February 8th by reopening closed businesses.

The acerbity which characterized Egyptian neoliberalism combined with the repressive state apparatus galvanized the working class into action on occasion before 2011. These instances often resulted in the state applying excessive punitive measures towards workers who organized independently of it. With the advent of a new revolutionary fervor, the apprehension which had previously enervated the working class began to wane and workers across Egypt saw an opportunity to take action on an unprecedented scale. What had before been a refractory challenge to the Mubarak regime now became a menacing force to its very existence as the organized working class began to preponderate as a social force. Although there were small organizations with limited scope calling for maximalist demands of social revolution based on working class principles, these did not materialize into a revolutionary organization with the social force capable of carrying them through. Given that revolutions are often long, complex processes and that important contradictions in Egyptian society have yet to be resolved, it is quite unlikely that the denouement of this particular historical process has been seen. While it may be true that there exists a general malaise afflicting the worldwide left, the following chapters demonstrate that a genuine discourse which places the Egyptian working class as a primary mover of history is necessary. While many would traduce any working class or Marxist analysis as antiquarian and anachronistic, the Egyptian revolution shows that a narrative positioning the working class as a historical subject is far from obsolete.

The Weeks before January 25th

Coming off the heels of the 2006 and 2008 Mahalla struggles and the resulting upswing in labor struggles across the country, contentious, working class militancy against the regime and its symbols were becoming increasingly evident prior the revolution. The weeks prior to January 25th had witnessed a marked increase in labor activity. A few examples of these activities include: a strike carried out by one-fifth of the railway workshop employees in Cairo, a strike of 300 workers in a wood factory in Dashna demanding unpaid wages, and a sit-in by al-Karakat Company workers in Ismailia and Port Said. Added to this was a sit-in by 1,500 Mansoura University Hospital temporary workers demanding permanent employment and a strike by 200 nurses and X-ray technicians at Ashmoun hospital protesting their benefits being cut. These last two examples foreshadowed the emergence of a new militancy in the medical sector in May.[1] Overall, some 42 economic struggles were documented in January.

Just as the April 6th Movement had its origins in the 2008 Mahalla strike, it is important to note this intensification of labor activity as it provides a backdrop to the January 25th uprising. While the case cannot be made that this augmentation of struggle led directly to the revolution, it ought to be understood that a general rise in the level of struggle, particularly in the context of the past decade, led to an atmosphere in which people were less fearful to challenge the establishment. Thus, this increase in labor activity should not be relegated as a penumbra outside the scope of the revolution. Instead, these seemingly desultory actions should be viewed, in a very general sort of way, as helping to create conditions propitious enough for an uprising to occur.

Workers as Individuals and the Emergence of Independent Trade Unionism

From the very beginning of the revolution workers took part as individuals in the protests calling for Mubarak to step down. However, even early in the course of the uprising some workers began taking collective, independent actions. A significant development came on January 30th as representatives from two independent trade unions representing workers from around a dozen major industrial areas organized a press conference announcing they were organizing an independent trade union federation.[2] In the coming weeks and months this trade union federation, the Egyptian Federation of Independent Trade Unions (EFITU), with help from the Center for Trade Union and Workers' Services (CTUWS), would begin to supplant the state-sponsored and controlled Egyptian Trade Union Federation (ETUF).

Although a few days earlier than most of their Western counterparts, the Socialist International announced on January 31 that they were relinquishing the membership of Mubarak's National Democratic Party. The letter to the NDP read, in part, "we consider that a party in government that does not listen, that does not move and that does not immediately initiate a process of meaningful change in these circumstances, cannot be a member of the Socialist International."[3] Apparently, the two decades of neoliberalism and smashing of collective working class action from 1989 onwards, when the NDP joined the International, meant little to those who ostensibly proclaim the mantle of "socialism" for themselves. Considering the privatization, repression, militarism, and capitalist nature of the party, any critical observer would question how the NDP even remotely resembled a party interested in propagating socialism. The obscenely late nature of this severance stands as a blatant demonstration of the ideological bankruptcy within the organization and a symptom of the wider affliction affecting the world left.

Even before Mubarak fell, the Revolutionary Socialists put forth their statement on how the Egyptian revolution ought to proceed. As one of the most notable organizations on the radical left, the group called for a massive redistribution of wealth, for the collectivization and re-nationalization of major industries, the development of revolutionary popular councils to manage society, and for the collective participation of the working class in the demonstrations. This, by far, was the most comprehensive call for a revolutionary reorganization of society at this point:

> What is happening today is the largest popular revolution in the history of our country and of the entire Arab world. The sacrifice of our martyrs has built our revolution and we have broken through all the barriers of fear. We will not back down until the criminal "leaders" and their criminal system is destroyed…
>
> Over the past three decades, this tyrannical regime corrupted the country's largest estates to a small handful of business leaders and foreign companies. One hundred families own more than 90 percent of the country's wealth.

They monopolize the wealth of the Egyptian people through policies of privatization, looting of power and the alliance with capital. They have turned the majority of the Egyptian people to the poor, landless and unemployed...We want the nationalization of companies, land and property looted by this bunch. As long as our resources remain in their hands we will not be able to completely get rid of this system. Economic slavery is the other face of political tyranny...

This system does not stand alone. As a dictator, Mubarak was a servant and client directly acting for the sake of the interests of America and Israel. Egypt acted as a colony of America, participated directly in the siege of the Palestinian people, made the Suez Canal and Egyptian airspace free zones for warships and fighter jets that destroyed and killed the Iraqi people, and sold gas to Israel dirt cheap while stifling the Egyptian people by soaring prices...

This is not a revolution of the elite, political parties or religious groups. Egypt's youth, students, workers and the poor are the owners of this revolution. In recent days, a lot of elites, parties and so-called symbols have begun trying to ride the wave of revolution and hijack it from their rightful owners...

This army is no longer the people's army. This army is not the one which defeated the Zionist enemy in October 1973. This army is closely associated with America and Israel. Its role is to protect Israel, not the people. Yes, we want to win the soldiers for the revolution. But we must not be fooled by slogans that "the army is on our side." The army will either suppress the demonstrations directly, or restructure the police to play this role...

What we need right now is to push for the socio-economic demands as part of our demands, so that the person sitting in his home knows that we are fighting for their rights... The demonstrations and protests have played a key role in igniting and continuing our revolution. Now we need the workers. They can seal the fate of the regime. Not only by participating in the demonstrations, but by organizing a

> general strike in all the vital industries and large corporations.
>
> The regime can afford to wait out the sit-ins and demonstrations for days and weeks, but it cannot last beyond a few hours if workers use strikes as a weapon. Strike on the railways, on public transport, the airports and large industrial companies! Egyptian workers, on behalf of the rebellious youth and on behalf of the blood of our martyrs, join the ranks of the revolution, use your power and victory will be ours![4]

It was clear, however, that while the left played a crucial role in the revolution it did not have the organizational structures in place to fully win over the hearts of minds of the Egyptian masses. The Revolutionary Socialists, while celebrating the inspiring and collective struggle of the Egyptian people, argued desperately that Egyptians could not let a new form of oppression and exploitation replace the old one. After decades of vicious austerity, they hoped a call to arms for Egyptian workers would secure an organic labor uprising capable of pushing the revolution forward. In what was to be a common phrase in the coming weeks, the Revolutionary Socialists urged workers to "take Tahrir to the factories." Such a move would be the only protection against any convalescence of counter-revolutionary forces. The party, with well below a thousand active members at the time, was in no position to implement its program or to protect against the co-opting of the popular movement by a disgruntled elite aiming at superficial reforms. Despite these limitations, within a week of the call to organize being issued the working class responded with a paroxysm of activity and entered the revolution as an immensely important collective force.

February 8: "Normalizing" Economic Relations and Labor's Response

Tuesday, February 8th saw scenes of mass protests all across Egypt similar to what had happened during the prior two weeks. Hundreds of thousands of people flooded Tahrir square once again and 1,000 protestors marched on Parliament, not far from Tahrir, to demand Mubarak's resignation. One protestor hung a sign on the Parliament building that read "Closed until the fall of the regime." Tents had been erected and some began referring to Tahrir square as "Tahrir Republic" or the "Tahrir Commune," representing a form of liberated, democratic space in an otherwise hostile state apparatus. The Egyptian people organized their own checkpoints, defense committees, street cleaners, medical teams, and various other services. In other words, Tahrir square was essentially functioning as its own mini-state, a liberated area which the Egyptian people not only passively occupied but actively ran on their own.

More importantly, however, the 8th saw the entrance of a new, percussive component into the movement. A full fourteen days of sustained activity by the Egyptian masses meant that the regime was already on the defensive, but as protests entered their third week the movement was beginning to find it harder to extract significant concessions, especially their demand for the removal of Mubarak. In response, EFITU called for a general strike on February 8th demanding that Mubarak step down. The 8th clearly displayed, for the first time, that the Egyptian working class was ready to forcefully impose itself upon the course of the revolution. Up until this point, workers had taken part in demonstrations primarily as individuals, as Egyptian citizens. Organized labor, acting as a collective, unified force, had been the sleeping giant and no one knew when, or if, it would wake. A week after the Revolutionary Socialists put out their call, working people began taking to the streets and going on strike in solidarity with the desires of the anti-Mubarak protestors. At the same time, they began formulating their own economic demands. The development, at least in part, was a response to the regime's attempt to "normalize" Egyptian society on February 6th by reopening closed institutions and workplaces. Prior to this, workers were unable to organize collectively because the capitalists had shut down production to avoid a massive plummet in the stock market due to the upheaval. "Only when the government tried to bring the country back to 'normal' on 8 February," explains Hossam El-Hamalawy, "did the workers return to their factories, discuss the current situation and start to organise en masse, moving as an independent block."[5] February 8th was the day the massive strike wave began. Khalid 'Ali explained that "The workers did not start the January 25 movement because they [had] no organizing structure. . . . [But] one of the important steps of this revolution was taken when they began to protest, giving the revolution an economic and social slant besides the political demands."[6]

In all, tens of thousands of workers would respond to the call, organizing over 60 strikes and protests before the Mubarak regime collapsed.[7] Suez Canal workers went out first and, by the next day, strikes had spread to various sectors of industry as independent labor unions called on their workers to not go into work. In an attempt to stave off the protests, the Mubarak regime promised government employees, around six million Egyptians, a fifteen percent pay increase scheduled to start in April. In spite of this paltry concession, by Februrary 10th some 20,000 factory workers across trade lines went on strike, as did many workers in involved industries such as textiles, tourism, iron and steel, chemical, cement, oil, and telecommunications.⁸ Similarly, postal workers, doctors, lawyers, transport workers, artists, teachers, electricians, and others all staged collective actions of one sort of another.⁹ Joel Beinin articulates how workers began to merge economic and political demands:

> Up until now, there has been relatively a low level of worker participation as workers—not as individuals, of course; people participated in various demonstrations—but there's been very low level of worker participation in the movement. But in the last few days what you've seen is tens of thousands of workers linking their economic demands to the political demand that the Mubarak regime step aside. And this means that what had been perceived as a gap between the mostly economic demands that were raised over the last decade and the political demands that were raised by the intelligentsia, that gap has been closed, and now these things are fused together.¹⁰

It should be noted that, originally, workers began to articulate demands that were sometimes sectional and pecuniary in nature. Yet, within a day or two workers began appropriating the political demands of the democratization movement. "Many of these workers who had returned to their jobs in the past days had participated in the demonstrations of the last two-and-a-half weeks, but as individuals," explained Mostafa Omar, "By the time they returned to the factories, they were radicalized enough to formulate their own economic demands. But they also support the political demands coming out of Tahrir Square."¹¹ The closure of the gap that Beinin speaks of could not have been articulated more clearly than by the statement put forth by the Iron and Steel workers, who adumbrated their demands as such:

> 1. Immediate resignation of the president and all men and symbols of the regime.
>
> 2. Confiscation of funds and property of all symbols of previous regime and everyone proved corrupt.
>
> 3. Iron and steel workers, who have given martyrs and militants, call upon all workers of Egypt to revolt from the regime's and ruling party workers' federation, to dismantle it and announce their independent union now, and to plan for their general assembly to freely establish their own

independent union without prior permission or consent of the regime, which has fallen and lost all legitimacy.

4. Confiscation of public-sector companies that have been sold or closed down or privatized, as well as the public sector which belongs to the people and its nationalization in the name of the people and formation of a new management by workers and technicians.

5. Formation of a workers' monitoring committee in all workplaces, monitoring production, prices, distribution and wages.

6. Call for a general assembly of all sectors and political trends of the people to develop a new constitution and elect real popular committees without waiting for the consent or negotiation with the regime.

A huge workers' demonstration will join the Tahrir Square on Friday, the 11th of February 2011 to join the revolution and announce the demands of the workers of Egypt.

Long live the revolution!
Long live Egypt's workers!
Long live the intifada of Egyptian youth--People's revolution for the people![12]

Echoing these sentiments, public bus workers also issued political demands in conjunction with their economic goals. A statement put out by the public transport workers called for abolishing the emergency law, removing NDP members from the state institutions, dissolving the parliament, drafting new constitution, forming a national unity government, setting a national minimum wage of 1200 Egyptian pounds, and prosecuting corrupt officials. Clearly, workers were not depoliticized or simply focused on narrow economic interests.[13]

The Working Class and its Economic Threat to the Regime

Aside from US military aid, which propped up the Mubarak regime, the Egyptian elite relied heavily upon two significant economic sources through which they generated their wealth. Tourism, which represents over 11% of Egypt's Gross Domestic Product,[14] despite the population only ever seeing a paltry fraction of that amount, had already been effectively shut down by a combination of tourist industry strikes and tourists fearing the reign of violence brought about by the Mubarak regime. Egyptian ministers estimated at the time that Egypt was losing over $300 million a day because of the deflating tourism industry. To get an idea of the magnitude of this phenomenon, by summer the finance minister Samir Radwan would claim that strikes and labor actions had cost the tourist industry 13.5 billion Egyptian pounds.[15]

A second major source of revenue for Egypt was the Suez Canal. Roughly 8% of world trade, nearly 100 ships per day, crossed through the Suez Canal. Its closure would have meant a significant loss to world trade and the revenue generated from it. The loyalties and consciousness of Egyptian canal workers, and especially the operators of the canal, were a point of contention. Egyptian workers had the power to not only shut their own economy down and halt the profits and exploitation imposed on them by the capitalist class, but also the potential to disrupt international trade. The organized power of the working class, and their pivotal role in bringing down Mubarak, was never more visible than when the canal workers went on strike and Western officials immediately clamored about its potential closing. Ultimately, the canal did not have to be closed for Mubarak to step down. However, even the specter of its closure remained an important leverage point for Egyptian workers. At this point, the future of Egyptian society and the extent to which the revolution was propagated remained in the hands of the Egyptian working class.

Mubarak Desperately Holds On

The exuberant entrance of the working class as a collective force into the struggle rejuvenated pro-democracy activists. Protestors continued their occupation not only of Tahrir, but also Parliament, the Presidential Palace, and the state media building. State-owned Channel 5 in Alexandria was even shut down by protestors. Those in more rural, provincial towns took action in solidarity with workers and youth. According to an Associated Press Report, "Some 8,000 protesters, mainly farmers, set barricades of flaming palm trees in the southern province of Assiut. They blocked the main highway and railway to Cairo to complain of bread shortages. They then drove off the governor by pelting his van with stones."[16]

In response to the entrance of labor into the revolution, the government responded with more concessions. The regime was forced by popular pressure to follow through on its amnesty for prisoners. They released some 1,840 prisoners on the 9th of February as signs of labor unrest continued. These included:

demonstrations by thousands of workers in Helwan, Kafr al-Dawwar and Kafr al-Zayyat; a demonstration by temporary employees in front of the General Authority of Health Insurance building in Cairo in demand of permanent employment; a demonstration by over 500 employees of the Red Crescent on behalf of temporary workers on provisional contracts for 20 years; a strike by the Boulaq railway workshop's workers who gathered to prevent trains from passing through; and a march by thousands of street cleaning personnel down Sudan Street in the Cairo neighborhood of Muhandisin to demand higher wages and better working conditions.[17]

A day later word began circulating that Mubarak was considering stepping down and handing power over to the military. Egyptians waited anxiously to hear what they thought would finally be the sound of their oppressor admitting defeat. They were woefully disappointed. Instead of resigning, Mubarak announced that "I have seen that it is required to delegate the powers and authorities of the president to the vice president as dictated in the constitution." He maintained that he would stay in Egypt and "continue to shoulder my responsibility to protect the constitution and safeguard the interests of the people ... until power is handed over to those elected in September by the people in free and fair elections in which all the guarantees of transparencies will be secured."[18]

The massive crowd in Tahrir responded with disgust, angrily shouting that Mubarak must leave and not accepting any conferral of power to the hand-chosen Suleiman. Egyptians understood well enough that the constitutional article that allowed him to delegate powers did not require his resignation. One protestor articulated the calls of many when he proclaimed that the old constitution was simply not adequate for a post-revolution Egypt and that Egyptians could "make a new one," adding that since January 25th Mubarak has "no authority over us." Another protestor explained that "the people have spoken...they want the whole regime to resign. They don't want Omar Suleiman or Hosni Mubarak or some other guy from the government. They said that they want the whole regime to go. This is just playing with the people's minds."[19] By this point most estimates placed the death toll of the revolution at above 300, a cost too steep for the Egyptian people to settle with piecemeal reforms. For many Egyptians, there was no turning back.

Mass Strikes and Mubarak's Resignation

The labor movement played an important role in bringing down Mubarak. Strikes all across Egypt continued as workers fought desperately not only to improve their own livelihoods but also to fight the oppressive nature of Mubarak's reign:

> In the industrial community of Kafr al-Dawwar—a historic center of working class militancy—hundreds of silk and textile workers participated in protests over inadequate pay and bad conditions. In Helwan, a Nile city south of Cairo, 4,000 workers from the Coke Coal and Basic Chemical Company announced a strike. While demanding higher pay, permanent contracts for temporary workers, and an end to corruption, the workers also declared their solidarity with protestors in the capital. In another significant protest action in Helwan, 2,000 silk workers participated in a demonstration that demanded the removal of their company's board of directors.
>
> In the city of Mahalla, located in the Nile Delta, 1,500 workers protested the late payment of wages and bonuses. In another struggle in that city, hundreds of workers at a spinning company participated in a sit-in demanding action on over-due promotions. In Quesna, also located in the Delta, 2,000 pharmaceutical workers went on strike.
>
> More than 6,000 workers employed by the Suez Canal Authority in Port Said, Ismailia and Suez staged sit-ins to demand adjustments in their pay. Also in Suez, 400 workers employed by the Misr National Steel Company initiated industrial action.[20]

During February 10th and 11th strikes continued throughout Egypt in key sectors. The question that remained at this juncture was not whether workers were willing to organize. Instead, it was how the various segments of the working class could be organized into an alternative political power. On February 11th, in conjunction with the nascent strike wave, millions of citizens participated in protests all across Egypt. Cairo, Alexandria, Suez, Mansoura, and Ismailia, Mahalla, Shebin el-Kom, El-Arish, Sohag, Minya, and many other cities and towns saw large-scale protests against Mubarak and the NDP. Two and a half weeks of collective action finally brought Mubarak to his knees, and Suleiman announced that Mubarak would step down and transfer power to a military junta that would rule in the transition period. According to the Egyptian NGO *Awlad al-Ard*, the economic stoppages were "one of the most important factors leading to the rapidity of... Mubarak's decision to leave."[21] February 11th became a day of celebration as the "dictatorship of fear" had been broken. A new upsurge in labor militancy characterized the rest of February.

Only one day after forcing Mubarak out, the next stage of the revolution was already in motion. Postal workers continued to strike calling for higher wages and the removal of overpaid military administrators.[22] Thousands of public transit workers staged protests in el-Gabal el-Ahmar, as did the steelworkers at the Helwan Steel Mills. Four thousand workers from the East Delta Flour Mills went on strike. Railway technicians brought trains to a halt and thousands of el-Hawamdiya Sugar Factory workers went on strike. Oil workers struck over their own economic demands with simultaneous political calls for the removal of Minister Sameh Fahmy and a stoppage of subsidized gas exports to Israel.[23]

The largely uncoordinated, wildcat nature of the workers struggles during this period had a percussive "disorganizing effort" on the regime, and made it impossible to "insulate the rest of society" from the protests at the heart of the revolution in Tahrir. Furthermore, in the following period these struggles served as a relentless attack on the return to "normality" that the post-Mubarak regime so desperately wanted. Workers played a pivotal role in shifting the "frontier of control" in their own favor, a process which Anne Alexander argues became "politically important as it coincided with a lull in the mass street mobilization."[24] At the time, Hossam El-Hamalawy articulated the prodigious importance of the working class to the revolution:

> All classes in Egypt took part in the uprising. In Tahrir Square you found sons and daughters of the Egyptian elite, together with the workers, middle class citizens, and the urban poor. Mubarak has managed to alienate all social classes in society including wide section of the bourgeoisie. But remember that it's only when the mass strikes started three days ago that's when the regime started crumbling and the army had to force Mubarak to resign because the system was about to collapse... At this point, the Tahrir Square occupation is likely to be suspended. But we have to take Tahrir to the factories now. As the revolution proceeds an inevitable class polarization is to happen. We

have to be vigilant. We shouldn't stop here... We hold the keys to the liberation of the entire region, not just Egypt... Onwards with a permanent revolution that will empower the people of this country with direct democracy from below...[25]

[1] Sallam, "Striking Back at Egyptian Workers."
[2] "Striking Egyptian Workers Fuel the Uprising After 10 Years of Labor Organizing."
[3] Luis Ayala (Secretary General of the Socialist International), "To the General Secretary of the National Democratic Party, NDP, Egypt." Last modified January 31, 2011. Accessed July 18, 2013. http://www.socialistinternational.org/images/dynamicImages/files/Letter NDP.pdf.
[4] English translation: Revolutionary Socialists, "A call from Egyptian socialists." Last modified February 07, 2011. Accessed July 18, 2013. http://socialistworker.org/2011/02/07/call-from-egyptian-socialists. Original text in Arabic: http://www.e-socialists.net/node/6445
[5] Hossam El-Hamalawy, "Egypt protests continue in the factories." *The Guardian*, February 14, 2011. http://www.guardian.co.uk/commentisfree/2011/feb/14/egypt-protests-democracy-generals (accessed July 18, 2013).
[6] Beinin, "The Rise of Egypt's Workers."
[7] Ibid.
[8] Mostafa Ali, "Workers take center stage." *Socialist Worker (US)*, February 10, 2011. http://socialistworker.org/2011/02/10/workers-take-center-stage (accessed July 18, 2013).
[9] "Workers to continue Egypt strikes," *Al-Jazeera English*, February 10, 2011. http://www.aljazeera.com/news/middleeast/2011/02/20112107944393156.html (accessed July 18, 2013).
[10] Beinin, "Striking Egyptian Workers Fuel the Uprising After 10 Years of Labor Organizing."
[11] Ali, "Workers take center stage."
[12] Ibid.
[13] Hossam El-Hamalawy, "Public transportation workers call for overthrowing Mubarak," *3arabawy* (blog), February 09, 2011, http://www.arabawy.org/2011/02/09/jan25-public-transportation-workers-call-for-overthrowing-mubarak/.
[14] "Egypt tourism faces blow, may only be short-term."*Reuters*, January 29, 2011. http://www.reuters.com/article/2011/01/29/egypt-protests-tourism-idUSLDE70S0EG20110129 (accessed July 18, 2013).
[15] Sallam, "Striking Back at Egyptian Workers."
[16] "Strikes in Egypt add to pressure from protests."*Associated Press*, February 09, 2011. http://m.fayobserver.com/articles?path=/articles/2011/02/09/1069935 (accessed July 18, 2013).
[17] Sallam, "Striking Back at Egyptian Workers."
[18] Michael Maggie, "Egypt's Mubarak transfers power to vice president." *Associated Press*, February 10, 2011. http://apnews.myway.com//article/20110210/D9LA5JD00.html (accessed July

18, 2013).

[19] "Exclusive Video: Protesters in Tahrir Square Voice Outrage After Mubarak Defiantly Refuses to Step Down," DemocracyNow!

[20] David North, "The Egyptian working class moves to the forefront." *World Socialist Web Site*, February 10, 2011. http://www.wsws.org/en/articles/2011/02/pers-f10.html?view=print (accessed July 18, 2013).

[21] Beinin, "The Rise of Egypt's Workers."

[22] In Arabic: Fatima Ramadan, "Egypt's Workers Continue Work Stoppages to Reclaim their Rights in the Era after the Deposed President," Tadamon Masr (blog), February 12, 2011, http://tadamonmasr.wordpress.com/2011/02/12/strikes/ (accessed July 18, 2013).

[23] Hossam El-Hamalawy, "The Workers, Middle Class, Military Junta, and the Permanent Revolution."*Jadaliyya*, February 12, 2011. http://www.jadaliyya.com/pages/index/629/the-workers-middle-class-military-junta-and-the-permanent-revolution (accessed July 18, 2013).

[24] Alexander, "The Egyptian workers' movement and the 25 January Revolution."

[25] El-Hamalawy, "The Workers, Middle Class, Military Junta, and the Permanent Revolution."

6

Labor Activity and Military Rule in February: "Let the Revolution in Egypt be Permanent!"

Not long after the fall of Mubarak, Egypt's ruling military clique began to utilize the "chaos and disorder" card[1] in order to "ban meetings by labour unions or professional syndicates, effectively forbidding strikes, and tell all Egyptians to get back to work after the unrest that toppled Hosni Mubarak."[2] Three days after Mubarak's resignation, the Supreme Council of the Armed Forces released a communique blasting economic stoppages of any sort. The military high command utilized nationalist rhetoric to try and break the class struggle erupting inside the country: "Noble Egyptians see that these strikes, at this delicate time, lead to negative results."[3] Egyptians, however, were quick to point out the similarities between the military controlled periods of 1952 and 2011, especially with the amount of strike activity during both periods. Workers were acutely aware of the role the military played in 1952 when thousands went on strike in Kafr al-Dawwar after the Free Officer coup. One of the first actions the military commanders took was to savagely crush the strike and, three weeks later, hang two of the strike leaders. The names of Mustafa Khamis and Ahmad al-Bakri were not lost to Egyptian workers.

"It Is the Fate of All Revolutions that This Union of Different Classes Cannot Subsist"

By this point, the loose alliance that was vital in organizing and maintaining the uprising began to deteriorate. The coalition, with its broad class-base that attempted to include members of the elite, spokespersons for the middle class, and the most exploited and oppressed of the working class, was no longer sustainable. As Friedrich Engels pointed out not long after the European revolutions of 1848:

> It is the fate of all revolutions that this union of different classes, which in some degree is always the necessary condition of any revolution, cannot subsist long. No sooner is the victory gained against the common enemy than the victors become divided amongst themselves into different camps and turn their weapons against each other. It is this rapid and passionate development of class antagonism which, in old and complicated social organisms, makes revolution such a powerful agent of social and political progress.[4]

One of the first schisms that arose was the decision by both the leadership of the Muslim Brotherhood and Mohamed ElBaradei to support the military takeover under the assumption that it was the only force capable of overseeing an "orderly transition."[5] Similarly, many of the middle class activists, especially those that composed the base of the secular liberal camp, accepted that the revolution's zenith had already passed and argued it was time to rebuild. The military took this opportunity to exploit and expand these splits in the coalition. They sowed the seeds of conflict by utilizing the rhetoric of "chaos and disorder" to create tension between the Islamists and secular liberals who supported the military council's attempts at slow, orderly reform and working class and left-wing elements who wanted to carry the revolution further.

The cohesion of the coalition could no longer be maintained. The organizing nexus, namely the objective to remove Mubarak, had been achieved. Subsequently, the various views on how the reorganization of society ought to occur began to arise, with some elements siding with the military in an attempt to see their vision concretized. The middle class activists were now at odds with the working class who desired to see their economic demands met. For instance, Wael Ghonim, touted repeatedly in Western media as one of the leaders of the revolution, called for protestors to simply trust the army and return to work. Richard Seymour explained these developments at the time:

> The focus, in the Anglophone media, on the Twitterati, may have overstated the relevance of the middle class, but they did not fabricate their role. In the current situation, it is often the small businessmen and middle class professionals (like the Google marketing head Wael Ghonim, currently in a meeting with the higher council of the armed forces) who are in a hurry to call an end to hostilities. They want to get back to earning money. The

accent is shifting far more clearly to the organised working class.⁶

The ruling class was able to capitalize on these middle class sentiments. This desire to "get back to earning money" was particularly true of the military elites involved in business endeavors that suffered from the revolutionary upheaval, such as tourism. The opening of the stock market, which had been closed at the end of January, had already been postponed until February 16th in fear that an early opening would lead to a plummet as uncertain investors pulled out their money. In the two days prior to the market closing in January, stocks had dropped by 17%.⁷ The ruling class was desperate to get back to its primary role as capital accumulators. Subsequently, they were more than willing to utilize the ideological rhetoric of "stability" and "prosperity" to simultaneously woo the middle class and suit their own needs.

The New Pejorative of the Military, the Media, and the Brotherhood: *Ihtijajat Fi'awiyya*

Immediately after Mubarak's resignation, with the increase in labor strife across Egypt, Egyptian authorities and media outlets began labeling labor protests pejoratively as *ihtijajat fi'awiyya*, or "small group protests." As Hesham Sallam explains:

> The Arabic term *fi'a* simply means "group," but has acquired negative connotations and might be compared with how the term "special interest" is used to disparage American labor. In post-Mubarak Egypt, officials have used its adjectival form *fi'awi* in reference to any demonstration, strike or sit-in advancing demands related to distribution of wealth, whether the protesters are blue- or white-collar employees, and whether they are calling for higher wages, greater benefits, improved working conditions or replacement of corrupt management personnel. The term's recent usage seems to encompass the public and private sectors and to apply to collective action as limited as a protest in a single state-owned enterprise and as broad as a national strike by disgruntled members of a professional syndicate... Before the release of the army's Communiqué 5, the mainstream media relied on terms like "demands-based protests" (*ihtijajat matlabiyya*) or labor sit-ins (*i'tisamat 'ummaliyya*) when discussing worker unrest.⁸

Subsequently, middle-class elements were quick to pick up the cue and act as the demobilizing buffer that would blunt the class dimension of the revolution. This included both the secular liberals and the Muslim Brotherhood, who largely drew their activist base from the Egyptian middle class. Only two days after SCAF issued the communique denouncing "*fi'awi* demands" as illegitimate, a spokesman for the Muslim Brotherhood accused *fi'awi* protests of "undermining national consensus" and expressed "understanding" for the army's position, while the editor-in-chief of the liberal *Wafd*'s daily paper warned that demonstrations could "destroy" the gains of the revolution.[9] Western media and the Egyptian elite alike sought to cloak the class composition of the revolution with the artificial, innocuous, and deceivingly-homogenous construct called the "youth."

For the workers around Egypt erupting in demands for improved economic conditions, the gains were minimal. New faces in government and fair elections were an improvement, no doubt, but such things provided little comfort when workers regularly faced a weekly wage incapable of providing a decent standard of living. "Activists can take some rest from the protest and go back to their well-paying jobs for six months, waiting for the military to give us salvation," explained Hossam El-Hamalawy, "but the worker can't go back to his factory and still get paid 250 pounds."[10] It was now clear that a major internal divide within the popular uprising was class polarization. As the Tahrir occupation was being dismantled and the army cleared out the square, many workers and socialists argued the working class must push the revolution forward through strikes and factory occupations. Hossam El-Hamalawy articulated this position rather succinctly: "We have to take Tahrir to the factories now."[11]

Mid-February: Taking Tahrir to the Factories

Some workers were already heeding the call to take Tahrir to the factories. Hundreds of public transportation workers demonstrated outside the state-media buildings demanding better pay, as did the Youth and Sports Organization workers in Tahrir square. Hundreds of ambulance drivers demanded better pay and permanent jobs by parking some 70 ambulances near the river, refusing to drive them. Likewise, hundreds of unemployed archaeology graduates, a relatively large field of study in Egypt, demonstrated outside the Supreme Council for Antiquities in Zamalek, calling for access to jobs. Workers went on strike at Cairo International Airport calling for more pay and better benefits, bringing EgyptAir's flight capacity down to 30% as strikes by workers spread to companies that provided support services for the Egyptian airlines as well. An order from the Central Bank of Egypt closed all banks after employees went on strike at the largest state-owned bank and many other financial institutions. Several hundred people protested outside the state-run Trade and Workers Federation demanding the dissolving of its board, which they accused of corruption.[12] Labor strife became so prominent that one businessman even hired thugs to fire on strikers and run them over with a car.[13]

Likewise, protests and strikes occurred outside of Cairo. Suez Canal workers organized a sit-in at the state-run union office in defiance of the Suez Canal Authority head, Admiral Ahmed Fadel, because of his refusal to acknowledge the demands of workers in the past.[14] The online version of *El Badil* estimated that strikes were affecting some fifty companies in Suez alone on February 13th.[15] In Alexandria, workers held demonstrations. Workers called for a strike at one of the world's largest gold mines near the city of Marsa Alam. Protests were not limited purely to strikes, however. In Beni Sweif, south of Cairo, thousands of poor workers and the unemployed demanded access to the state-built, low-cost apartments that party officials regularly dished out to friends and relatives. Some, tired of waiting, took direct action and seized around 60,000 empty units in the cities of Cairo, Beni Sweif and Qalioubiya.[16] Other workers on strike included electrical workers, cement laborers, phosphate miners, textile workers, and municipal employees.[17] Demands were centered on five main objectives:

> First, workers want a 1,200-pound ($204) monthly minimum wage. Second, they want to replace corrupt CEOs--many of them are also members of Mubarak's National Democratic Party. Third, the strikers, many of whom have been working on temporary contracts for years, want job security. Fourth, many workers are demanding that privatization and outsourcing be reversed, and that they become government employees again. Fifth, among many strikers, there is a desire to get rid of pro-regime union officials and sympathy for the formation of new, independent unions.[18]

Although it was obvious that class struggle was intensifying, the largest problem was that no central organization was in place to coordinate worker actions. Spontaneous eruptions and wildcat strikes seemed to occur all over Egypt, but they lacked a coordinated plan of action incorporating the goals of the working class as a whole. Without such an organizational structure to unite around, it would be a challenge for the workers to push through their class demands and articulate wider demands, such as a significant redistribution of wealth and the democratization of the economy.

Thus far, working class and radical organizations were excluded entirely from talks with the ruling military junta. Instead, representatives of the popular movement came primarily from the Islamist and Secular Liberal camps, including the Muslim Brotherhood, the National Association for Change, members of the April 6th Movement, and the Democratic Front. Some of these middle-class representatives of the so-called "youth movement" in Egypt, who relied upon the percussive power of labor to bring down Mubarak, now betrayed working class movement and sided with the military. They claimed it was not the time to strike since eighteen days of upheaval had already caused economic problems for Egypt. For the middle class and the elites, the revolution had to be tamed. Middle-class representatives wanted their freedom of speech and expression, but fundamental economic restructuring was out of the question.

"The workers must drive the proposals of the democrats to their logical extreme (the democrats will in any case act in a reformist and not a revolutionary manner) and transform these proposals into direct attacks on private property," explained Karl Marx on the role of workers in a revolution.[19] The military sent a text message to every Egyptian cell phone that read: "We urge citizens and members of professional and labor unions to go back to their positions and each play their part."[20] Defying the second military warning in three days, workers took to the streets and factories on Wednesday the 16th to "drive the proposals of the democrats to their logical extreme." In Mahalla, some 20,000 workers were on strike calling for higher pay and an investigation of corruption at the main factory there. In Cairo, airport employees called for better wages and benefits. Teachers demonstrated in front of the education ministry. By this time, workers were beginning to develop the notion that "it is [their] interest and [their] task to make the revolution permanent until all the more or less propertied classes have been driven from their ruling positions."[21]

On Thursday the 17th, the US tried desperately to maintain control over the situation by promising the military leaders an immediate $150 million, ostensibly to help "pay for the transition period." Meanwhile, the military hoped to placate the protestors aiming to fill Tahrir on Friday by ordering the arrests of two former officials accused of misusing public funds - a steel tycoon named Ahmad 'Izz who dominated two-thirds of the steel industry, and the Interior Minister, Habib el-Adli, for his role in orchestrating both the repression of protestors and the bombing of a Coptic church in Alexandria during December. Egyptian workers across the country continued to test the limits imposed by the military regime, calling for higher wages, better working conditions, the removal of corrupt leaders in the state-controlled trade unions, the right to form independent unions, and an increase in the minimum wage. Teachers tried to storm the Education Ministry. Mahalla workers continued striking. Trains were delayed as railway workers went on strike, calling for a 50% pay increase. Nurses and doctors demanded the removal of their directors for mismanagement. Oil workers called for a fairer distribution of wages, increased pay, and the prosecution of corrupt officials who raked in large sums of money.[22] The staff striking at Menoufia University in Shibin el Kom numbered around 2,000 and demanded permanent employment and higher wages.[23] Labor lawyer Khaled 'Ali estimated that anywhere between thirty to sixty strikes occurred every day from Februrary 12th until the 17th. He articulated the importance of collective workers actions in both the foundation and continuation of the revolution:

> The workers actions right now are the best means of preserving the gains of the revolution… You can't deny the role of middle class youth in the revolution and you can't deny that youth are the ones who sparked this revolution. But there is a big difference between those who sparked the revolution and those who continued on with the revolution and are still continuing on until all its demands are met… The workers have successfully launched and sustained the largest wave of labor mobilization this county has seen from 2004 until 2011. The workers are the ones who brought down the structures of this regime in the past years. They are the ones that have been fighting for independent organizing on the ground and they are the ones who created Egypt's first de facto independent trade union. And they insisted on the right to have pluralistic trade unions, not just unions that are stacked with government supporters. They are the ones who brought their grievances to the streets. Last spring workers were protesting in large numbers in front of the upper and lower houses of the Egyptian Parliament… Workers laid the ground for the emergence of this revolution…[24]

Hundreds of thousands of people flooded Tahrir Square on the 18th of February, one week after the downfall of Mubarak, in what became known as the "Friday of Victory and Continuation."

While Friday was largely celebratory, those who came to Tahrir also knew that they had to put pressure on the military to see through their demands, including the enactment of swift reforms and the release of thousands of political prisoners. Furthermore, many understood the revolution was no longer simply about bringing down Mubarak and the nepotism surrounding the NDP, but about formulating political and economic alternatives to the neoliberal project itself. Sharif Abdel Kouddous explicated upon the atmosphere:

> It is been one week since Mubarak stepped down. And we've seen strikes across the city, across the country, even when you are driving around Egypt, you drive past a fancy hotel and you'll see hotel workers out on strike. You drive past a sporting Club, you will see the workers there are on strike. You drive past a bank, you'll see workers on strike too. And so people are calling for reforms, better wages, for the resignation of officials who have been tied to the regime and corruption.[25]

Strikes continued all across the country, a high concentration of them in Cairo and Alexandria. Many strikes also occurred in the heavily industrialized northern Delta region and more sporadically through the south. Workers, regardless of the localized nuances of their demands, had four primary goals in mind: (1) cleansing, or the removal from positions of power all corrupt CEOs appointed by Mubarak or tied to the NDP; (2) the end to the "temporary worker status" for millions of workers that allowed employers to hire and fire at will; (3) the increase of wages and benefits, especially the implementation of a minimum and maximum wage; (4) the re-nationalization of companies sold far below market prices to wealthy investors.

These demands were consistently repeated in one form or another regardless of the sector in question. At the state-owned al-Ahram newspaper company, hundreds of journalists and employees called for the resignation of the pro-Mubarak managers. Taxi cab drivers staged a demonstration in front of a government building in Hurghada until military police dispersed the drivers by firing gunshots into the air. What happened in Hurghada was part of a wider strategy by the military that aimed at dismantling the worker-led movement to win further gains from the revolution. On the same day, while watching over the celebrations in Tahrir, the military warned that it would begin to take action to halt strikes and worker actions. The military council stated that strikes would "be confronted" and "illegitimate practices" like work stoppage and the seizure of government land and property would not be tolerated. According to the junta, those who have "organised stoppages and protests, disrupting (economic) interests, halting the wheels of production and creating difficult economic conditions that could lead to the deterioration of the nation's economy" were to be stopped "to protect the security of the nation and citizens."[26] Apparently, for the military apparatus those within the Egyptian working class did not constitute part of the "nation."

It was far too late, however, for the military leaders to roll back the revolution without a fight. A century ago Rosa Luxemburg described the dynamic relationship between political and economic struggle during a revolutionary process, explaining that with every political concession granted by elites "the political struggle is transformed into a powerful impetus for the economic struggle." As economic gains are made, the "workers' condition of ceaseless economic struggle with the capitalists keeps their fighting spirit alive in every political interval."[27] Successive waves of political and economic demands become merged, each one reinforcing the other. Although the mass strike – the single phenomenon which could have fully paralyzed the economy, broke the dictatorship of the military regime, and pushed the revolution to new heights – never occurred in Egypt, the increasingly spontaneous strike wave which gripped the nation in February was the greatest challenge to the military regime, and the only major social force propelling the revolution forward.

Working Class Organizations: The Proliferation of New Political Parties

The first attempt to develop a centralized apparatus through which the working class movement could operate was underway as socialists, activists, and union members came together and laid the ground work for the establishment of the Democratic Labor Party of Egypt. Inspired in large part by the Revolutionary Socialists and other segments of the left, delegates articulated a general framework for the party and discussion of the party platform was open to representatives from important sectors of the Egyptian working class, including workers from Mahalla, Kafr El-Dawar, Suez, Helwan, and several other areas. Sameh Naguib of the Revolutionary Socialists noted at the time:

> We have built contacts and close relationships in the working class over the previous years of struggle. At the same time, we are focusing on central sectors of the economy: workers in textiles, post office, railways, transportation, communications and cement industries. I also think that the new movement to form independent militant unions to replace the pro-government unions will succeed, and this will aid our effort to build a worker's party.[28]

Various trades were represented, including factory and cement workers, tax collectors, public transport and railways workers, workers employed by the military, nurses and health professionals, leaders of unions, as well as many other occupations. Conference delegates agreed to begin the necessary work for the establishment of the DLP, agreeing on a draft of the founding statement for the party. Kamal Khalil, a seasoned socialist veteran and spokesperson for the new party, explained that "Our ideology is the same as the revolution's; we only paraphrase its demands of freedom, social justice and civil state from the point of view of workers… Existing parties are state-made and have never adopted or defended workers in their struggle; so under the pressure of workers we decided to form a party of our own."[29]

The following week, the DLP held a more extensive meeting where delegates adumbrated a general outline of the party's program and ideas. Delegates finalized their founding statement, declaring that the Democratic Labor Party was the party of all of salaried workers, employees, professionals and agricultural workers, and that the party was open to all students, intellectuals, and writers in the community who sympathize and defend the rights of the workers. Furthermore, they emphasized their openness to the rural elements of society, proclaiming that the DLP also represented the basic demands of the peasants. These included a radical agrarian reform in the Egyptian countryside, the reduction of agricultural rents, and support for the agricultural requirements such as seeds and fertilizers. In this way they hoped for the DLP to become a mass party for all rural workers and peasants. They similarly argued the need for the DLP to "permanently and continuously" defend the three principles of the Egyptian revolution: freedom, social justice, and civilian government. Founders also drafted program positions calling to overturn the Camp David Accords, stop the exportation of natural gas to Israel and drop the QIZ requirements linking trade the "Zionist entity," and support Palestinian, Lebanese, and Iraqi forces for the liberation of Palestine and Iraq. For them, the struggle against colonialism and Zionism was inseparable from the issues of freedom, social justice and a democratic, civil state. Finally, they argued for the inclusion and augmenting of the "Committees for the Defense of the Revolution," [Popular Committees] which were formed in various districts and provinces to protect and further the revolution.[30] As one Revolutionary Socialist later lamented, the DLP was "not as radical as we had hoped, but its formation adds to the workers' political front."[31]

Meanwhile, streams of the old left, centered on dissidents from the Al-Tagammu party, formed the Socialist Popular Alliance Party (*Al-Tahaluf al-sha'abi al-ishtiraki*). This was meant to act as a new platform for leftists to organize around issues of social justice and a rolling back of the neoliberal agenda. The founding statement proclaimed the "people's will for change was aligned with leftist streams" which represented "the heritage of people's struggle for democracy and social justice during the revolution."

The organization aimed to draw the public into political life, unite various leftist currents, and organize heavily among the youth instead of focusing on the older, official leftist figureheads. "We are a democratic, open party whose decisions and policies aren't imposed but coordinated among its streams allowing for diversity of opinions," the statement read. Similarly, the Muslim Brotherhood announced the formation of its own Freedom and Justice Party, while more liberal Islamists who had split from the Muslim Brotherhood in the 1990s finally gained legal recognition for their *al-Wasat* ("Center") Party.[32]

The Movement towards Independent Trade Unionism

It was not only the formation of radical political parties that drove the post-Mubarak revolutionary fervor. On February 19th a coalition of independent trade unionists meeting in Cairo released a declaration titled "Demands of the Workers in the Revolution":

> O heroes of the 25 January revolution! We, workers and trade unionists from different workplaces which have seen strikes, occupations and demonstrations by hundreds of thousands of workers across Egypt during the current period, feel it is right to unite the demands of striking workers that they may become an integral part of the goals of our revolution, which the people of Egypt made, and for which the martyrs shed their blood. We present to you a workers' program which brings together our just demands, in order to reaffirm the social aspect of this revolution and to prevent the revolution being taken away from at its base who should be its beneficiaries.
>
> The workers' demands which we raised before the 25 January revolution and were part of the prelude to this glorious revolution are:
>
> 1. Raising the national minimum wage and pension, and a narrowing of the gap between minimum and maximum wages so that the maximum is no more than 15 times the minimum in order to achieve the principle of social justice which the revolution gave birth to; payment of unemployment benefit, and a regular increment which will increase with rising prices.

2. The freedom to organize independent trade unions without conditions or restrictions, and the protection of trade unions and their leaders.

3. The right of manual workers and clerical workers, peasant farmers and professionals, to job security and protection from dismissal. Temporary workers must be made permanent, and dismissed workers to be returned to their jobs. We must do away with all excuses for employing workers on temporary contracts.

4. Renationalization of all privatized enterprises and a complete stop to the infamous privatization program which wrecked our national economy under the defunct regime

5. * Complete removal of corrupt managers who were imposed on companies in order to run them down and sell them off.

* Curbing the employment of consultants who are past the age of retirement and who eat up 3 billion of the national income, in order to open up employment opportunities for the young.

* Return to the enforcement of price controls on goods and services in order to keep prices down and not to burden the poor.

6. The right of Egyptian workers to strike, organize sit-ins, and demonstrate peacefully, including those striking now against the remnants of the failed regime, those who were imposed on their companies in order to run them down prior to a sell-off. It is our opinion that if this revolution does not lead to the fair distribution of wealth it is not worth anything. Freedoms are not complete without social freedoms. The right to vote is naturally dependent on the right to a loaf of bread.

7. Health care is a necessary condition for increasing production.

> 8. Dissolution of the Egyptian Trade Union Federation which was one of the most important symbols of corruption under the defunct regime. Execution of the legal judgments issued against it and seizure of its financial assets and documents. Seizure of the assets of the leaders of the ETUF and its member unions and their investigation.[33]

In direct violation of the orders given by both the military council and the leading officials within the Egyptian Trade Union Federation, workers in Egypt's largest gold mine struck and cab drivers refused to work in protest. The class-collaborationist secretary general of the official ETUF, Ibrahim El-Azhari, seethed in indignation: "Stop these protests. Most of the protests are asking for wage rise, or the removal of chairmen and so on. This is a kind of extremism."[34]

Workers not only ignored the proclamations of the official union, they augmented their "extremism" by proposing "direct attacks on private property," just as Marx had argued for a century and a half earlier. The next day, representatives from a multifaceted coalition of labor organizations, including the pensioners' union, the tax collectors' union, iron and steel workers, textile and mill workers, pharmaceutical and healthcare workers, oil workers, and teachers met and released another set of demands. This set of demands was even more radical than the one that preceded it:

> 1 - The implementation of the six demands of the revolution not yet carried out.[35]
>
> 2 – The adoption of a minimum and maximum wage of a 1 to 10 ratio, with rates linked directly to inflation and the real increase in prices.
>
> 3 – The immediate inclusion of all temporary workers into the seniority ladder, including more than half a million workers and staff within the state apparatus.
>
> 4 – The end of the privatization program, including an investigation into all the corrupt sales of public sector workplaces and the recovery of these companies to be operated and run by the workers.
>
> 5 - The seizure of all the companies that the owners have shut down to be opened and run by the workers.

6 – The removal of the new labor codes instituted in 2003, which permitted separation and displacement, and to make slaves of workers have employer.

7 – Begin the process of providing employment opportunities for the unemployed and pass a law providing unemployment benefits equal to half the minimum wage

8 - Remove the insurance law, which undermined the rights of all wage earners, and increased the burden on them.

9 - Recovery funds, insurance and pension funds seized by the government of Hosni Mubarak.

10 – Stoppage of the privatization projects aimed at health institutions and extending the right treatment to every citizen.

11 – Cleanse remnants of the corrupt regime from the government and all institutions, putting the former leaders on trial.[36]

Both statements suggest that working people were making their demands clear: a stringent minimum and maximum real wage in direct correlation with the cost of living, extension of unemployment benefits to those who cannot find work, the extension of public, universal healthcare for all citizens, the freedom to organize independent labor unions that represent workers' interests, the right to strike without consent of the state, the immediate end of the "temporary worker" status and the adaptation of permanent contracts, the removal of all symbols and figures in the old regime, including corrupt managers and the state-run unions, an end to the privatization schemes, as well as a re-nationalization of all privatized companies, and most importantly the direct democratic control by workers of these companies and other workplaces shut down by owners.

These demands, radical in both their economic, political, and social content, represented a significant departure from the modest, reform oriented demands of free and fair elections. The holistic nature of the statements represented something radical beyond the specificity of the demands; namely, it was apparent that significant portions of the Egyptian working class were not fragmented by trade and occupation or factional economic interests. Working people, acting as a collective unit and recognizing themselves as an organic whole within the sphere of social relations, articulated their own class demands. They did not argue for a new set of rulers or for one faction of the capitalist class over another. Instead, they put forth a vision for a radically different set of social relations, one in which the exploitation of the capitalist class could be dramatically reduced through the democratic control of publicly owned places of work.

Making the Revolution Permanent

The Egyptian working class was now fighting for a better life, not only politically, but socially and economically. Mubarak was not solely responsible for the deprivation that had enervated the Egyptian masses. Such economic disparity was and continues to be part of a wider, global system, resulting not from a single government but from the international capitalist system and the imperialist mechanisms which sustain it. Egypt was a prototype for the neoliberal order. Even with the revolutionary overthrow of Mubarak, the chasm between rich and poor did not vanish. As one commentator noted, it was still the case that "the Sawiris family, estimated wealth over $20 billion, coexists with millions in slums and abject poverty," and nothing yet had fundamentally altered "the contrast between the rich luxuriating in Zamalek or Heliopolis and wage slaves of Mahalla or Helwan or the poor of Shubra or the Cities of the Dead." While US and European elites may have dumped Mubarak at the midnight hour and expressed "false solidarity and fake approval of the Revolution," their primary desire was to see that no serious challenge to the economic order would advance.[37] Egyptians, at least revolutionaries hailing from the working class and radical left, understood the dynamic interrelationship of political oppression, economic exploitation, and foreign imperialism all too well. Many understood that a political revolution severed from the leveling spirit of economic restructuring could be nothing more than a hollow shadow of reform.

This was not simply a matter of abstract principles, however. Workers were seeing concrete results from their struggles. At Ghazl al-Mahalla, workers led a successful three-day strike which only ended when all of their demands were met, including the firing of the director and a 25% wage increase. This victory did not subside the tide of activism, however; it emboldened it. Workers went on to publish a statement defending the revolution, asserting their right to organize independently and represent their own interests in whatever form they saw fit, be that strikes or protest. They then announced their plan to create an independent syndicate, breaking with the Egyptian Trade Union Federation, a direct violation of the labor law which stipulated only one union could represent workers in a particular sector. This example spread as postal workers, public transit workers, and nurses all declared similar intentions to organize independently. The official union responded with paternalistic disdain, claiming Egyptian workers were not ready for independent trade unions: "The pluralism will separate the workers and will break their union, besides the law doesn't allow it."[38] The media played its part as well, amplifying the rhetoric of the military regime and claiming workers were elevating their selfish interests above the rest of Egypt. On top of this ideological backlash, the military took an increasingly hard line with workers, arresting seven strikers at the Adamiya Port in Suez on Februrary 22nd and, later that day, reportedly killed a woman who had been among the protesters trying to free the arrested strikers.[39] Despite the tri-fold hostility of the official unions, the media and the military, workers continued their call for the formation of militant, independent unions and working class organizations.[40]

Rural Egyptians were also explicit in their calls for reform. On the 24th, three thousand *fellaheen* from the villages surrounding Mansoura gathered to protest the takeover of rural land by large agriculturalists, a process fueled by the exploitative, export-oriented shift in Egyptian agriculture that has stripped peasants of both their land rights and means of subsistence. They outlined a program that, among other things, called for: (1) ownership of the land by those who work and live on it; (2) restructured land contracts for farmers based on agrarian reform; (3) a cancellation of all public and private land auctions which stripped peasants of their land and housing; (4) the waiving of all debt accumulated through rent increases.[41] In Ismailia, some three thousand peasants gathered on the 21st and called on the government to recognize ownership of the land on which their homes were built. The following week, when demands had not yet been met, the protests grew to include over five thousand demonstrators.[42] Rural Egyptians, who constitute roughly half of the population, were organizing on behalf of their own interests despite the logistical difficulties non-urban communities face. It appeared that some potential existed for a working class and peasant front to be established that could push forward with a revolutionary restructuring of social relations.

Both workers and peasants had severe economic grievances against the regime. Attempts to form an alliance between workers and peasants were being actively pursued by the founding of the Democratic Labor Party, which openly advocated on behalf of both groups. The question that remained was how far workers, strategically aligned with the peasants, would push this call for "permanent revolution." The left was trying to augment this process:

> Socialists and the left are organizing popular committees to defend the revolution in factories and in city neighborhoods and villages--the goal is to mobilize forces that can confront the regime on a local basis. In Cairo

alone, 16 such neighborhood committees have been formed and are active. Socialists have printed thousands of bulletins titled "Egypt the Revolution" with the aim of recruiting new members.[43]

Although it did not occur on a large enough scale, councils such as these could have acted as the organizational apparatus through which the working class would become versed in the day-to-day requirements and forms of direct democracy needed to rebuild society.

The pursuance of a "permanent revolution" by a united working class, with the aid of the *fellaheen*, was the only force capable of making a qualitative break from the neoliberal model and instituting collective, democratic control over the economy. The February 19th document "Demands of the Workers in the Revolution" was to become influential in the coming months as hundreds of thousands of workers across a wide array of sectors would raise the core demands found in it. Critically, it reinforced the notion of social justice as a principle demand of the revolution: "If this revolution does not lead to a fair distribution of wealth and to the establishment of social justice then it will be as if nothing changed. Political freedoms cannot be complete without social freedoms. The right to a loaf of bread is the natural precursor of the right to a ballot."

In mid-February Egyptians faced a critical juncture in the revolutionary process. Without the aforementioned redistribution of wealth, the Egyptian revolution was delivered dead on arrival – a neoliberal corpse with the trappings of political reform. An Egypt functioning under the same economic rules of the past forty years would mean little more than a superficial change in political structure, whether the face of that structure was Mubarak, ElBaradei, or Morsi. As the Revolutionary Socialists wrote at the time:

> The revolution quickly transformed from the political stage to the social, as always happens in the great revolutions. The revolution will not win in the end without the entry of millions of workers and peasants onto the battlefield and the explosion of their demands for justice and the rights they have been deprived of for decades. It is not strange for members of the Supreme Council of the Armed Forces to call for a halt to strikes and demonstrations. They want to empty the revolution of its social content, to stop in the middle of the road… The revolution… is what is being done today by workers, peasants and the poor of Egypt in the form of strikes, demonstrations and sit-ins… Egypt's workers and peasants

alone are in the position through their self-organization to deepen and broaden the scope of the Egyptian revolution and achieve the glorious revolutionary society that we dream about.[44]

Pacification, Repression, and Resistance

The military apparatus, with its tentacles gripping nearly every sector of the Egyptian economy, hoped to maintain some variation of the old economic order. On Tuesday the 22nd the military council attempted a half-hearted "reform" in the form of a cabinet reshuffle. The realignment did include a few opposition figures but the most important positions, such as the ministers of interior and defense, as well as the justice and foreign ministers, remained in the hands of Mubarak loyalists. In response, one hundred thousand protestors gathered once again in Tahrir square on Friday, February 25th to demand the dismantling of the old regime and the National Democratic Party. Included in these demands were the dissolution of the Ahmed Shafiq government, the ending of the secret police, a lifting of the state of emergency, the immediate release of all political prisoners, the freezing and returning to the national treasury all assets held by figures from the old regime, and for authorities to put these former leaders on trial.

This protest came one day after a massive wave of labor demonstrations and strikes, as well as rural unrest, including: hundreds of Bahariya Oasis mine workers protesting poor working conditions, a thousand graduates, workers, and teachers from Beni Suef attempting to storm the Education Ministry building, over one thousand steel workers blocking Al-Adabiya-Ain Sokhna road, bus drivers striking in Kafr al-Sheikh to protest insurance hikes, 1,500 farmers protesting government officials who had sold off the land they had lived on for 70 years to private investors in Daqahlia, and 700 workers from the Al-Nasr mining company in Aswan presenting a memorandum to the state-owned mining union demanding a temporary administrative committee composed of workers and the removal of the old union committee leadership.[45]

As labor unrest coupled with a resurgence in Tahrir square militancy, the SCAF made the decision to forcefully remove those occupying the square by nightfall. Soldiers shut off all light from the lamp posts, fired shots into the air, and moved in to disperse the crowd. The military also forcefully dispersed protestors in front of parliament, taking on the roll previously held by the hated state security forces. Military police surrounded a group of a couple hundred protestors and then attacked them, beating them with clubs and using tasers to break up the protest. Some protestors were arrested at gunpoint. One of the arrested was quickly tried by a military tribunal and sentenced to five years in prison for "attacking a public servant."[46] Grandiose illusions of the army's neutrality had already been set on a dangerous precipice before this attack. Now these illusions were shattered. Ashraf Omar, one of the occupants, succinctly articulated this emerging consciousness: "There is no more unity between the people and the army."[47]

In line with the military's approach, the carrot came not long after the stick. The next day, the council issued an official apology for the attack and announced it had frozen Mubarak's assets and issued the arrest of a number of ministers and businessmen close to ex-dictator. Despite these weak attempts at pacification, labor struggles continued to develop in number and intensify. The educational sector in particular was on fire. Roughly 6,000 teachers protested in Alexandria[48] on March 1st following major demonstrations by educators in Helwan, Marsa Matrouh and Ismaïlia.[49] Teachers all across Egypt announced a planned strike on March 6th with wide-ranging demands: fair wages, a purging of the public symbols of corruption in school councils and official unions, trials for those who siphoned off and mismanaged school funds, the parity of wages and benefits between private and public school teachers, a reduction in class sizes, and the right to form independent unions.

It was not simply within the realm of education, however, as employees at Egypt's Principal Bank for Development and Agricultural Credit continued their strike over work conditions and called for the removal of the bank director for corruption. Over a thousand cement workers staged a sit-in demanding the retirement benefits that were promised to them.[50] Around 1,500 Helwan workers at the Arab Organization for Industrialization factories, owned by the Ministry of Defense, sat-in to raise pay, attain meal allowances, and call for the removal of overpaid administrators who allegedly siphoned hundreds of thousands of Egyptian pounds every month from the company. Workers at the Al-Nasr Company for Coke and Chemicals went on strike demanding the resignation of the chairman, an improvement of working conditions, and distribution of the massive profits made by the company to workers.[51] Some 1,200 railway workers went on strike and factory workers continued indefinite strikes, work stoppages, and sit-ins across the country.[52] Medical workers also organized, as Manshiyet el-Bakri Hospital workers struck over poor working conditions and managerial corruption, and the right to form an independent labor union.[53] Elsewhere, emergency medical rescue workers also went on strike to protest poor wages and privatization.[54] Steel workers went on strike and closed the gates of one steel company, claiming the director ought to be removed for corruption and nepotism.[55] Overall, some 10,000 workers, including a large portion of postal workers, struck in Alexandria on March 1st.[56] On the same day, 10,000 peasants from the villages surrounding Mansoura gathered to articulate their grievances to the military junta. Peaceful protestors were met with rough treatment by the military, which led to brief clashes.[57] The Egyptian ruling class was so fearful that it yet again postponed the reopening of the stock market from March 1st to the 6th, hoping labor unrest would wither away in due time.[58]

While the spontaneous eruption of wildcat strikes that characterized February slowed in March, working class action did not disappear. A twelve-point program of demands had been articulated by 3,500 Iron and Steel workers who continued sitting-in for the twelfth day straight. Some of these demands included the renaming of the factory to "National Iron and Steel," a proclamation of their desire for public ownership, the removal over overpaid engineers taking home 150,000 Egyptian pounds a month, annual increases to keep up with inflation, an equitable distribution of wages and profits in accordance with a national minimum and maximum wage, and an overall increase in benefits.[59] Over 2,000 oil workers continued their eighth day of picketing in Suez over issues of job security.[60] Meanwhile, protestors stormed the office of the Minister of Petroleum as other oil workers went on a hunger strike calling for increased pay.[61] Hundreds protested in Ismailia to demand the resignation of the corrupt governor, Abdul Jalil. Similarly, in Menoufia, hundreds gathered to demand the dismantling of the state security apparatus.[62]

Egyptian natural gas resources were still not flowing into Israel as late as early March. Natural gas exports to Israel had been nonexistent since February 5th when the pipelines were sabotaged in an attack. Egyptian natural gas accounted for over 40% of Israel's supplies.[63] Israeli officials accused their Egyptian counterparts of caving into public opinion, which overwhelmingly opposed Egyptian natural gas resources being sold at highly subsidized rates. For Israeli leaders, "democracy" constituted doing the opposite of what the public wanted. Many within the Egyptian labor movement supported a complete cut-off. In this way workers were not only becoming more militant, they were fusing political, economic, and geopolitical demands together. It was within this context that the new independent trade union federation was built.

A New Era for Trade Unionism: The Egyptian Federation of Independent Trade Unions

As wildcat strikes sprung up all throughout the country, a new level of working class organization appeared on the economic front. Although the formation of the Egyptian Federation of Independent Trade Unions (EFITU) came about informally in Tahrir Square on January 30th, it was not until March 2nd that EFITU formally launched with its founding conference. At this point, EFITU was centered on four primary independent organizations: the Health Professionals Union, the Real Estate Tax Authority Employee Union, the Federation of Pensioners, and the Independent Teachers Syndicate. At the conference, labor leader Kamal Abu 'Aita announced that EFITU's primarily goal was for all workers to remove themselves from the 4-million strong ETUF and any other state-sponsored unions. Kamal Abbas, of the Centre for Trade Union and Worker Services, was clear that workers ought to no longer rely upon the regime for legitimacy:

> They gave a statement after their conference yesterday announcing that they accepted the right for us to form our own unions. Come now, come now, brother! This is too little too late. It is we who now say that we don't accept your right to exist from this day forward![64]

People were heeding that call. Workers from all over Egypt proclaimed their intention to join the ranks of EFITU, including tens of thousands of Mahalla Textile workers, the bus drivers, conductors, mechanics, engineers, employees of the Public Transport Authority, the national postal workers, the Helwan Iron and Steel workers, and industrial workers from Naga' Hamadi. Thousands of industrial workers in the private sector from the cities of Tenth of Ramadan and Sadat also expressed their desire to unionize and organize with EFITU. Elsewhere, workers were forming independent syndicates and unions not yet associated with the new independent federation.[65]

As Ashraf Omar of the Revolutionary Socialists explained, Mubarak was the head of "a dictatorship of an entire system," a system which, even after the dictator's fall, would continue to impoverish the masses through "policies of privatization, and policies that continue the alliance with the Zionist entity…[and] American interests." Omar wrote at the time:

> …millions of Egyptian revolutionaries did not come out in the streets and in the workplace only to remove a tyrant or win a handful of democratic demands that have not even been implemented yet. In the end, the millions who live below the poverty line cannot return to their homes after the revolution to feed their children with "freedom" and "democracy." Indeed, poverty, inflation and unemployment were the main reasons that prompted Egyptians in this revolution… [If we do not continue the revolution to make radical changes in the economic structure and the distribution of social wealth… [it] will be as if we toppled Mubarak only to face 100,000 Mubaraks

singing the praises of revolution, democracy and reform, but continuing policies of tyranny and impoverishment.[66]

One unanswered question was whether or not the Egyptian workers, struggling for an independent alternative to the decades of corrupt ETUF hegemony, would remain clear of the imperial co-optation that often accompanies working class movements. For instance, the National Endowment for Democracy (NED), a privately owned but US tax-payer funded organization, funds both private capitalists and workers organizations in other countries in order to dictate the way they function and blunt the potential radicalization of workers. A major union in the US, the AFL-CIO, uses its "Solidarity Center" to act as the intermediary between the NED and the working classes movements around the world, providing aid and support for reform but largely trying to direct and control the movements as to avoid emancipatory radicalization.[67] This was the case in Poland, Nicaragua, and South Africa, where the collapse of radicalism lead to a disastrous form of globalization and privatization. More recently, the Solidarity Center actively attempted to undermine the "Bolivarian Revolution" in Venezuela.

Regarding Egypt, the AFL-CIO's Solidarity Center states in its policy that harmonization of "the ETUF, Egyptian NGOs, the Egyptian government, the US government, the international labor and human rights communities, and the US corporations" is necessary. The Solidarity Center cites both public and private non-profit sources for its funding, including "the U.S. Agency for International Development, the National Endowment for Democracy, the U.S. Department of State, the U.S. Department of Labor, the AFL-CIO, private foundations, and national and international labor organizations." In 2009 alone, the NED spent $318,757 co-opting labor unions in Egypt while simultaneously giving $187,569 to the Center for International Private Enterprise, an organization which funds and trains the very people engaging in the process of privatization and exploitation that Egyptian workers are fighting against.[68] As Philip Marfleet points out:

> Revolutionary activists also point to what they call the "infatuation" of some union leaders with international trade union federations. The emergence of Egypt's independent unions has been tracked closely by organisations such as the International Trade Union Confederation (ITUC) and the European Trade Union Confederation (ETUC). In 2010 the national trade union federation in the US, the AFL-CIO, presented its George Meany-Lane Kirkland Award for Human Rights jointly to Abu-Eita and Abbas. Never slow to co-opt new union

leaderships, ITUC and other international networks have since been courting the Egyptian federations. One revolutionary activist in Cairo says: "We can do without constant invitations to Egyptian trade unionists to attend conferences at which they will be 'taught how to negotiate'. We need to develop strong organisation of the rank and file, not to train more bureaucrats."[69]

Up to this point the demands for reform articulated by independent trade unionists had been relatively broad and far-reaching in nature. At the beginning of March, when EFITU was officially announced, they called for strict opposition to the ETUF.[70] Still, it was not clear if or for how long they could maintain their independence. Some workers and revolutionaries were actively agitating for the permanence of revolutionary struggle. Cooptation of the independent movement was a real fear among revolutionary elements, a fear that had historical precedent in other parts of the world. In spite of these fears, it was evident that the Egyptian working class had awoken. Although the limits to the independent movement could be seen in the following months, in the midst of this initial upswing the Revolutionary Socialists rightly called for the permanence of the revolution: "Let the revolution in Egypt be permanent! Let our revolution in the Arab region be permanent! Let there be a permanent revolution in the factories and neighborhoods and universities until we achieve all our demands!"[71]

[1] Ironically, the hated police, who just days before had beaten and terrorized pro-democracy protestors, had the nerve to go on strike Sunday the 13th in demand of higher pay. They were met with harsh criticism by protestors. Hossam El-Hamalawy, who was there, recorded what must have been one of the finer examples of Egyptian humor. He reports that as the police chanted, "The police, the army, and the people are one," an elderly woman tailed them and followed every chant with "Since When?"
[2] Marwa Awad, "Egypt's military to warn against "chaos and disorder"." *Reuters*, February 13, 2011. http://uk.reuters.com/article/2011/02/13/uk-egypt-warning-idUKTRE71C1OG20110213 (accessed July 19, 2013).
[3] Donald MacIntyre, "Egyptian military calls for 'damaging' strikes and protests to end." *The Guardian*, February 15, 2011. http://www.independent.co.uk/news/world/africa/egyptian-military-calls-for-damaging-strikes-and-protests-to-end-2215073.html (accessed July 19, 2013).
[4] Frederick Engels, "V. The Vienna Insurrection" in *Revolution and Counter-Revolution in Germany*, (New York Tribune, 1851) http://www.marxists.org/archive/marx/works/1852/germany/ (accessed July 19, 2013).
[5] Chris McGreal, "How Hosni Mubarak misread his military men." *The Guardian*, Saturday 12, 2011. http://www.guardian.co.uk/world/2011/feb/12/hosni-mubarak-misread-military-men (accessed July 19, 2013).
[6] Richard Seymour, "Egyptian army moves to preserve its power ," *Lenin's Tomb* (blog), February 13, 2011, http://www.leninology.com/2011/02/egyptian-army-moves-to-preserve-its.html.
[7] "Egypt government struggles to finance itself." *Business Today*, http://www.businesstoday-eg.com/management/africa/egypt-government-struggles-to-finance-itself.html (accessed July 19, 2013).
[8] Sallam, "Striking Back at Egyptian Workers."
[9] Ibid.
[10] Hossam El-Hamalawy quoted in Paul Schemm, "Veteran Egypt activist sees revolution as ongoing." *UT San Diego*, February 19, 2011. http://www.utsandiego.com/news/2011/feb/19/veteran-egypt-activist-sees-revolution-as-ongoing/all/ (accessed July 19, 2013).
[11] El-Hamalawy, "Egypt protests continue in the factories."
[12] Strike information found on Salon.com, http://www.salon.com/wires/allwires/2011/02/14/D9LCPNUG0_ml_egypt/index.html
[13] In Arabic: Fatima Abu Shanab, "Airline travel prevented, hired thugs run over the employees with car," *Al-Masry Al-Youm*, February 27, 2011, 19:39. Found at: http://www.almasryalyoum.com/news/ (accessed 2011).
[14] In Arabic: *Al-Dostor*, February 15, 2011,

http://www.dostor.org/politics/egypt/11/february/15/36323 (accessed 2011).
[15] In Arabic: Abdella, *El-Badil*, February 13, 2011.
[16] Tarek El-Tablawy and Sarah El-Deeb. "Strikes spread after Egypt uprising, worrying army." *Associated Press*, February 14, 2011. http://www.utsandiego.com/news/2011/feb/14/strikes-spread-after-egypt-uprising-worrying-army/all/?print (accessed July 19, 2013).
[17] Tamer El-Ghobashy, Margaret Coker, and Charles Levinson. "Strikes Worry Egypt's Military, Youth." *Wall Street Journal*, February 15, 2011. http://online.wsj.com/article/SB10001424052748703584804576143824048718898.html
[18] Mostafa Ali, "Egypt's spreading strikes." *Socialist Worker (US)*, February 18, 2011. http://socialistworker.org/2011/02/18/egypts-spreading-strikes (accessed July 21, 2013).
[19] Karl Marx, "Address of the Central Committee to the Communist League." Last modified March 1850. Accessed July 21, 2013. http://www.marxists.org/archive/marx/works/1847/communist-league/1850-ad1.htm.
[20] Maggie Michael, "Egyptians Defy Military Rulers With More Protests." *CBS*, February 16, 2011. http://www.cbsnews.com/2100-501713_162-7355456.html (accessed July 21, 2013).
[21] Marx, "Address of the Central Committee to the Communist League."
[22] In Arabic: Reports in *Al-Ahram*, dated mid-February, originally available here: http://www.ahram.org.eg/Inner.aspx?ContentID=63373&typeid=27
[23] In Arabic: Ayman Hassanein, *El-Badil*, February 17, 2011.
[24] Khaled 'Ali, "Striking Egyptian Workers Fuel the Uprising After 10 Years of Labor Organizin," DemocracyNow!.
[25] Sharif Abdel Kouddos, "'A Celebration, Not a Protest': Massive Crowd Packs Cairo's Tahrir Square to Mark One Week Since Mubarak's Ouster," Web, http://www.democracynow.org/2011/2/18/a_celebration_not_a_protest_massive.

[26] Carol Williams, "EGYPT: Military says strikes hurting economy, won't be tolerated." *Los Angeles Times*, February 18, 2011. http://latimesblogs.latimes.com/babylonbeyond/2011/02/egypt-protests-1.html (accessed July 21, 2013).
[27] Rosa Luxemburg quoted in: David McNally, "Transformed by the revolution." *Socialist Worker (US)*, February 15, 2011. http://socialistworker.org/2011/02/15/transformed-by-revolution?quicktabs_sw-recent-articles=6-14 (accessed July 21, 2013).
[28] Sameh Naguib, interview by Mostafa Ali, "Conversation with an Egyptian socialist," February 23, 2011, July 21, 2013, http://socialistworker.org/2011/02/23/interview-with-egyptian-socialist.
[29] Tamim Elyan, "Workers, leftists to form new parties." *Daily News Egypt*, February 27, 2011. http://www.thedailynewsegypt.com/egypt/workers-leftists-to-form-new-parties.html (accessed July 21, 2013).
[30] ""Draft Program of the Democratic Labor Party - Under Construction"." Last

modified February 25, 2011. Accessed July 21, 2013. http://www.e-socialists.net/node/6545.

[31] Mohammed Hamama, interview by Peter Manson, "Unity across the Arab world," March 31, 2011, July 21, 2013, http://www.cpgb.org.uk/home/weekly-worker/859/unity-across-the-arab-world.

[32] Elyan, "Workers, leftists to form new parties."

[33] "Egyptian independent trade unionists' declaration."*3arabawy* (blog), February 19, 2011. http://www.arabawy.org/2011/02/21/jan25-egyworkers-egyptian-independent-trade-unionists'-declaration/ (accessed July 21, 2013). Original in Arabic here: http://www.e-socialists.net/node/6509.

[34] Marwa Hussein, "Revolution fuels Egypt labour movement." *Ahram Online*, February 25, 2011. http://english.ahram.org.eg/News/6383.aspx (accessed July 21, 2013).

[35] Although it is not entirely clear these six demands were specifically, an educated guess would be what protestors gathered in Tahrir to call for on Friday, the 25th: (1) The dissolution of the Ahmed Shafiq government, (2) cancellation of the country's state security intelligence, (3) lifting the state of emergency, (4) the immediate release of all political prisoners, (5) Mubarak to be put on trial, and (6) the freezing and returning to the national treasury of all assets from key figures in the old regime, including Mubarak and his family, Safwat El Sherif, Fathy Sorour, Zakria Azmy, Mofeed Shehab, and Ahmed Fathy Srour among others.

[36] "Min 'Amal Masr." *Al-Ishtiraki*, February 20, 2011. http://www.e-socialists.net/node/6518 (accessed July 21, 2013).

[37] Molyneux, John. "Hail the Egyptian Revolution." February 12, 2011. http://johnmolyneux.blogspot.com/2011/02/hail-egyptian-revolution.html?spref=fb (accessed July 21, 2013).

[38] Hussein, "Revolution fuels Egypt labour movement."

[39] Mosafa Ali, "The struggle that lies ahead in Egypt." *Socialist Worker (US)*, February 28, 2011. http://socialistworker.org/2011/02/28/the-struggle-that-lies-ahead-in-egypt (accessed July 21, 2013).

[40] Meanwhile, masquerading under a sort of phony-labor struggle, police continued their refusal to work, as they had been doing since the downfall of Mubarak. They called for increased pay and more respect. This attempted to polish their tarnished image with the Egyptian masses did not go over very well. In what was a testament to both the transformative power of revolution and the newfound ability of the Egyptian masses to control their destiny, Egypt did not break into lawlessness or chaos via the absence of a repressive police force patrolling the streets.

[41] In Arabic: "Villages in Mansoura and Dakahlia demonstrate," Tadamon Masr (blog), February 24, 2011, http://tadamonmasr.wordpress.com/2011/02/24/peasants-19/

[42] In Arabic: "Peasants in Ismailia and the east participate in protest," Tadamon (blog), February 28, 2011, http://tadamon.katib.org/2011/02/28/

[43] Ali, "The struggle that lies ahead in Egypt.

[44] "Our Revolution Continues Because the System Did Not Fall." *Al-Ishtiraki*, February 25, 2011. http://www.e-socialists.net/node/6539 (accessed July 21, 2013).

[45] "Labor protests escalate throughout Egypt." *Signalfire*, February 25, 2011. http://www.signalfire.org/?p=7851 (accessed July 21, 2013).

[46] Laila Mustafa Soueif, Comment in Reem Abdellatif, "Testimonial to arrest & assault of Amr Abdullah in Cairo,"*Reporting Live* (blog), February 27, 2011, http://reemabdellatif.wordpress.com/2011/02/27/testimonial-to-arrest-assault-of-amr-abdullah-in-cairo/.

[47] "Egypt protesters dispersed by force." *Al-Jazeera English*, February 26, 2011. http://www.aljazeera.com/news/middleeast/2011/02/2011226221957428.html (accessed July 21, 2013).

[48] In Arabic: Suha Masoud, Laila Nur al-Din, Khalid Amir and Shaimaa Othman, *El-Badil*, March 1, 2011.

[49] In Arabic: "Hundreds of Teachers Protest in Ismailia." *Al-Wafd*, March 01, 2011. http://www.alwafd.org/index.php?option=com_content&view=article&id=19996 (accessed July 21, 2013).

[50] In Arabic: Tadamon Masr (blog), February 27, 2011, http://tadamonmasr.wordpress.com/2011/02/27/torah/

[51] "Helwan employees protest working conditions, bad pay and corruption." *Egypt Independent*, February 28, 2011. http://www.egyptindependent.com/news/helwan-employees-protest-working-conditions-bad-pay-and-corruption (accessed July 21, 2013). In Arabic: http://www.ctuws.com/default.aspx?item=823

[52] In Arabic: Hesham Fouad, "Workers' Struggles Continue." *Al-Ishtiraki*, February 27, 2011. http://www.e-socialists.net/node/6547 (accessed July 21, 2013).

[53] Hossam El-Hamalawy, "Hospital Workers for Unionization," 3arabawy (blog), March 01, 2011, http://www.arabawy.org/2011/03/01/hospital-workers-for-unionization

[54] In Arabic: Tadamon Masr (blog), March 01, 2011, http://tadamonmasr.wordpress.com/2011/03/01/ambulance-2/

[55] In Arabic: "Workers' Strike at Arab Company for Special Steel" Tadamon Masr (blog), March 01, 2011, http://tadamonmasr.wordpress.com/2011/03/01/arabiya-steel-2/

[56] In Arabic: Masoud et al., *El-Badil*, March 1, 2011.

[57] In Arabic: "Ten thousand peasants knocking on the door of Dakahlia governor," Tadamon (blog), March 01, 2011, http://tadamon.katib.org/2011/03/01/

[58] "Egypt delays expected reopening of stock market." *Business Week*, March 01, 2011. http://www.businessweek.com/ap/financialnews/D9LMBCDG0.htm (accessed July 21, 2013).

[59] In Arabic: "Ezz Steel workers continue sit-in," Tadamon Masr (blog), March

02, 2011, http://tadamonmasr.wordpress.com/2011/03/02/ezz/
[60] In Arabic: "Workers picket Suez Petroleum Co.," Tadamon Masr (blog), March 02, 2011, http://tadamonmasr.wordpress.com/2011/03/02/suez/
[61] In Arabic: Lubna Salah al-Din, Nismah Ali, and Muhammad Al-Malhi, "Protestors storm Ministry of Petroluem building," *Al-Masry al-Youm*, March 02, 2011, http://www.almasryalyoum.com/node/336862
[62] In Arabic: Allaa Al-Bulk and Abdullah Al-'Arini, "Demonstrations call for dismissal of governor in Ismailia," *Al-Masry al-Youm*, March 04, 2011, http://www.almasryalyoum.com/node/339473
[63] Ahmed Belal, "Egypt gas still not flowing to Israel." *Egypt Independent*, March 04, 2011. http://www.almasryalyoum.com/en/node/338959 (accessed July 21, 2013).
[64] Yassin Gaber, "Egypt workers lay down demands at new trade union conference." *Ahram Online*, March 03, 2011. http://english.ahram.org.eg/News/6901.aspx (accessed July 21, 2013).
[65] Jano Charbel, "After 50-year hiatus, Egypt's first independent labor union is born." *Egypt Independent*, March 03, 2011. http://www.egyptindependent.com/news/after-50-year-hiatus-egypts-first-independent-labor-union-born (accessed July 21, 2013).
[66] Ashraf Omar, "Making the revolution permanent," *Socialist Worker* (US), March 15, 2011, http://socialistworker.org/2011/03/15/making-the-revolution-permanent. Orginially published in *Al-Ishtiraki*, translated by Mostafa Omar.
[67] Author and political scientist Michael Parenti once jokingly referred to the AFL-CIO as the "AFL-CIA," noting how it has basically appropriated certain propaganda techniques that were previously carried out covertly by the CIA.
[68] K.R. Bolton, Global Research, Center for Research on Globalization, "Is Egypt's Labor Movement Being Co-opted by Globalists?" Last modified February 21, 2011. Accessed July 21, 2013. http://www.globalresearch.ca/is-egypt-s-labor-movement-being-co-opted-by-globalists/23305.
[69] Philip Marfleet, "Egypt: The workers advance," *International Socialism* (139), July 4, 2013, http://www.isj.org.uk/index.php4?id=904&issue=139.
[70] Hesham Fouad, "Annoucing the Establishment of the Egyptian Federation of Independent Trade Unions," Al-Ishtiraki, March 3, 2011, http://www.e-socialists.net/node/6573.
[71] Omar, "Making the revolution permanent."

7

Action and Reaction: "The People Want another Wheel of Production"

On March 2nd the military council announced that a tentative date had been set for a referendum to decide whether mild constitutional reforms would move forward. On the same day, protestors outside the interior ministry demanding the purging and reformation of the security apparatus were dispersed by Egyptian troops who fired into the air and threatened force.[1] Increasing attacks on labor took place as well. Aside from the media smear campaigns and various communiqués denouncing workers and strikes, military police forcefully broke up a sit-in of 1,000 teachers in the city of Sohag on March 2nd.[2] Likewise, the military forcefully dismantled a demonstration of 2,000 oil workers protesting in front of the Ministry of Petroleum in Nasr City and arrested twenty of the strikers.[3] This pattern of concession and repression was repeated in the coming months. These reactions, whether marginal reforms or acts of force, were by and large responses to workers, peasants, and other protestors organizing across Egypt. While the SCAF still held state power, the people in the streets often dictated the tempo of this continuing cycle of action and reaction.

The Collapse of State Security and Continuation of Popular Struggles

March 5th marked the beginning of the end for the reign of state security after protestors stormed their offices all across the country. This was similar to the crumbling of the Iranian Shah's infamous SAVAK secret police over three decades earlier. On March 7th, close to fifty officers were charged by the attorney general for burning documents and tampering with potentially incriminating evidence. Furthermore, the military junta took the unprecedented step of removing all state security police from university campuses. This was significant as for years the state security had been responsible for repressing dissent, targeting political activists, and limiting academic freedom at universities.

In the midst of the crumbling state security forces, the unrelenting student, peasant, and labor struggles continued. One of the most significant new fronts for the revolutionary struggle materialized as the army reopened schools and universities. On March 6th students, faculty, and staff gathered in the tens of thousands in an effort to oust the all NDP-linked administrators, including the University of Cairo President Hossam Kamel, brother of the Mubarak-appointed telecommunications minister. Protestors also called for the abolition of restrictions on political activism, free and fair elections for both student government and administrative positions, more student control and input, and an increase of academic freedom for professors. Students protested against increased tuition and fees, professors against low wages, and staff for higher pay and better working conditions.[4] One female student leading the chants exclaimed, "We will run the university. The university will not run us."[5] Similarly, at the Ain Shams University in Cairo, students and faculty echoed these calls by demonstrating throughout the campus.[6] This student uprising was not isolated to Cairo. Thousands of protestors held demonstrations, with some overarching and some localized demands, in various private and public institutions all across Egypt. Cites of protest included the universities of Assiut, Minia, Tanta, Sohag, and the Sixth of October.[7] High school students and teachers even articulated their demands, calling for the end to corporal punishment and the removal of curriculum with hagiographic Mubarak content.

The *fellaheen* also continued organizing at an unprecedented level. In perhaps the most impressive display of peasant organization, it was reported that ten thousand peasants were "knocking on the doors" of the Dakahlia governor in Mansoura on February 28th. The peasants came from villages south of the city and insisted the governor listen to their demands. The army shot into the air, hoping to scare the demonstrators, which only succeeded in angering them more. Eventually, the peasants forced the army to back down and chose five representatives to present their demands to the governor, threatening to repeat the demonstration if they did not hear a response within the week.[8]

Labor struggles were even more expansive. In Cairo 700 oil and gas workers struck calling for the return of laid off workers.[9] Employees shut down a number of Ahli United Bank branches, demanding improvements in their salaries and health insurance policy.[10] In Ismailia, 700 canal workers went on a hunger strike for better working conditions.[11] In Giza, 50 laid-off ambulance workers called for reemployment.[12] In Shibin al-Kom, spinners intensified their weeks-long protest by calling for a full strike in order to achieve a change in their companies management, increased wages, a return of laid off workers, and the installation of a 1,200 pound minimum wage.[13] Postal workers in Kafr al-Sheikh and Fayoum protested for better wages and bonuses. Fayoum also saw demonstrations by hospital workers calling for better working conditions, increased pay, the removal of parasitic administrators, and permanent employment.[14] In Helwan, Subway Authority workers, some of whom had been on temporary contracts for fifteen years, wanted permanent contracts. Mine workers from the Baharia Oasis demanded increased wages and safer working conditions.[15] Roughly 600 Tora Cement workers conducted a sit-in[16] for a larger distribution of the company's profits, which had increased nearly 30% from 2009 to 2010 with little benefit to the workers.[17] Staff from the Faisal Islamic Bank protested in front of the central bank demanding an overall increase in salaries and oversight of union committees to ensure more parity in wages between the lowest salaried workers and the administrators.[18]

Strikers representing some 10,000 employees at insurance companies all across Egypt called for an increase in pay, better working conditions, and permanent employment.[19] Nearly 3000 Aviation Ministry workers demanded the resignation of Ibrahim Manna and Atef Abdel Hamid, the NDP appointed Aviation and Transportation ministers. Workers feared the maintenance of their power would mean that other NDP officials could be granted safe passage out of the country with their unjustly garnered wealth.[20] EgyptAir workers also threatened to stop work if Yousry Gamal Eldin Mamdouh, the chairman and the managing director of the company, did not resign. Workers at the Egyptian Pharmaceuticals Trading Company similarly called for the removal of all symbols of the old regime, as well as increased pay.[21] Journalists demonstrated in front of major media outlets for a freer and open media, as well as the removal of NDP figures from media control.[22] Dozens of librarians and library workers at the massive library in Alexandria linked their economic demands of better wages and benefits with political demands, waving banners that read "No to Corruption" and argued against normalization of relations with Israel.[23] Hundreds of agricultural researchers at the National Center for Agricultural Research performed a sit-in to try and improve their economic conditions.[24]

Repression was never far away, however. In Fayoum, the army suspended the postal workers strike by force and arrested three of its organizers.[25] The same scene was repeated in Nasr City, where workers protested in front of the Petrotrade Company.[26] Some 400 service workers surrounded the parliament building, protesting the corruption of the general secretary. Police used dogs to disperse the demonstrators.[27] The leader of the Democratic Labor Party, Kamal Khalil, cited the repression at Fayoum as a "dangerous development" and called on workers to "continue the revolution in order to eliminate symbols of corruption and improve living standards."[28] EFITU likewise condemned the attacks, attaching the signatures of a broad cross section of Egyptian revolutionary organizations, including the Democratic Labor Party, the Revolutionary Youth Coalition, the Egyptian Committee for the Protection of Labor Rights, the April 6th Movement, the Democratic Lawyers Group, and 15 other unions, organizations, and political parties.[29]

The Social Revolution Lags Behind the Political

As sporadic labor struggles intensified and multiplied, key turning points in the revolution were occurring as the social revolution clearly lagged behind the political one. Sectarian tension and patriarchy resurfaced to break the cohesiveness and solidarity displayed during the original uprising. On March 8th a demonstration for women's equality ended in violence as men harassed and attempted to strike some of the women in a wanton display of sexist violence.[30]

A few days later 13 people were killed and over 100 wounded in clashes between Coptic Christians and Muslims in Cairo after the bombing of a church in the working-class Mokattam district. Some 1,000 Coptic Christians had organized a rally demanding an end of discrimination by the state when Salafists from a neighboring area attacked the protestors.[31] While it is possible that, as some commentators suggested, remnants of the state security apparatus were a factor in the attacks, it is not at all evident they was the primary culprit. Instead, it is likely that many of the Salafi leaders, especially those who benefited from the Mubarak regime and had garnered significant wealth under it, were attempting to shore up their support during what was a large social crisis for them.

Historically, Salafi leaders had issued *fatwas* against their followers participating in strikes and other forms of labor activity. This created tension between them and many of their poor or working class adherents. As strikes were erupting all across Egypt, and the regime which they had urged their followers not to struggle against had crumbled, the Salafi leadership found itself in a difficult space. It is likely that these attacks on Coptic Christians were meant to diffuse the militancy of their followers by unleashing it in a totally different direction. This scene would repeat itself again later in May.

These incidents were revealing. While the Democratic Labor Party put forward calls for solidarity between Muslims and Christians and called for equality between men and women, they in no way exercised political hegemony over the entirety of the working class. The most progressive and class-conscious elements of the working class lacked the decisive leadership position needed to push the revolution forward and marginalize the divisive, counter-revolutionary ideologies espoused by Salafi ideologues and others.

"There Are So Many Strikes that we've Lost Count"

Notwithstanding these counter-revolutionary activities, labor struggles kept pace over the next week. March 12th saw the ushering in of a new wave of strikes all across Egypt. Strikes by workers in various sectors such as aviation, cement, and education, as well as in the postal service and the Suez Canal, continued unabated.[32] Calls for a Petrol Station Workers' Association were put forth and centered on a guaranteed minimum wage, increased social benefits, protection against job risks, and a percentage of sales to be redirected back to the workers.[33] Tora Cement workers demanded the renationalization of their company, which had been privatized and sold to an Italian firm prior to the revolution. LaFarge cement workers also continued their strike in Suez. Some 3,000 iron and steel workers also struck, with another 10,000 joining the following day.[34]

A perceived victory came when reports that Ahmed al-Borai, recently appointed Minister of Manpower after workers pressured the neoliberal Ismail Ibrahim Fahmi out of office, announced "that the ministry is working on drafting a new law to replace the restrictive Trade Union Law 35/1976." The revisions would be "based on the recommendations put forth by the independent Center for Trade Union and Workers' Services (CTUWS)" and "conform to International Labor Organization's (ILO) conventions, which Egypt has ratified but failed to uphold for over five decades."[35] These recommendations included a higher minimum wage, the right to collective bargaining, and the right to strike – key demands which had lacked legal sanction for decades. Officials hoped such an announcement would temporarily stifle labor discontent, and Borai desperately continued calling for a cessation of strikes. This was an indication that the still sporadic but increasingly militant and organized labor activity was having an impact.

As these announcements were made, thousands of workers from all over the country proclaimed their intent to join EFITU, including national postal workers, workers from the Mahalla Textile Company, the Public Transport Authority, the Helwan Iron and Steel Complex, industries in the town of Naga Hamadi, as well as the industrial sites Sadat City and the Tenth of Ramadan. These workers would join those already at the core of the new federation: the Real Estate Tax Authority Employee's Union, the Egyptian Health Technologists' Syndicate, the independent Teachers' Syndicate, and the Federation of Pensioners. Other workers, such as electricity workers, street cleaners, and employees at the Media Production city also announced their intention to unionize and join.[36]

Even as the military junta made a successful attempt to control the domestic political scene with a referendum superimposing mild cosmetic changes on top of the constitution, labor activity continued to surface. As the results of the referendum came in, 2,000 oil workers continued their strike while another 150 Petrojet workers held a labor protest.[37] In Cairo, workers, engineers, and technicians from the Ministry of Military Production held a demonstration against their temporary labor status.[38] Radio workers at the Maspero building went on strike. Librarians closed the library doors after receiving notification that no increase would be made to their paltry wages.[39] Some 3,000 teachers refused to administer exams without assurance they would be able to form an independent union.[40] Hundreds of employees at Masr Insurance protested in front of the headquarters to stop the company from separating into eight different subsidiaries, which would allow for a reduction in their wages.[41] Around 1,200 public employees demonstrated in front of the parliament calling for an end to corruption and a negation of their old, exploitative contract. They were also joined by electricity workers and engineers, Egyptian women married to Palestinian men demanding Egyptian nationality for their children, and dozens of farmers calling for ownership over the lands they worked and an end to high rents.[42] In what was probably the biggest and most disconcerting strike for the military regime, despite it only lasting two hours, train workers stopped all the trains at Cairo running to and from the provinces of Beni Suef, Minya, and Assiut. The workers were protesting the fact that they had not received the overtime pay they had worked for. They further condemned the official state union, claiming it did not represent them.[43] Delegates from the military council immediately met with striking workers to convince them to return to work, and promised they would respond to their demands.[44]

Kamal Abu 'Aita, president of the Property Tax Collectors Union and later president of EFITU, remarked that since the strikes began to spread "there are so many that we've lost count." As he explained, two of the main demands of the revolution - fair wages and independent unions - were in the process of being met. By this time, in an effort to neutralize the increasing militancy of Egyptian workers, the new finance and labor ministers had set up a committee to evaluate the minimum wage and discuss anti-trade union laws. Another demand, that of the maximum wage, continued to fall on deaf ears. As Abu 'Aita explains, their slogan was "A maximum wage for those who live in palaces, a minimum wage for those who live in the graveyards." He went on to call for the cessation of subsidized gas sales to Israel, for the ending of subsidies to big companies run by Mubarak cronies, and a new tax on stock market transactions. "Our victory is a victory for the workers of the world against the whole system of capitalist and imperialist globalization," he proclaimed, "It is a step towards a new kind of globalisation, the globalisation of humanity in the name of the oppressed everywhere."[45]

Making Strikes Illegal: The Military Pushes Back

One day after the statement was published by Abu 'Aita, and in a complete reversal of the hopes of and promises given to Egyptian workers by al-Borai, the Cabinet declared Law 34, previously Military Decree 34 issued by the SCAF, criminalizing protests and strikes. Under Law 34, anyone organizing or calling for a strike would face a possible year in prison and fines of up to half a million Egyptian pounds. It would apply to "anyone inciting, urging, promoting or participating in a protest or strike that hampers or delays work at any private or public establishments." The new labor law was to be enforced as long as the emergency law remained in place, which it had since 1981.[46] The text of the law read:

> The cabinet reasserted the necessity of immediate stoppage of all demonstrations and strikes witnessed nationwide... the cabinet has received huge amount of legal demands... the government is working to prepare a complete [framework] to deal with policies of employment and incomes. In this concern, the cabinet approved the draft law criminalizing some strikes, demonstrations and mobs included the following;
>
> a-   Who make or participate in any demonstration or strike that lead to hindering of private or public authorities.
>
> b-   Who incite, call or promote to the mentioned crimes.
>
> c-   Taking the mentioned crimes while running of emergency case.
>
> d-   Penalties includes; imprisonment [a maximum of one year] and fines either both or one of them, and fines may reach EGP 500,000.[47]

The reasons for this law were clear. A massive propaganda campaign had been in full swing for weeks. It was aimed against Egyptian workers and derided their legitimate calls for improved living conditions as selfish "special interest" demands. The liberal elite, the leadership of the Muslim Brotherhood, and the Supreme Council of the Armed Forces, led by "Mubarak's Poodle" Tantawi, all agreed that "the wheels of production must turn." Indeed, bread-and-butter demands were "presented as a major challenge to Egypt's economic prosperity and, therefore, national security." In one instance, Finance Minister Samir Radwan claimed that *fi'awi* demonstrations cost the treasury 7 billion Egyptian pounds and the tourism sector 13.5 billion pounds, placing the blame for Egypt's budget deficit on the "illegitimate demands" of Egyptian workers.[48] In response, the Revolutionary Socialists produced a statement smashing the anti-strike law and calling out the military junta and "a number of political forces, most importantly the Muslim Brotherhood and the liberals," for orchestrating a campaign against the strikes and demonizing workers for "stopping the wheel of production and causing the destabilization of the economy." They argued that all "sincere political forces" should "stand up against this law, and against all the decisions and actions that aim to discharge the revolution of its content," and dismiss the "demands of the toiling majority of the Egyptian people."[49]

The "toiling majority" responded to the anti-strike law in force. EFITU immediately called for demonstrations to be held in front of the Ministers' Council, with workers from Cairo, Mahala, Helwan, the Tenth of Ramadan, and other cities participating. More than thirty rights organizations and political groups also signed on to a statement condemning the "undemocratic" law as a "retreat from the revolution's values."[50] One labor activist, Nagy Rashad, explained that "protests will continue and we will challenge this decision. We are not afraid of being imprisoned or fined. Our slogan will be unity for Egyptian workers and we will show solidarity and support for every worker protest or sit-in."[51] Kamal Abbas, General Coordinator of the Center for Trade Unions and Workers Services (CTUWS), called the decision "terrible," with the CTUWS publishing a punctual response. In a statement that was part conciliation, part condemnation, they made overtures toward the government which had just betrayed them, explaining they "do not deny the difficulties that the government of Dr. Essam Sharaf has confronted," and "do not deny the efforts" of the government in "dialogue and negotiations with workers," but that there needed to be the "participation of all social parties in serious negotiations" that could reach a "clear cut map of the road" by ensuring "sufficient stability and better economic conditions." While this language was somewhat appeasing in nature, especially towards a government which just rendered workers impotent, the statement was unequivocal in support of the right to strike:

> The Egyptian workers have struggled for decades to maintain the right to strike. They paid the price when they were imprisoned, transferred or killed. There were martyrs

in the Iron and Steel strikes of 1989, Kafr el Dawar strikes of 1994 and Mehalla el Kobra strikes of 2008.

Article 124 of the Egyptian Penal Law which criminalizes the right to strike is a witness that the regime was reactionary and had the fingerprints of the 19th century. It violated the international labour conventions which are ratified by the Egyptian government and put in the waste basket.

Article 124 of the Egyptian Penal Law which is not different from the suggested draft law was a curse in the history of the regime in Egypt. When the railway workers went in strike in 1986 Mubarak's regime asked to apply that infamous Article against them. But the Egyptian judiciary ruled that Article 124 is automatically annulled since the date of ratification by the government of Egypt on the International Convention of Economic, Social and Cultural Rights.

The government was obliged to abide by the ILO Conventions and to confirm in the Labour Law No. 12/2003 the workers right to strike. In spite of the restrictions which made the application of the right to strike next to impossible, the labour movement utilized this right extensively during the last four years.

The Egyptian workers did not start to move after 25th January 2011. On the contrary, they were on the vanguard of the revolution until it reached its summit and would not stop until the realization of the workers demands or at least the workers are assured that their demands are on the way for achievement.

It was unfortunate that the Egyptian transitional governments after the revolution could not read the Egyptian labour movement or recognize its features and fair demands. Their stance was not much different from that of the regime of Mubarak and exceeded it when they called our strikes "categorical movements which hinder transformation to the required democratic society". It is worrying that democracy is summarized in parliamentary

> and presidential elections under the supervision of the judiciary and opening towards the Muslim Brotherhood while they disregard the liberation of the civil society and the workers' rights to develop their stances and negotiate for gaining their rights...the government of Egypt is still far from dealing with the Egyptian workers as citizens and partners in decision making who have the right to access knowledge and discuss their conditions.
>
> Real democracy does not stop at the level of representation; it is not a parliament or a consultative council. It is the independent unions and the civil society organizations which express the real demands of the workers and lobby for their realization. They are active democratic mechanisms for negotiations, participation in decision making and social supervision of the social resources which were being stolen for many years in the absence of democracy...[52]

The statement was by no means militant, but given the history of marginalization workers and working class representatives faced by the Egyptian state, it did match the tone and mood of many workers who were not ready to carry forward with "permanent revolution" but still hoped for significant reforms in the economic order. As this battle went down over the proposed strike law, in Bani Suweif and Fayoum 500 railway workers formed an independent union and many leading railway activists signed on to the Democratic Labor Party. The Independent Union of Public Transport Authority Workers was officially established the day after the new law was announced, bringing together 60,000 bus-drivers, conductors, mechanics, and engineers employed in the Public Transport Authority and joining the other four major unions in EFITU.[53]

Alternative Political Parties Grow: the Democratic Labor Party

Meanwhile, workers participation on the political front also increased. Proliferating new left-wing, worker-oriented political parties surfaced during the months after Mubarak's fall. Most lacked the 5,000 members and the hundreds of thousands of Egyptian pounds required to form a new political party. However, by October one new left-wing party, was realized. The Socialist Popular Alliance Party (SPA) originated when over 70 dissident members of Tagammu walked out of a party conference in March because of disagreements over a variety of issues, including past political positions, some leaders coziness with Mubarak-era figures, and the hierarchical structure of the party.⁵⁴ The SPA developed a platform focusing primarily upon political reforms, government investment and oversight of the market, stemming the flow of privatization, and the implementation of a progressive tax reform.⁵⁵ The SPA's main achievement was being the first left-wing party to be granted recognition after the fall of Mubarak. It participated in and helped organize various left-wing coalitions throughout 2011 and 2012.

Meanwhile, the Democratic Labor Party was making modest but important advancements as well. Mohammad Hamama, a member of the Revolutionary Socialists, estimated that the membership of the organization rose from an initial 6,000 to 15,000 members by the end of March.⁵⁶ The development coincided with the articulation of the party's program, which was released on March 24th. The program, although only in draft form at this point, was extensive and covered a wide range of topics, specifically with regard to its statement of principles and its demands for freedom and social justice for all oppressed groups in society. Composed of five parts – an introduction to the party, an explanation of who the party represented, a declaration of principles, an introduction to the demands, and the demands themselves – the program was a huge departure from any of the officially recognized parties.

In the introduction, the DLP situated itself within the revolution of 2011 but traced its historical trajectory back as far as the 1899 cigarette rollers strike and the 1919 popular revolution against the British occupation. The program also cites the formation of the National Committee of Workers and Students in 1946 and the 2008 uprising at Mahalla al-Kubra. They put forth the call for Egyptians to "join the struggle" against "all forms of class exploitation and oppression," calling the formation of the DLP an "urgent need and historical inevitability" which will advance the struggle for "freedom, democracy, human dignity, and social justice." "Workers are the builders of progress and civilization," it explains; and, as such, the party was to have a "workers' identity." Hamama commented on this aspect of the program, explaining that "one of the main conditions they want to apply is that the majority should be workers - it certainly makes sense that a majority of the members of a workers' party should be workers."⁵⁷ While the party is open to all "peasants and politicians, intellectuals and students who wish to engage in the party ranks and defend the interests of working people," it was to be composed primarily of workers to maintain its legitimacy as representative of workers' interests. The program continues by adumbrating a list of 23 principles which members must agree to: a non-discrimination clause based on religion, color, and sex; the aim of a civil, secular state; anti-colonialism and anti-Zionism; and the call for a region-wide "comprehensive Arab revolution against all the Arab dictatorships," among other things. The DLP explains that it would "constantly strive to improve work conditions" in order to "make the workplace a fundamental area to enhance creativity rather than more and more misery," since "labor laws do not just reflect economic relationships between workers and employers, but also directly affect social and family relationships." Therefore, the DLP advocated "fair wages, a seven-hour work day, ensuring the right to work," unemployment and pension benefits, the building of independent unions and peasant collectives, and a variety of other economic and social goals.

After asserting their principles, the document paid tribute to "the revolutionaries of Egypt" and proclaimed the party's intention to destroy the "looting system known as capitalism" and "build a society of equality between human beings, Copts and Muslims, men and women." They explained that "poverty, repression, and oppression" do not "distinguish between a Muslim and a Christian, or between a man and a woman," and therefore the only distinction to be made during a "social revolution" was between "oppressors and the oppressed." They situated the former "corrupt regime" within the geopolitical context of "colonialism and Zionism," and called for Egyptians to "stand by the people struggling for freedom and independence" from the "Americans and the Zionists," especially the Palestinian people. They went on to lay out a three-part program articulating immediate demands of the "workers struggle for freedom," "social justice," and "the national cause." The political freedoms advocated were: a new constitution which "repeals the dictatorial presidential system" and establishes the "masses as the source of all authority," and "protects all economic and social rights of the popular classes and ensures a decent life for every citizen"; the immediate release of political prisoners; the trial of Mubarak and all corrupt NDP associates; the trial of all those responsible for torture; the prosecution of those behind sectarian crimes; the dissolution of the National Federation of Trade Unions; and the freedom to form political parties, trade unions, syndicates, student unions, and people's committees; and the right to publish newspapers, to organize strikes, sit-ins, and demonstrations.

The second set of demands was composed of six primary topics: workers, peasants, health and education, housing, people of the Sinai, the Nubians. The first topic was the longest and dealt directly with Egyptian workers. Naturally, the initial demand was for a national minimum wage of 1,500 LE ($270) that regularly increases in direct proportion to inflation. This demand, which was meant to include private sector workers and has been a constant issue raised by Egyptians, remains well above the 700 LE minimum wage that was guaranteed only to public sector workers in June 2011.[58] They also called for a minimum monthly pension connected to price increases, unemployment benefits, and permanent employment for those temporarily employed. Additionally, they put forth a call for "nationalization of large companies that were sold cheaply to businessmen and foreign companies... without compensation, and... under workers' democratic control." They demanded an end to all privatization and liberalization policies, and concluded by calling for increased taxes on the wealthy and large corporations so the state could return "to its central role in development and investment for the benefit of the masses." Regarding the other five areas, the DLP called the cancellation of all debts owed to banks by peasants and agricultural workers, the renationalization of the production and distribution of water and agricultural equipment, the capping of all residential and agricultural rents, the "radical redistribution of land" in favor of the peasantry, a universal healthcare system with an increase in health spending, "real, free education" and a doubling of the educational budget with "popular control over the implementation of educational investment plans" and curriculum, and the nationalization of the largest private real estate companies.

The DLP's program is significant in large part because it specifically reached out to ethnic minorities in Egypt, including the native Bedouin people of the Sinai who inhabit the eastern side of the Suez Canal on a small peninsula bordering Gaza and Israel. This peninsula of around 23,500 square miles links Africa and Asia and is of extensive geopolitical importance. The area is composed of two separate worlds, with wealthy, tourist resorts like Sharm el Sheikh, reserved for the pleasure of Egyptian capitalists and the world's ruling class, juxtaposed with the nearly 400,000 strong, semi-sedentary Bedouins who do not share equal citizenship rights with the rest of Egyptians.[59] For decades, Bedouins faced and continue to face systematic political, economic, and social discrimination institutionalized by government policies and private business. While their land is utilized for extensive tourism, they reap almost none of the benefits from the industry and are regularly denied employment in tourism. It is within this context that the DLP demanded the abolition of restrictions on investment in the Sinai, the adoption of citizenship and equal rights, the release of detainees and compensation to Bedouins imprisoned for activism on the community's behalf, and trials for those responsible for attacks on the people of the Sinai and the "squandering of funds earmarked for development projects" in the region. The second people addressed in the program are the Nubians, an indigenous group native to Southern Egypt and northern Sudan. The Nubians, darker than most of the Egyptian Arabs, face systematic discrimination and are treated as second class citizens in Egypt, especially in relation to government jobs and services. The demands included reparations for the 50,000 to 60,000 Nubians displaced in 1964 by the creation of the Aswan High Dam, jobs for unemployed Nubians, and the development of Nubian heritage projects to commemorate Nubian culture and secure their collective displacement in Egyptian historical memory for future generations. Strangely, the roughly

12 to 16 million Coptic Christians, who make up anywhere from 16-18% of the population officially (and much more by some accounts), are noticeably absent from the program. While equality between Christians and Muslims is assured on occasion, the DLP noticeably neglected to provide significant political space for Christians within the document.

The last plank of the program specifically identified the role of workers in the national cause and addressed the "colonial and Zionist schemes" disrupting Egypt's sovereignty. They argue for a "just and lasting peace agreement" for all states, principally including Sudan and Ethiopia, but also presumably Uganda, Kenya, Tanzania, Burundi, and Rwanda, regarding the water resources of the Nile River. The DLP calls for the cessation of "all forms of normalization with the Zionist enemy in all areas of political, military, cultural, diplomatic, and commercial" life. This position essentially endorsed the Palestinian Boycott, Divestment, and Sanctions call put forth in 2005. They emphasized the importance of stopping the subsidized gas scheme providing Israel with prodigious amounts of cheap natural gas, and argued for the abolition of Qualified Industrial Zones which stipulate that the Egyptian textile sector must import Israeli components to be used in the industry. Likewise, they called for the abolition of the Camp David agreement and an open Rafah border with Gaza, thereby breaking the siege on Gaza and initiating a "policy of solidarity with the heroic resistance" in Palestine. Likewise, they demanded the cessation of all joint exercises and cooperation with the US military. Finally, they end with the demand that all Suez Canal revenues should be redirected towards providing a "dignified life" for Egyptian citizens, which includes "solving the unemployment and housing crises" and other "problems stifling the popular classes." They note that Egypt's duty should be to prevent any warships from passing through whose intentions are the "destruction and occupation of Arab land, as happened in the case of American aggression against Iraq." The DLP closes its program by arguing that "the time has come for the workers and the poor of Egypt to develop an independent voice and independent political party," a political party which could "complete the glorious Egyptian revolution" and strive for a "revolutionary government which truly reflects the interests of the majority of the Egyptian masses."[60]

Notwithstanding this comprehensive program, beyond 2011 the DLP failed to capitalize on the upsurge in labor militancy. While the party was intended both to coordinate labor actions and as a parliamentary political base, in the years following its launch it failed to attract a substantial mass base akin to labor parties in other parts of the world, such as the Workers' Party of Brazil in the 1980s. A more detailed analysis is required, but there are a few possible reasons for this inability of the DLP to become a mass party. Philip Marfleet suggests the DLP "suffered from lack of clarity as to key strategic aims," which may have contributed to this failure. On top of this, Marfleet points out that "even networks of solidarity are undeveloped," the result of state domination of the unions and no real, independent working class movement after Nasser came to power.[61] Yet, there are other factors peculiar to Egypt that could have played a role as well, including the legacy of Nasserism which continues to dominate large sections of the left. Coupled with the ideological hegemony that the Muslim Brotherhood exercised over a significant minority of the population, especially in its capacity to act as the primary oppositional force to the Mubarak regime, any political party attempting to secure a mass-base was working within a highly delimited political space. In this context, much of the dominant discourse of Egyptian politics was and is subsumed by a secular-Islamist binary that has historically enervated class politics. In contrast, during the decades prior to the Workers' Party formation, Brazil had witnessed an exuberant entrance of Catholic liberation theology onto the political scene, which contributed to a political culture capable of transcending the secular-religious debate and opening space for the formation of a Workers' Party with a mass base. Intellectually, the closest corresponding phenomenon in Islam is probably the work of Ali Shariati. An Iranian Shi'ite who attempted to bridge Marxism and Islam, Shariati enjoys very little cultural capital in Egypt, where the vast majority of Muslims are Sunni. It is important to note that it took some ten years for the Workers' Party of Brazil, from its inception in 1980 to its electoral successes in 1990, to become a major force in Brazilian politics. With this understanding, it would be a mistake to rule out the emergence of a mass labor party in Egypt in the future. In all likelihood such a party would draw on the historical legacy of Nasser and Arab socialism, unless there is some dramatic development in Sunni political Islam that allows a significant space for class politics. If such a space develops in the future, the DLP's model – an amalgamation of principles with a demands-based program – may provide a base from which a mass political party could be born.

Contentious Labor Action under the Anti-Strike Law

Despite the ultimate inefficacy of the DLP, the call for workers to "complete the glorious revolution" did not seem so farfetched at the time. The week following the passage of the anti-strike law and the release of the DLP's program not only saw modest gains for the party, it saw a prodigious wave of independent labor activity with many workers being drawn into the orbit of EFITU. Every day fresh strikes in new sectors and different cities were announced. Workers at a Suez fertilizer company were on strike for increased wages and 10% profit sharing.[62] Hundreds of temporary workers at the Suez Canal, some of whom had been on intermittent contracts for 20 years, went on strike demanding permanent contracts. Around 5,000 workers at the Cleopatra Ceramics company in Suez struck for the implementation of demands the company had previously agreed upon. Hundreds of workers at the Helwan Cement Company also went on strike.[63] 400 workers at a paper company in Qena engaged in a sit-down strike, occupying their workplace.[64] In Cairo, 1,000 employees of the Ministry of Housing continued striking for three days straight, while another 500 public service workers demanded better wages. In Kafr El-Sheikh, 500 temporary workers at the Sakha Agricultural Research Center demanded permanent employment, while 400 factory workers in Al Jawhara demanded wage increases and a reduction in the work day from 12 to 8 hours.[65] Strikes were also noted in the New Valley, South Sinai, Damietta, and Port Said governorates.[66]

In a piece titled "The People Want another Wheel of Production," Egyptian writer Wael Gamal emphasized that "Egyptians have revolted to replace the old wheel of production because it is oppressive and creates poverty, ignorance and illness." The sheer amount of workers engaged in labor activity suggests this was the case. By the end of February, it is safe to assume that the number of workers involved in collective labor action of one sort or another reached at least 150,000.[67] In Cairo, dozens of strikes and other labor actions that critics derided as *fi'awi* took place with upwards of 50,000 workers participating. Suez saw an enormous number of strikes as well, with at least 20,000 workers participating. In Mahalla, some 20,000 workers participated in a number of large-scale strikes, while at least 16,000 workers engaged in collective labor action in Helwan and nearly 10,000 in Helwarn. The number of workers engaged in labor activity in Mansoura, Ismailia, Helwan, Quesna, Shibin al-Kom, Port Said, Kafr al-Sheikh, Kafr al-Dawwar, Beni Suef, and Daqahlia reached into the thousands, while hundreds of workers were involved in labor action in Aswan, Marsa Matrouh, Menoufia, Fayoum, and Qena. In Mansoura, if peasants are included in those taking part in collective action, this number was closer to 15,000. These numbers are by no means conclusive, as they are based purely on the limited number of reports available. In all likelihood, the number of workers partaking in labor struggles throughout the two month period of February and March was significantly higher. *Awlad al-Ard*,[68] an Egyptian NGO, cites 123 different forms of collective labor action with 83,000 workers taking part in March.[69] In contrast, some 489 different actions were reported in February, implying that we can expect the number of workers participating to be at least double, and possibly quadruple the 83,000 that were active in March.[70] Therefore, one could assume a more accurate figure would place the number of workers engaging in collective action during February somewhere between 166,000 to 332,000.

This tremendous upsurge is even more inspiring given that workers prior to 2011 had almost no nationally recognized leadership, a paucity of organizational infrastructure, paltry financial resources, almost no political program, and only a skeletal economic one. Yet, the revolutionary conditions in Egypt created a space where workers could mobilize; and that is what they did. While the labor upsurge in February was impetuous, responding to the revolution conditions, by the last half of the year this changed dramatically. In September of 2011 workers organized at an unprecedented level and coordinated actions in a manner not seen since the uprisings against the British occupation.

[1] "Egypt PM appoints new key ministers." *Al-Jazeera*, March 06, 2011. http://www.aljazeera.com/news/middleeast/2011/03/2011365436227288.html (accessed July 22, 2013).
[2] In Arabic: *Al-Shorouk*, March, 2011, http://www.shorouknews.com/ContentData.aspx?id=400594
[3] In Arabic: *Al-Dostor*, March 03, 2011, http://www.dostor.org/politics/egypt/11/march/3/37383
[4] In Arabic: Osama Ahmed, "Demonstrations Sweep Cairo University to Remove Director," March 6, 2011, http://www.e-socialists.net/node/6594.
[5] Hossam El-Hamalawy, "Cairo U students continue their protests," *3arabawy* (blog), March 8, 2011, http://www.arabawy.org/2011/03/08/students-5/.
[6] In Arabic: Muhammed Al-Weeshi, "Demonstrations at Ain Shams University Call for Dismissal of it's President," *Al-Wafd*, March 8, 2011, http://www.alwafd.org/index.php?option=com_content&view=article&id=21790:
[7] In Arabic: Abu Al-Saud Muhammad, Muhammad Kamal, Baant Zein Al-Deen, and Waleed Majdi, "University Uprisings," *Al-Masry Al-Youm*, March 8, 2011, http://www.almasryalyoum.com/node/344573.
[8] "Ten thousand peasants knocking on the door of Dakahlia governor," *Tadamon*.
[9] In Arabic: *Tadamon Masr*, March 06, 2011, http://tadamonmasr.wordpress.com/2011/03/06/petrotrade-30/.
[10] "Nationwide labor protests continue in Egypt," Egypt Independent, March 06, 2011, http://www.almasryalyoum.com/en/node/341691.
[11] "700 Suez Canal workers reported on hunger strike," *Egypt Workers' Solidarity* (blog), March 07, 2011, http://www.egyptworkersolidarity.org/?p=338.
[12] In Arabic: *Tadamon Masr*, March 06, 2011, http://tadamonmasr.wordpress.com/2011/03/06/ambulence/.
[13] In Arabic: *Al-Dostor*, March 05, 2011, http://www.dostor.org/society-and-people/variety/11/march/5/37525.
[14] In Arabic: *Al-Shoruk*, March, 2011, http://www.shorouknews.com/ContentData.aspx?id=403100.
[15] "Egyptian labor protests continue," Egypt Independent, March 07, 2011, http://www.almasryalyoum.com/en/node/341691
[16] In Arabic: Tadamon Masr, March 06, 2011, http://tadamonmasr.wordpress.com/2011/03/06/tora/.
[17] "Egypt's Torah Cement 2010 profit rises 29.6 pct," *Reuters*, February 24, 2011, http://in.reuters.com/article/2011/02/24/torahcement-results-idINLDE70A10V20110224.
[18] In Arabic: *Al-Dostor*, March 05, 2011, http://www.dostor.org/politics/egypt/11/march/5/37553.
[19] "Nationwide labor protests continue in Egypt," Egypt Independent.
[20] In Arabic: Youssef Al-'Awmi, *Al-Masry al-Youm*, March 08, 2011,

http://www.almasryalyoum.com/node/344747.

[21] In Arabic: *Al-Ishtiraki*, March 08, 2011, http://www.e-socialists.net/node/6630.

[22] In Arabic: *Al-Dostor*, March 05, 2011, http://www.dostor.org/society-and-people/variety/11/march/5/37548.

[23] In Arabic: *Al-Shorouk*, March, 2011, http://www.shorouknews.com/ContentData.aspx?ID=403498.

[24] In Arabic: *Al-Dostor*, March 06, 2011, http://www.dostor.org/society-and-people/variety/11/march/6/37630.

[25] In Arabic: Hesham Fouad, "Army arrests 3 striking postal workers," *Al-Ishtiraki*, March 07, 2011, http://www.e-socialists.net/node/6600.

[26] In Arabic: "Statement of Unions and Political Forces Against the Military Assault on Postal Workers and Petrotrade," *Tadamon Masr*, March 07, 2011, http://tadamonmasr.wordpress.com/2011/03/07/statement-9/

[27] In Arabic: Gamal Essam El-Din, "Army intervenes to protect Secretary General of Parliament," *Al-Ahram*, March 07, 2011, http://gate.ahram.org.eg/News/46854.aspx

[28] In Arabic: Fouad, "Army arrests 3 striking postal workers."

[29] "Statement of Unions and Political Forces Against the Military Assault on Postal Workers and Petrotrade," *Tadamon Masr*.

[30] Ali Abd al-Mohsen, "Women suffer assault and derision at Tahrir march," *Egypt Independent*, March 08, 2011, http://www.egyptindependent.com/news/women-suffer-assault-and-derision-tahrir-march.

[31] "Copts and Muslims clash in Cairo," Al-Jazeera English, March 09, 2011, http://www.aljazeera.com/news/middleeast/2011/03/201138211326148908.html.

[32] Hesham Fouad, "Sit-ins sweep aviation, medicine, education, cement, and Suez Canal sectors," *Al-Ishtiraki*, March 13, 2011, http://www.e-socialists.net/node/6651.

[33] *Al-Ishtiraki*, March 12, 2011, http://www.e-socialists.net/node/6644.

[34] Hesham Fouad, *Al-Ishtiraki*, March 15, 2011, http://www.e-socialists.net/node/6658.

[35] Jano Charbel, "A new era for trade unions," *Egypt Independent*, March 15, 2011, http://www.egyptindependent.com/news/new-era-trade-unions.

[36] Charbel, "A new era for trade unions."

[37] In Arabic: *Tadamon Masr*, March 22, 2011, http://tadamonmasr.wordpress.com/2011/03/22/petroget/.

[38] In Arabic: *Tadamon Masr*, March 22, 2011, http://tadamonmasr.wordpress.com/2011/03/22/military-prod/.

[39] In Arabic: *Al-Wafd*, March 22, 2011, http://www.alwafd.org/index.php?option=com_content&view=article&id=26031.

[40] In Arabic: Khalif Ali Hassen, *Al-Masry al-Youm*, March 22, 2011, http://www.almasryalyoum.com/node/369518.

⁴¹ In Arabic: Yasser Ibrahim, *Al-Wafd*, March 23, 2011, http://www.alwafd.org/index.php?option=com_content&view=article&id=26375.

⁴² In Arabic: Muhammad Ahmed Saadani, Yasser Shameese, Hesham Omar Abd al-Halim, and Ahmed al-Buhairi, *Al-Masry al-Youm*, March 21, 2011, http://www.almasryalyoum.com/node/368508.

⁴³ In Arabic: Ayman Ibrahim, "Strike stops train lines," *Al-Wafd*, March 22, 2011, http://www.alwafd.org/index.php?option=com_content&view=article&id=26246.

⁴⁴ In Arabic: Ayman Ibrahim, "Train lines back to work," *Al-Wafd*, March 22, 2011, http://www.alwafd.org/index.php?option=com_content&view=article&id=26251.

⁴⁵ Kamal Abu 'Aita, "Egyptian worker: 'Our victor is a victor for workers of the world'," Socialist Worker (UK), March 22, 2011, http://www.socialistworker.co.uk/art.php?id=24326.

⁴⁶ Mohamed Abdel Ghany, "New Egyptian law criminalizes protests," *Egypt Independent*, March 23, 2011, http://www.egyptindependent.com/news/new-egyptian-law-criminalizes-protests.

⁴⁷ "Strikes, sit-ins and protests made illegal by Egyptian government," *Egypt Workers' Solidarity* (blog), March 23, 2011, http://www.egyptworkersolidarity.org/?p=420.

⁴⁸ Sallam, "Striking Back at Egyptian Workers."

⁴⁹ In Arabic: *Al-Ishtiraki*, March 23, 2011, http://www.e-socialists.net/node/6692.

⁵⁰ "Egypt's independent labour unions to protest anti-strike law," *Ahram Online*, March 26, 2011, http://english.ahram.org.eg/News/8602.aspx.

⁵¹ Tmim Elyan, "Workers refuse draft bill criminalizing protests, say sector protests will continue," Daily News Egypt, March 24, 2011, http://www.masress.com/en/dailynews/128571.

⁵² "CTUWS statement on anti-strike law," *Egypt Workers' Solidarity*, March 30, 2011, http://www.egyptworkersolidarity.org/?p=444.

⁵³ "Public Transport Workers Establish Independent Union!" *Sheqiq* (blog), July 22, 2013, http://she2i2.blogspot.com/2011/03/public-transport-workers-establish.html. The four unions joined by the Public Transit Authority were the Real Estate Tax Authority Employees' Union, The Independent Teachers' Syndicate, Egyptian Health Technologists' Syndicate, Pensioners' Federation

⁵⁴ Alastair Beach, "What's left of Egypt's left," *Egypt Independent*, March 26, 2011, http://www.egyptindependent.com/news/whats-left-egypts-left.

⁵⁵ "Guide to Egypt's Transition – Socialist Popular Alliance Party (Al-Tahaluf al-sha'abi al-ishtiraki)," Carnegie Endowment for International Peace, http://egyptelections.carnegieendowment.org/2011/10/19/socialist-popular-alliance-party-al-tahaluf-al-sha%E2%80%99abi-al-ishtiraki.

⁵⁶ Manson, "Unity across the Arab world."

⁵⁷ Ibid.
⁵⁸ Bassem Abo Alabass, "A dream for millions of Egyptian workers: A minimum wage," *Ahram Online*, July 27, 2012, http://english.ahram.org.eg/NewsContent/3/12/48780/Business/Economy/A-dream-for-millions-of-Egyptian-workers-A-minimum.aspx.
⁵⁹ "EGYPT: Bedouins begin to demand equal citizenship rights," IRIN, July 16, 2011, http://www.irinnews.org/report/92998/egypt-bedouins-begin-to-demand-equal-citizenship-rights.
⁶⁰ Translated by Rania Abu Alhana. Original in Arabic: "'Alaan Mubaada' Hizb al-'Amal al-Dimaqratiyyah, (Democratic Labor Party's Declaration of Principles)," http://www.e-socialists.net/node/6702.
⁶¹ Philip Marfleet, "Never going back: Egypt's continuing revolution," *International Socialism* (137), January 9, 2013, http://www.isj.org.uk/?id=866.
⁶² In Arabic: *Tadamon Masr*, March 27, 2011, http://tadamonmasr.wordpress.com/2011/03/27/suez-2/.
⁶³ In Arabic: Amani Zaki, *Al-Wafd*, March 28, 2011, http://www.alwafd.org/index.php?option=com_content&view=article&id=28086.
⁶⁴ In Arabic: *Tadamon Masr*, March 30, 2011, http://tadamonmasr.wordpress.com/2011/03/30/papers/.
⁶⁵ Khalil 'Abaadi et al., "Labor protests in Suez, Port Said, Kafr el-Sheikh, and Damanhur," *Al-Masry al-Youm*, March 31, 2011, http://www.almasryalyoum.com/node/381757.
⁶⁶ "Labor protests continue in Cairo and other governorates," March 30, 2011, http://www.egyptindependent.com/news/labor-protests-continue-cairo-and-other-governorates.
⁶⁷ Beinin, "The Rise of Egypt's Workers."
⁶⁸ Awlad al-Ard translates roughly into "Children of the Earth" or "Sons of the Land."
⁶⁹ Alexander, "The Egyptian workers' movement and the 25 January Revolution."
⁷⁰ "Egypt: Strike statistics for 2009-2011," *Middle East and North African Solidarity Network*, August 9, 2011, http://menasolidaritynetwork.com/2011/08/09/egypt-strike-statistics-for-2009-2011/.

8

April 2011 and Beyond: "The Union is a Shield and Our Sword is the Strike"

The tidal wave of labor activity continued throughout 2011, signifying that the people truly did want "another wheel of production." This desire expressed itself via two central tenants: social justice, in the form of living wages, improved working conditions, permanent employment, etc., and *tathir*, the cleansing of public institutions from the old regime. By the end of March, 2011, the total number of collective labor actions had already reached a record high of 612.[1] In contrast, the number of labor actions for the entire year of 2009 and 2010 were 478 and 530, respectively. In other words, this two month period in 2011 saw 22% more incidents of labor unrest than the entire year of 2009 and a 14% increase over the entire year of 2010. Halfway through 2011 incidents of labor unrest reached 956 and by the end of the year nearly 1,400 work stoppages or other labor protests had occurred.[2] This was almost three times the annual amount counted in any year during the previous decade. The number of workers involved in work stoppages and other actions would steadily decrease from April to August, hitting a low point of 76 incidents involving 33,000 workers in July. Still, in total some 280,000 workers engaged in "stopping the wheel of production" between April and August, near the same or less than in February and March. These numbers only paint a partial picture, however, as the consolidation of organizational capacity within and between individual workplaces during this period facilitated the struggle that detonated in September.[3]

April to August (2011): Obstacles for Egyptian Labor

The battles that preceded the September upsurge, those from April to August, were important less for their numbers than the qualitative developments that occurred within the labor movement. To take just a few examples, in Sadat City, categorized as a Qualified Industrial Zone, some 50,000 workers were employed in some two hundred firms. Before 2011 there was almost no union representation. Sadat City was the bastion of Ahmad 'Izz's iron and steel magnate and over the years the NDP had forcibly maintained a low union presence to attract capital investment. By the end of 2011, twelve new unions and a city-wide labor council appeared in Sadat City, all affiliated with EFITU. These unions were formed in the heat of struggle 9,000 Beshay Steel workers, 5,000 workers at the Mega Textile factory, and as hundreds of Ceramics workers went on strike and won many of their demands. In these months alone, at least 30% of Sadat City workers had engaged in labor activity.

By mid-May contention over control of the professional syndicates was evident, despite their being a historic stronghold of the Muslim Brotherhood. Thousands of doctors, who occupy a fundamentally different economic space in Egypt than in places like the United States and had felt the pinch of decades-long economic and educational decline, went on strike. During this process they opened up arguments about the function and role of unions for professionals. Mohammed Shafiq, referring to the June Doctors' syndicate elections after the strike, articulated the changing social reality:

> The Independence List put up six candidates for the young doctors' seats on the general council who are elected across the entire country. I was one of them. It is well known that I am a communist. The list got ten thousand votes. I got twelve thousand votes in total. Those extra two thousand votes came from the Brotherhood. I was putting forward the view that the union should be a fighting union; that the union is a shield and our sword is the strike.[4]

Thus, even doctors were beginning to radicalize as hundreds of thousands of workers around them were donning their shields and unsheathing their swords for the first time. Yet, with every step forward there was reaction as well. At Beshay Steel, 1,500 temporary workers lost their jobs due to the strike, even as the others won their demands. At the Mega Textile factory, managers dismissed 43 members from the newly formed union there, and a sit-in was attacked by military police. On June 29, a military court sentenced five workers at Petrojet under Law 34 to one-year prison sentences after workers occupied the public space in front of the ministry for two weeks demanding permanent employment status. These examples from Sadat City and Petrojet highlight the turbulent nature of the labor struggle in Egypt, and the obstacles that workers faced when taking collective action.[5]

The Mass Strike-wave of September: "A Shift from the Defensive to the Offensive"

September saw a drastic turnaround, marking a prodigious augmentation of struggle by Egyptian workers in the form of major strikes in four sectors. Postal workers, teachers, sugar workers, and public transit workers all engaged in coordinated, mass action during September. While there were only 56 recorded incidents of collective action in September, this number is misleading since some 500,000 to 700,000 workers were involved in the highly concentrated sector strikes. Compare this to all of 2008, where only 540,000 workers participated in labor activity. In other words, the number of workers who waged social struggle in September 2011 alone nearly met or exceeded the number in all of 2008.[6] These four strikes paralyzed the Supreme Council of the Armed Forces, still ruling Egypt throughout 2011, and set the stage for mass protests in November of that year.

The primary difference between the eclectic explosion of labor activity in February and the immense strike wave in September was the level of organization and coordination involved. In February, labor militancy was largely uncoordinated, spontaneous, and sectional. After years of political and economic repression, coupled with a dearth of independent labor organizations capable of uniting large groups of workers, this "many-headed hydra"[7] model matched the revolutionary climate as the Mubarak regime collapsed. By September, however, conditions were qualitatively different. Workers had formed dozens of independent unions, many linked together by EFITU, and many more worked in conjunction with other support networks. Despite the severity of the military junta's attacks on labor, which may partially explain the decline of activity from March through August, the revolutionary conditions were far more conducive to independent labor organizing than before. Workers seized this opportunity, and the September strike wave marked a dramatic shift apropos to the new level of coordination. Of the major strikes which took place in September, the teachers' strike was the largest, with some 250,000 to 500,000 teachers taking part. Another six strikes involved roughly 160,000 workers.[8] The concentration of workers in fewer but significantly larger strikes symbolized the higher level of organization on behalf of Egyptian workers.

The second dominant proclivity that distinguishes September from February is that a large amount of workers were engaged in battles against state institutions and employers in September, while in February workers were more likely to be fighting private employers. In March, over one-third of all workers engaged in collective struggle during March did so at a single workplace, while only fifteen percent engaged in nationally coordinated strikes. In September a complete reversal took place, with three-fourths of workers involved in strikes that took place at the national level.[9] These two factors, the concentration of workers into larger strikes with greater coordination and the shift in targets from private employers to state ones, were accompanied by the evolution of workers' demands into calls for large-scale social changes that transcended individual grievances. While examples of this could be seen in February, where generalized political and economic demands were being fused with local requests pertinent to individual workplaces, this phenomenon was significantly more widespread during September. These social demands, beyond the capacity of any individual employer to deliver upon, could be seen in many of the nationwide strikes. Alexander explains that:

> Collectively, they articulate one of the organized working class' most significant ideological challenges to neo-liberalism in the current economic crisis. The strikes in Egypt differ from the defensive strikes against austerity measures in Greece and strikes in Britain. The Egyptian strikes, by and large, represent the workers' movement's direct offensive against the "successes" of neo-liberalism, rather than its failure and crisis, with relentless rises in the cost of living actually driving the movement.[10]

Two major components of the demands articulated by workers were the implementation of a minimum wage of 1,200 Egyptian pounds per month and the dissolution and discontinuation of temporary contracts. This last issue was particularly important, as temporary contracts allowed Egyptian employers to keep wages low and easily dismiss any workers daring enough to try and collectively improve working conditions or wages. Various nationwide strikes adumbrated some variation of this demand calling for the immediate, mass transfer of workers from temporary to permanent employment. Strikes against the privatization of state companies formed another central component of this wave of unrest. Some small-scale victories, such as court decisions to annul the selling-off of a department store and a textile factory, were of enormous significance in terms of refreshing workers hopes that the wave of privatization could not only be stopped but potentially reversed. These shifts represented what Alexander calls a "shift from the defensive to the offensive." During September, workers began to seriously challenge the despondence caused from decades of rebarbative neoliberalism, articulating their own collective demands for dramatic social change. Even if these demands fell short of calling for a fundamental social transformation of society, a new consciousness had developed in Egyptian workers that could not easily be bottled back up.

This "shift from the defensive to the offensive" could be seen most clearly in the teachers' strike. The nationwide teachers' strike, the first of its kind since 1951, was coordinated by two new independent unions. The 80,000-strong Independent School Teachers' Union was founded in July 2010, before the revolution, and became affiliated with EFITU after its creation in 2011.[11] The Egyptian Teachers' Federation, based out of Giza, was also a key participant. The official state-sponsored union associated with the ETUF, which Muslim Brother candidates had just won control of, refused to support the strike. The demands that teachers made were broad and social in nature: the removal of the NDP-affiliated minister of education Ahmed Gamal Eddin Moussa, massive investment in public education equaling 6.5% of GDP, a minimum monthly wage for teachers of at least 1,200 Egyptian pounds, a large-scale school-building program, a reduction in class sizes to no more than 30 (where before 60 or more was common), and permanent contracts for fixed-term and supply teachers.[12] As one teacher explained, "I have been working for 28 years as a teacher, and I earn less than 1000 Egyptian pounds a month. The Education ministry is stuffed full of consultants on huge...earning 100,000 Egyptian pounds while teachers are paid so little." Another participant reinforced this narrative, "I have been working for 16 years, I have a family and children of my own, and I make LE900. Everyone knows that no one in Egypt can live on less than 1200-1500 pounds per month."[13] Hala Talaat, a leading organizer of the Egyptian Teachers' Federation union committee in Giza, maintains that teachers went on strike to "win a decent wage and allow them to live in dignity." She recalls an anecdote from her time in a small town: "A very large number of teachers do all kinds of jobs you would never imagine. For example I was in a town called Al-Fashan which is in Beni Sueif, there was a village there where the teacher used to sell watermelons from a barrow in the summer, because he didn't make enough money from his salary."[14]

Still, the demands of the teachers were not relegated to "narrow" economic demands. On the contrary, many of the demands dealt directly with rebuilding the decrepit and inadequate public education system. In Egypt, like many places in the Middle East, public schools serve as institutions where those too poor to afford private institutions are dumped. The teachers' strike was about improving conditions for both students and teachers. While government statistics claim that only 0.6% of teachers responded to the strike, independent analyses from journalists and activists indicated that about 65 to 75% of teachers did not report to their classrooms in various parts of the country. Even without the approval of the ETUF teachers' union, estimates place the number of striking teachers at over 250,000.[15] A solidarity protest by school students in Mahalla al-Kubra, notorious for the massive textile workers struggle of 2008, saw students chanting 'the teachers want the downfall of the minister', while "11 schools shut down in Wadi al-Gadid, 49 in Aswan, 16 in Luxor, 29 in

Minya, 26 in Sohag, and all schools shut in Minufiyya governorate." As a report from the Middle East and North Africa Solidarity Network explains, these statistics are not "a complete picture, but they give a sense of how wide the geographical spread of action is across the country."[16] While the Muslim Brother dominated ETUF teachers' union denounced the strike, so too did the minister of education Moussa, who condemned strikers in a familiar tone for "prioritizing sectional interests over the national good."[17] The teachers' strike was yet another clear example of the Muslim Brotherhood aligning itself with figures from the old regime.

It was not just teachers that organized large, coordinated protests. In Mahalla, cite of the historic 2006 strike and the bloody battle against the Mubarak regime in 2008, 22,000 workers announced they were beginning an open-ended strike on September 10, demanding increased wages and benefits as well as state investment in the main textile factory there. Thousands of low paid postal workers struck over both economic and political demands, shutting down 50% of Egypt's post offices in ten different governorates and demanding that corrupt officials and overpaid consultants be removed from their positions, and that a 7% annual pay increase be implemented in tandem with inflation. The recently formed Independent Postal Workers' Union was imperative in facilitating this nationwide strike.[18] Tens of thousands of public transport workers, organized by the Independent Public Transport Authority Worker's Union, went on strike as well. Sector-wide sugar refinery strikes were organized by a nascent formation called the Sugar Factories' Front for Change, a coordination committee with the intention of developing an independent union. Pay, work conditions, and the purging of Mubarak regime remnants from company management were the prioritized demands of the thousands of strikers. As El-Hamalawy explained at the time, "the current mass strikes are political" and not just economic:

> While activists are mobilizing thousands in Tahrir to denounce the military tribunals, the workers in the hundreds of thousands are in effect breaking the anti-strike law which refers strikes to military courts. The common denominator between all the strikes, though they still lack a centralized command or coordinating body, is the purging of the company management from corrupt, regime affiliated figures. The strikers are even raising questions about global politics, anti-imperialism and anti-Zionism, during their industrial actions.[19]

Thus, September represented a clear convergence of political and economic demands on a level previously unseen in Egypt. As El-Hamalawy noted, however, no nationwide coordinating body or centralized nexus connected these strikes. While EFITU was attempting to play that role, its own organizational limitations, external obstacles, and its ambiguous relationship to politics prevented it from fulfilling that function. Therefore, while gains were being made and a new level of consciousness was developing within Egyptian workers, both of these developments remained uneven and inconsistent.

Gains Thus Far

By this point the most immediate gains made were improvements in compensation and the development of a large, independent organizational infrastructure for workers. In July, 2011, before the massive strike wave in September, the first post-Mubarak interim cabinet increased the minimum wage for public sector workers to EGP 700, about $116, per month. In October 2011, right after the tempest of labor activity in September, the first-ever private sector minimum wage was established at EGP 700 as well.[20] While this was just over half of what Egyptian workers had been calling for, it was an enormous step forward and a reminder that collective class struggle could force social change.

There were problems, however. Namely, the private-sector minimum wage was never enforced. As late as July 2012, Ahmed Sadeq, a member of the Freedom and Justice Party and part of the parliament's planning and budget committee in 2011, explained that while private sector workers were promised a minimum wage and an "emergency allowance" if their pay did not meet 700 EGP, this simply was not accepted by businessmen and, subsequently, remained unenforced.[21] Furthermore, the minimum wage did not apply to workers with less than ten employees, which characterizes the majority of workplaces. Likewise, any enterprise that could present "sufficient proof" – which was not clearly defined – that they could not afford to raise wages was also exempt. Moreover, somewhere between 40% and 58% of workers are employed in the informal sector, rendering them unaffected by any state regulation.[22]

Thus, while the basic principle of establishing a minimum wage was a step forward from the Mubarak era, the failure to enforce it meant that very few workers would actually benefit from it. Instead, as Al-Ahram notes, "the minimum wage issue is being dealt with by governmental and private bodies on an ad hoc basis... with temporary bonuses and wage increases being issued when workers voice discontent in order to silence calls for a national minimum and maximum wage."[23] The struggle for wages became so intense that, in one instance, former Mansura-España textile workers went out in the street to protest back wages owed to them. A police man urged a truck driver to run through the mostly female crowd of workers, murdering one of the women, Mariam Hawas, a forty-four year old mother of three. Despite this atrocity, ten days later the workers received a collective total of $62,000 in severance pay and wages owed to them.[24]

EFITU Rapidly Expands in Spite of Challenges

While some ground had been gained on the wage front, the formation of independent unions was at best a partial success story. For the first time since the 1950s, independent unions blossomed in post-Mubarak Egypt. By October 2011, EFITU claimed 72 affiliated unions, with the largest amount of workers forming independent unions in the following sectors: transportation (15), the civil service (10), oil and gas (8), manufacturing (7), crafts (6), and food production and distribution (5), among over a dozen other trades and industrial sectors. [25] By the first year anniversary of Mubarak's downfall in February 2012, the number of unions affiliated with EFITU grew to around 200, with some two million blue and white collar workers represented.[26] By October 2012, these numbers had swelled to 261 unions, with 2.4 million workers linked to EFITU – some 8.8% of the total Egyptian workforce.[27] The most important affiliates remained the Independent General Union of Real Estate Tax Authority Workers (IGURETA), the independent teachers' unions, and unions representing workers from the Cairo Public Transport Authority, Egypt Telecom, the postal service, and those in the aviation sector.[28] This was an astonishing development, especially since prior to 2011 labor movements appeared mostly as what Nadine Abdalla calls "islands" that were:

> …isolated and with no structural ties linking one strike or demonstration to another. Every labor movement focused on demands related to its own sector, and engaged in protests and strikes separately. In consequence, collective actions never led to the formation of an overarching social movement encompassing several smaller labor movements – not even in one single industrial sector… The integration of the different unions into an effective federation will therefore require tremendous efforts, as it cannot rely on any organizational linkages or prior cooperation experience.[29]

This lack of democratic trade union experience was a serious impediment to the development of a national, coordinated union movement that could challenge whichever representative of the Egyptian ruling elite happened to be in power at the time.

In light of the repression of labor organizers in Sadat City, where bosses divided workers by temporary and permanent status and summarily dismissed union members from their jobs, this new level of organization was not without risk. Legal and organizational obstacles also existed, as companies could simply refuse to negotiate with newly formed unions, since no legal mechanism forced them to. One instance of this surfaced when Ismail Ibrahim Fahmi, recently appointed as an ETUF bureaucrat, pressed a lawsuit against CTUWS leader Kamal 'Abbas, which lead to a sentence of six months in prison for "insulting a public officer." Another legal challenge developed when the Socialist Popular Alliance Party (SPA) and EFITU member Fatma Ramadan attempted to run as a "worker" for the People's Assembly and the court refused to recognize EFITU-issued documents certifying her union status. She was subsequently unable to run for office.[30]

Similarly, in November the new Minister of Manpower al-Borai reinstated, with one exception, the entirety of the Mubarak-era ETUF leadership to their positions. The pluralistic trade union law that al-Borai drafted was never enacted, as the SCAF refused to allow its passage. Instead, the Muslim Brotherhood's Freedom and Justice Party, which held the most seats in the post-Mubarak parliament, circulated a draft law that allowed for one union per firm and gave an enormous advantage to the ETUF, since they already had some 1,400 to 1,800 enterprise level unions under their 23 national affiliates. EFITU and other independent labor organizations denounced the new legislation for this reason. They also cited the fact that it did not protect the rights of civil servants and professionals to form new unions, a particularly contentious issue given the enormous teachers' strike of September. Likewise, the law failed to concentrate power and decision making in local unions, instead continuing the centralized, top-down ETUF structure. Lastly, the law completely ignored the issue of social funds already accumulated by ETUF, which meant that workers leaving the ETUF to form an independent union would lose all social funds earned during their previous employment, including their pensions, insurance, etc.[31] Alongside this, the collection of dues from members remained arduous as the ETUF continued to automatically deduct dues from workers' wages even if the worker resigned from the state-sponsored federation and joined EFITU. Struggle over control of dues and social funds used for pensions and other benefits, which the ETUF maintains a monopoly on, remained an immense challenge for incipient unions.[32]

The First Schism in the New Labor Movement: The Egyptian Democratic Labor Congress

Exacerbating these external pressures, the nascent labor movement quickly developed internal schisms, manifest primarily in the relationship between EFITU, whose elected president was Kamal Abu 'Aita, and the CTUWS, represented by the coordinator Kamal 'Abbas. Abu 'Aita was also the president of IGURETA and a leading member of the Nasserist *Karama* (Dignity) Party, while 'Abbas, who took part in the illegal People's Revolutionary Party in the 1990s, had largely abandoned politics for grassroots trade unionism. The schism surrounding these two leading figures in the labor movement is partially personal, but also ideological, as 'Aita sought to position himself and other EFITU leaders as spokespersons for the largest number of workers possible in an attempt to enter parliamentary politics, while 'Abbas articulated the need for a slow educational process through which workers learned the fundamentals of trade union activism. While Abu 'Aita's *Karama* worked with the Muslim Brotherhood in the 2011 parliamentary elections, 'Abbas rejected organizing with the *Ikhwaan* given their long history of betraying trade union movements.

From this tension arose the founding of the Egyptian Democratic Labor Congress (EDLC) in October of 2011. Some 149 unions were represented in the EDLC from the start, and by January 2012, the EDLC claimed 214 affiliated unions with 1 million members, far short of EFITU but still a sizeable number of workers. Originally, the EDLC did not technically consider itself a labor federation, as it included a broad coalition of unions, NGOs, and individuals. Following the ideological dispositions of their respective leaders, EFITU positioned itself as an institution capable of representing broad layers of Egyptian workers in a somewhat top-down manner via various mechanisms such as the political and electoral arenas, whereas the EDLC focused on capacity-building from bottom-up trade union education and practice.

While this tension did not cause any serious discord within the independent labor movement, the potential existed and the division of resources – including time, people, and money – was detrimental to workers and organizers who had to decide where to align themselves. However, by mid-2012 the two organizations had come together to agree on a four point program, which included immediate enactment of the trade union pluralism law drafted by al-Borai's ministry, freedom of trade union activity, reinstatement of workers fired for organizing trade unions, and a monthly minimum wage of 1,200 Egyptian pounds to replace the current minimum of 700.[33] By 2013, at the EDLC's official launch as a trade union federation, EFITU president Abu 'Aita was present and proclaimed that "both unions represent the democratic labour movement. Our goal is to attain the freedom to form unions."[34] Yet, while the two labor formations claimed a collective membership of some 3 million workers by 2012, as Beinin explains, this:

> ...impressive number compared to ETUF's 3.8 million members in the Mubarak era... is surely an exaggeration. ETUF's membership was based on over 1,800 unions, an average membership of about 2,000 per union. Three million members in 400 unions would mean an average local union membership of 7,500, far too many given the small size of the great majority of Egyptian workplaces.[35]

Thus, neither union was strong enough on its own to challenge ETUF. Even combined it was not clear if their numbers and collective strength were enough to dislodge the decades-long monopoly of power the old union exercised.

As the trade union movement was facing internal schisms, exciting developments began to emerge regarding the socialist left. In May of 2011, the Democratic Labor Party entered into a socialist front with four other Egyptian leftist groups, which included the Revolutionary Socialists, the Egyptian Communist Party (ECP), the Socialist Party of Egypt (SPE), and the Socialist Popular Alliance Party (SPA). This formation, which came to be known as the Coalition of Socialist Forces (CSF), played an important role in both providing a limited amount of political leadership for the working class during the tumultuous wave of strikes and galvanizing the social base which provided support for Hamdeen Sabahi's 2012 presidential campaign. While not all of these parties were explicitly revolutionary, the process of developing some basic level of unity on the left was an important step, especially given the fragmented and often sectarian nature of its organizations. Still, the reach of this coalition, while extending wider than any singular component within it, remained relatively small and its membership continued to be dwarfed by the larger political parties.

Labor and Party Politics in the Egyptian Elections

In the face of these obstacles, workers still continued engaging in militant labor activity throughout the first half of 2012 in direct opposition to the laws enacted and atmosphere created by the SCAF. A few of the high-profile strikes were in the postal service, the Cairo public transport, the Railway Authority, court and prosecution services, the ceramic, iron, and steel sectors, and the ports of Alexandria and 'Ayn Sukhna. Roughly 480 collective labor actions were initiated from January to April of 2012,[36] and over 250 collective actions were taken by workers' during two two-week periods in April and May 2012.[37] By the end of June, some 1,000 labor actions took place, a riveting number in and of itself but one that would only set the stage for an even larger upsurge of struggle after the end of presidential elections on June 30th.[38]

Despite all of this activity, workers and their interests were hardly represented in Egypt's first post-Mubarak parliament or the government of Mohamed Morsi brought to power in mid-2012. Throughout all of 2011, the independent labor movement faced stark opposition vis-à-vis the ETUF leadership, the SCAF, and the Muslim Brotherhood. Even other electoral alliances were devotedly anti-labor. Both Tagammu (The National Progressive Unionist Party) and the Social Democratic Party (SDP), which ostensibly represented workers, partnered with the liberal Free Egyptians Party to form the Egyptian Bloc alliance. The Free Egyptians Party, headed by Egypt's wealthiest tycoon, Nagib Sawiris, supported the government's anti-strike law, and was at best ambivalent towards the NDP. While the Socialist Popular Alliance Party (SPA) and the Socialist Party of Egypt (SPE) both left the electoral bloc for this reason, *Tagammu* and the SDP decided to stay. At best, only a paltry 25 members of the total 508 elected seats in the first pro-Mubarak People's Assembly were consistently pro-labor. The Labor Committee in the People's Assembly was chaired by a manager in the oil sector, Sabr Abu al-Futtuh of the Freedom and Justice Party. As Beinin explains, this underrepresentation of workers and workers' interests "reflected the broader phenomenon that the forces who worked longest and hardest to overthrow Mubarak did not reap commensurate political rewards."[39]

This phenomenon was exacerbated when Mohamed Morsi of the Freedom and Justice Party (FJP), the Muslim Brotherhood's political wing, won the presidential elections in 2012 and seemed bent on continuing the neoliberal economic policies of his predecessors. During the first round of voting in May, Morsi won 5.7 million votes, roughly 24.8% of those cast, compared to the NDP old-guard Ahmed Shafiq's 5.5 million, or 23.7%. Neither candidate had a tincture of legitimacy with regard to representing workers. In fact, both were vehemently anti-labor. The one silver lining in the first round of elections was the close third place finish of Hamdeen Sabahi, of the *Karama* Party, who won 20.7% for a total of 4.8 million votes. Sabahi's platform was significantly more amiable to workers' interests than that of either Morsi or Shafiq. In the fourth and fifth place were Abdel Moneim Abu al-Fotouh and Amr Moussa, who won 17.5% and 11.1% respectively. Abdel Moneim Abu al-Futouh, a liberal Islamist politician who contrasts Morsi's conservatism, was expelled from the Muslim Brotherhood along with many other dissidents inside the organization. During this period of expulsions, many former Muslim Brothers regrouped around the Egyptian Current Party.

Sabahi's Nasserist ideology was particularly appealing to public sector workers given the legacy of Nasser's massive expansion of the public sector, including the job opportunities and security that accompanied it. The unexpected turnout for Sabahi was clearly class-based, and did away with the trite orientalist binary pitting authoritarian secularism against socially conservative Islamism. Sabahi advocated renationalizing public firms that had been privatized and proposed to expand the public sector in order to create jobs. He also called for a one-time tax on 20% of the wealth held by the richest 1% of the population, and argued for increased fees on real estate and stock transactions, all ideas which were met with wide acceptance by Egypt's workers. While there are obvious shortcomings with Sabahi's program, his was the only competitive candidacy that offered a serious alternative to the Morsi and Shafiq campaigns, both of whom shared similar neoliberal economic ideologies despite differing on political and social issues.[40] Such popularity explains how Sabahi managed to win the most votes in major cities such as Cairo and Alexandria, as well as the northern industrial governorate of Kafr el-Sheikh. Sabahi won nearly 1 million votes in Cairo, almost 28% of the total vote there, as well as 572,000 votes, nearly 32%, in Alexandria. In Kafr el-Sheikh, Sabahi won an outstanding 62% of the vote, close to half a million votes, which was one of the only two governorates where a majority of votes cast went to one candidate.[41] He also managed to make a strong showing in other industrial areas, taking second place in Gharbia, whose largest industrial city is al-Mahalla al-Kubra, with 23% of the vote, Dakahlia with 23%, Damietta with 24%, and Suez with 22%. After losing, Sabahi went on to play a prominent role in the National Salvation Front (NSF), a broad coalition united against Morsi, and helped launch a campaign with the SPA and NGOs to cancel Egypt's $35 billion foreign debt.

Despite these impressive showings by Sabahi, Morsi and Shafiq were able to narrowly secure the first and second place spots, guaranteeing them a position in the run-off elections scheduled for June, which Morsi won by an even narrower margin of 51.7% to Shafiq's 48.2%, a difference of less than one million votes. With a roughly 52% turnout, Morsi won some 13 million total votes in the run-off, about 26% of the total Egyptian voting age population. Many of these votes were secured by various revolutionary currents throwing their weight behind Morsi, despite initially opposing him, in order to ensure that a remnant from the old regime could not come to power. In this sense, much of Morsi's support in the second round was not an acceptance of his platform of the Muslim Brotherhood as much as a rejection of Shafiq and the old regime. Even far left organizations such as the Revolutionary Socialists provided critical support to Morsi's election in

June, citing the "accomplishment of the millions of voters from the poor, the workers, the peasants... who backed Hamdeen Sabahi," while simultaneously calling for "all the reformist and revolutionary forces and the remainder of the revolutionary candidates to form a national front which stands against the candidate of counter-revolution." In doing so, they also called on the Muslim Brotherhood to accept a set of conditions, including the formation of a "presidential coalition" which would include Hamdeen Sabbahi and Abd-al-Moneim Abu-al-Fotouh as Vice-Presidents, the selection of the Prime Minister from outside the ranks of the Brotherhood and the FJP, the approval of a pluralistic trade union law, and an agreement with other political forces on a civil constitution which guarantees a variety of social rights.[42] Aside from the appointment of an independent prime minister, a condition only partially met as his cabinet was quickly filled with technocrats and various representatives from Islamist parties, none of these demands were met under Morsi. Almost immediately after the elections Morsi lost the support of the bloc and the social base that had simply voted against Shafiq.

The Muslim Brotherhood in Power

The hope of wide-spread social change was quickly dashed not long after Morsi assumed office on June 30th, 2012. By continuing the most nefarious policies of the Sadat-Mubarak era, the stage was set for an increase in tensions between his administration and the working class. By so fully accepting the neoliberal paradigm that it even rejected renationalizing factories when court-ordered to do so, the first elected post-Mubarak government ignored the millions of Egyptian workers who struggled in the revolution but gained very little from his election. Indeed, while nearly 1,000 labor protests occurred in 2012 prior to Morsi's inauguration, a staggering 2,400 erupted from July until the end of the year. Roughly the same amount occurred during the first quarter of 2013.[43] Morsi did his best to extinguish the desire for far-reaching change, betraying the ideology and historical trajectory of the party from which Morsi ascended:

> The Muslim Brothers embrace the same neoliberal policies favored by the Mubarak regime and, if anything, envision an even more expansive program of privatization of public assets. The Brothers' leadership also has a history of opposing militant labor action. Some Brothers who happen to work in industrial or clerical jobs have been more sympathetic to local workers' issues. But they have not received support from the Guidance Bureau, which directs the organization and presumably has strong

influence over the positions of the Mursi government. Since Mursi assumed office, physical and legal attacks on trade union activists have increased. Hundreds of workers have been fired for trade union activities and thugs have beaten many others.[44]

Although there are competing and contentious ideologies within the Muslim Brothers, the opportunistic nature of the conservative leadership became increasingly apparent. While social protest could be a political tool used sparingly by the organization when marginalized by the state, it became an object of scorn and ridicule as soon as the group maneuvered its way into a position of power. This was a logical extension of the Brotherhood's history. The mythology of their revolutionary credentials could only be maintained so long as the Brotherhood was an oppositional movement. Once in a position to actually govern, their ideology was utterly inadequate for addressing the needs of the masses.

The historically conservative discourse which animated the Muslim Brotherhood became reactionary. Financier and second-in-command, Khairat el-Shater, was more akin to what Ali Shariati described decades ago as the "legitimations of false religion" than the social justice oriented rhetoric of equality that many rank-and-file members attributed to *Sharī'a*:

> Have patience, my religious brother. Leave the world to those who are of it. Let hunger be the capital for the pardon of your sins. Forebear the hell of life for the rewards of paradise in the Hereafter. If you only knew the reward of people who tolerate oppression and poverty in this world! Keep your stomach empty of food, O brother, in order to see the light of wisdom in it. What is the remedy? Whatever befalls us. The pen of destiny has written on our foreheads from before: The prosperous are prosperous from their mother's womb and the wretched are wretched from their mother's womb. Every protest is a protest against the Will of God. Give thanks for His giving or non-giving. Let the deeds of everyone be accounted for on the Day of Reckoning. Be patient with oppression and give thanks for poverty. Do not breathe a word so that you do not lose the reward of the patient in the Hereafter. Release your body so as not to require clothes! Do not forget that the protest of a creature is protest against the Creator. The accounting of Truth and justice is the work

of God, not the masses. In death, not in life. Do not pass judgment for the Judge of the judgment is God. Do not be shamed on the Day of Resurrection when you see that God, the Merciful, the Compassionate forgives the oppressor who you had not forgiven in this world. Everyone is responsible for his own deeds.[45]

While el-Shater could continue accumulating wealth from the exploitation of Egyptian labor and catering goods to the wealthiest Egyptians, workers were expected to let "hunger be their capital" and "tolerate poverty." Their stomachs "empty of food" stood in stark juxtaposition with el-Shater's wealth. Despite their history as an opposition movement, once the Muslim Brothers came to power it seemed that "every protest was a protest against the Will of God" and the "accounting of truth and justice was the work of God, not the masses." One pernicious manifestation of this phenomenon transpired in September when a court in Alexandria sentenced five union leaders to three years in prison for leading a strike at the Alexandria Port Containers Company the previous year. Similarly, Morsi refused to recognize either EFITU or the EDLC. Instead, Morsi met only with leaders of the ETUF, whose vacant positions had been filled largely with supporters of his party. After Morsi met with ETUF leaders and promised to establish more channels of communication with them, a "war of statements" ensued between the ETUF and the EFITU, both accusing the other of illegitimacy.[46]

Meanwhile, Morsi rapidly sought out help from the IMF, hoping to secure a $4.8 billion loan coupled with billions more in economic aid from Europe and the US. The social price for such a loan was to be paid by Egypt's workers and the poor, as it required higher costs for basic foodstuffs, more regressive taxation via new sales taxes, and more cuts in jobs targeting state employees. Because a large outcry of public disdain already existed following Morsi's decisions to temporarily grant himself unlimited executive power and push through a controversial new constitution, he was forced to retreat from immediately accepting the loan.

The November 22nd decree allowed Morsi to force through the constitution, drafted largely by members of his own and other Islamist parties as other parties refused to participate. The new constitution was also utilized to smash any form of dissent, particularly labor activity. A law to "protect the revolution" contained clauses creating a special prosecutor's office to deal with "crimes" such as participating or inciting a strike. Mass protests, the largest since the downfall of Mubarak, forced Morsi to rescind many of the powers he granted himself. However, the law institutionalizing the prosecution of those inciting or participating in a strike remained on the books. Another law – Decree 97 – granted Morsi enormous control over the ETUF, allowing the new Minister of Manpower FJP member Khalid al-Azhari to appoint dozens of key ETUF positions. The Brotherhood also continued its collaboration with holdovers from the Mubarak era, placing their own representatives on the ETUF executive board where possible and working in tandem with the ETUF bureaucrats to constrict the growth of the nascent independent trade union movement. Similarly, the constitution that went into effect in December failed to provide any serious protection to independent labor activity, connecting the "right to form unions" to the notorious Law 35, giving the ETUF a monopoly on trade union organization, permitting the dissolution of unions by judicial order, and failing to link wages to inflation.

Economic Protests Explode During Morsi's Tenure

It was this heavy-handedness towards labor, and the continuation of policies reminiscent of the Sadat-Mubarak era in other areas, that fostered such hostility on behalf of the independent trade union movement towards Morsi and his government. Morsi did next to nothing to ameliorate the economic conditions that continued to strangle Egyptian workers. It was within this context that some 2,400 forms of labor activity took place during the last half of 2012. This crescendo of labor action came even as the ETUF leader Ahmed Abdul-Zaher assured Morsi during meetings that there would be a one-year moratorium on strike action. According to the Egyptian Center for Economic and Social Rights, some 566 strikes and economically-motivated social protests took place in July, 410 in August, 615 in September, 507 in October, and 508 in November.[47] As Philip Marfleet explains, "These figures should be addressed with some care: ECESR records not only collective withdrawals of labour and workplace occupations but also vigils, demonstrations, blockades and hunger strikes among which some have been 'citizen actions' including protests over rising prices, lack of fuel and clean water, and power cuts."[48]

Still, the general trend showed that the quantity, frequency, and intensity of class struggle was moving upward. Hatem Tallima of the Revolutionary Socialists argued this phenomenon, involving a "greater readiness now to use the strike as a default strategy," was a result of the "fast learning" on behalf of workers after decades of political repression, and as such was part of the "political generalization within the revolutionary process."[49] One example clearly captured the escalating tensions and the willingness of workers to challenge Egypt's military establishment. Chemical workers at the Nasr Company, a subsidiary of the military-owned National Service Project Organization (NSPO), went on strike to demand that the director of the NSPO be sacked.⁵⁰ Meanwhile, doctors struck from October 1ˢᵗ to December 21ˢᵗ in order to demand higher salaries, an increase in the Ministry of Health budget, and more security in hospitals. At the beginning of the 2012 academic year, teachers repeated the nationwide protests they organized in September of 2011, citing the same list of demands that remained unmet. Public-sector industrial workers also battled for control of ETUF affiliated unions since their pensions and other benefits were linked to their membership in the federation.

By September, ten separate left-wing political organizations came together to form the Democratic Revolutionary Coalition (DRC), building off the momentum from the earlier attempt at left unity, the Coalition of Socialist Forces. While the CSF eventually fell apart, four of the five parties joined the DRC, including the Egyptian Socialist Party, the Socialist Popular Alliance, the Egyptian Communist Party, and the Democratic Labor Party. They were joined by the largest but increasingly enervated left-wing party Tagammu, as well as the Socialist Revolutionary Movement (January), the Egyptian Coalition to Fight Corruption, the Socialist Youth Union, the Workers and Peasants Party, and the Democratic Popular Movement. The DRC announced its intentions to ally with Sabahi's Popular Current Party and form a united front against the Morsi government. Yet, by 2013, the Popular Current party was in partial disarray, as many prominent activists in the party resigned, citing Sabahi's decision to join with elements of the *feloul* (elements from the old regime) in the National Salvation Front. Notably, the Revolutionary Socialists refused to participate in this coalition, primarily due to the presence of Tagammu, with Revolutionary Socialist member Hesham Fouad explaining that "even though the principle of having a united left is essential for us, we don't think that working with the Tagammu Party is acceptable" given some of the leadership's opportunistic dealings with figures from the Mubarak regime.⁵¹ It should be noted here that the position by the Revolutionary Socialists was a principled one, given that Tagammu supported the SCAF candidate Ahmed Shafiq in the run-off election against Morsi. Despite these reservations, the DRC was at this point the largest coalition of left-wing organizations in Egypt. It helped organize the mass protests against Morsi in November of 2012.

The continuing decline in living standards for Egyptians coupled with the Morsi government's inability to address the needs of Egypt's workers meant that militant labor activity was the only route forward for many workers. In February 2013, over one thousand dock workers at Ain Sukhna port maintained a 16-day strike where "not a single shipping container moved into or out of Egypt's principal port for Asian trade." That same month, workers at Kouta Steel in Tenth of Ramadan City, after having won a legal victory allowing them to run the factory when its owner fled, sent a letter to

Vio.Me steel workers in Salonika, Greece who had established their own self-managed cooperative:

> Though a thousand miles away from Greece, we send our strongest expression of solidarity and support to the workers of Vio.Me and to their newborn experiment in self-management. We also declare our absolute rejection of the austerity measures that affect first and foremost the working class, whether in Greece or here in Egypt.
>
> We invite Vio.Me workers to start and [sic] exchange of our experiences in struggle, so that we can benefit from lessons learned from both experiments in self-management. Millions of workers are looking at us as a concrete reality and an awaited dream.[52]

While there are obvious limitations to self-managed firms and worker cooperatives which are forced to abide by the dictates of the market, experiments such as these represented a clear development of agency and class consciousness on behalf of Egyptian workers. March saw widespread transport worker strikes in Mahalla al-Kubra, Alexandria, and Giza over fuel shortages, with drivers parking buses in squares and on railway lines. In April, 73,000 rail workers took part in the largest railroad sector stoppage in three decades. The military responded by attempting to conscript striking workers, threatening prison if workers refused. In a stunning act of solidarity, Cairo Metro workers threatened to go on strike and the army backed off.[53]

Morsi: Mubarak with a *Zibiba*

The reality for millions of Egyptians was that life under Morsi had not changed from life under Mubarak. Morsi was not a Mossadegh, a Nasser, or an Allende, and he failed to provide leadership, open up Egyptian society, improve economic conditions, or secure a stable social base. Indeed, as Adel Iskandar explains:

> In the absence of any vision... the Brotherhood regime has desperately stumbled back toward the tried and tested, albeit flawed, policies of the Mubarak era. Whether it is accepting World Bank and International Monetary Fund money without safeguards, maintaining strong and collaborative relations with an oppressive Israeli state at the expense of Palestinians (despite the Brotherhood's hostile domestic rhetoric), failing to improve wages or

create a conducive environment for tourism, attacking labor action, asphyxiating anti-government expression, [or] reducing subsidies on basic necessities... the Brotherhood are essentially a Mubarak regime with a *zibiba* ('raisin,' or prayer mark) on their foreheads... Whether they are hidden behind Gamal Mubarak's accentless English or Morsi's beard and *zibiba*, the policies are indistinguishably counter-revolutionary... This is an administration whose rhetoric is adorned with Qur'anic verses, anecdotes from the Hadith, and religious salutations accenting every expression... but tone and vernacular don't feed the hungry, treat the sick, educate children, or pay the bills.[54]

It was this complete failure to govern and the Brotherhood's immeasurable capacity to alienate large sectors of Egyptian society that would lead to Morsi's removal in July of 2013. As the desired social and economic gains failed to materialize in post-revolutionary Egypt, many workers became disillusioned with the slow pace of change and continued policies of the past. This development of an independent trajectory representing Egypt's workers set the stage for working class participation on a scale not seen in decades. Subsequently, workers composed one of the main social forces in the massive June 30th, 2013 protests. These enormous demonstrations initiated the military coup that ended in the ouster of Egypt's first democratically elected president, only one year after his coming to power.

Table 8.1 – Incidents of Labor Activity by Year[55]						
Year	Sit-in	Strike	Demonstration	Rally	Gathering	Total
2009	184	123	79	65	27	478
2010	209	135	80	83	23	530
2011 (Jan-June)	338	158	259	161	40	956
2011 (Total)	-	-	-	-	-	1,400
2012 (Total)	-	-	-	-	-	3,818

Table 8.2 – Number of Workers Involved in Labor Activity by Year[56]	
Year	Number of Workers
2005	141,000
2006	198,000
2007	475,000
2008	541,000
2011	1,045,000 – 1,461,000*

Table 8.3 – Incidents of Labor Activity by Month in 2011[57]						
Month	Sit-in	Strike	Demonstration	Rally	Gathering	Total
Jan	22	5	6	9	0	42
February	186	77	151	48	27	489
March	48	17	32	23	2	122
April	26	14	26	24	0	90
May	26	30	25	21	4	106
June	30	15	19	36	7	107
July	22	19	20	10	4	75
August	21	11	19	12	6	69
September	20	17	6	11	2	56
TOTAL	401	205	304	194	52	1156

Table 8.4 – Numbers of Workers Involved in Labor Activity by Month in 2011[58]	
Month	Number of Workers
January	20,000+
February	166,000 to 332,000+
March	82,000
April	65,000
May	57,000
June	57,000
July	33,000
August	65,000
September	500,000 – 750,000

Table 8.5 – Incidents of Labor Activity by Month in 2012[59]

Month	Incidents
January	186
February	119
March	170
April	270
May	206
June	157
July	566
August	410
September	615
October	507
November	508
December	104
TOTAL	3818

Table 8.6 – Number of Unions and Workers Affiliated with Labor Federations as of October 2012[60]

Name of Federation	Number of Affiliated Unions	Number of Workers (millions)	% of Labor force (27.2 million total)
ETUF	23	3.8	13.9%
EFITU	261	2.4	8.8%
EDLC	246	1.0+*	3.6%

1 "Egypt: Strike statistics for 2009-2011," *Middle East and North African Solidarity Network.*
2 Beinin, "Workers, Trade Unions and Egypt's Political Future."
3 Alexander, "The Egyptian workers' movement and the 25 January Revolution."
4 Mohammed Shafiq, interviewed by Anne Alexander, "The union is a shield and our sword is the strike," *Socialist Review*, December 2011, http://www.socialistreview.org.uk/article.php?articlenumber=11845.
5 Beinin, "The Rise of Egypt's Workers."
6 Anne Alexander, "The Strike Wave and the Crisis of the Egyptian State," *Jadaliyya*, December 10, 2011, http://www.jadaliyya.com/pages/index/3464/the-strike-wave-and-the-crisis-of-the-egyptian-sta.
7 For my borrowing of the term, see Peter Linebaugh and Marcus Rediker, *The Many-Headed Hydra: Sailors, Slaves, Commoners, and the Hidden History of the Revolutionary Atlantic* (Beacon Press, 2001).
8 Alexander, "The Strike Wave and the Crisis of the Egyptian State."
9 Ibid.
10 Ibid.
11 Tom Dale, "Draft law threatens independent unions, but workers vow to fight," *Egypt Independent*, March 14, 2012, http://www.egyptindependent.com/news/draft-law-threatens-independent-unions-workers-vow-fight.
12 "Egypt: Teachers' strike enters third day with strong support," *Middle East and North Africa Solidarity Network*, September 19, 2011, http://menasolidaritynetwork.com/2011/09/19/egypt-teachers-strike-enters-third-day-with-strong-support/.
13 Mostafa Ali, "Egypt teachers strike for the first time since 1951," *Ahram Online*, September 19, 2011, http://english.ahram.org.eg/NewsContent/1/64/21568/Egypt/Politics-/Egypt-teachers-strike-for-the-first-time-since-.aspx.
14 Hala Talaat, "Egypt: Women workers speak out – Teachers' unions build unity from below," Middle East and North Africa Solidarity Network, September 2011, http://menasolidaritynetwork.com/egyptwomen4/.
15 Alexander, "The Strike Wave and the Crisis of the Egyptian State."
16 "Egypt: Teachers' strike enters third day with strong support," *Middle East and North Africa Solidarity Network.*
17 Ali, "Egypt teachers strike for the first time since 1951."
18 Mostafa Ali, "Egyptian Postal workers strike a big headache for SCAF," *Ahram Online*, September 7, 2011, http://english.ahram.org.eg/News/20499.aspx.
19 "Egypt: Thousands of Sugar Workers on Strike," Middle East and North

Africa Solidarity Network, September 17, 2011, http://menasolidaritynetwork.com/2011/09/17/549/.

[20] Beinin, "The Rise of Egypt's Workers."

[21] Alabass, "A dream for millions of Egyptian workers: A minimum wage."

[22] The Egyptian Center for Economic and Social Rights cites 58% in "Report: ECESR Submits Report to the UN Committee on Economic and Social Rights" (May 21, 2013, http://ecesr.com/en/2013/05/21/ecesr-presents-a-report-to-the-un-economic-social-counsil/), while Beinin cites 40% in "The Rise of Egypt's Workers."

[23] Alabass, "A dream for millions of Egyptian workers: A minimum wage."

[24] Beinin, "The Rise of Egypt's Workers."

[25] Alexander, "The Egyptian workers' movement and the 25 January Revolution."

[26] Beinin, "The Rise of Egypt's Workers."

[27] Abdalla, "Egypt's Workers – From Protest Movement to Organized Labor."

[28] Beinin, "The Rise of Egypt's Workers."

[29] Abdalla, "Egypt's Workers – From Protest Movement to Organized Labor."

[30] Beinin, "The Rise of Egypt's Workers."

[31] Abdalla, "Egypt's Workers – From Protest Movement to Organized Labor."

[32] Beinin, "The Rise of Egypt's Workers."

[33] Beinin, "Workers, Trade Unions and Egypt's Political Future."

[34] Ayat Al-Tawy, "Egyptian Democratic Labour Congress officially launches," Ahram Online, April 25, 2011, http://english.ahram.org.eg/NewsContent/1/64/70102/Egypt/Politics-/Egyptian-Democratic-Labour-Congress-officially-lau.aspx.

[35] Beinin, "The Rise of Egypt's Workers."

[36] Abdalla, "Egypt's Workers – From Protest Movement to Organized Labor." Abdalla does not actually provide the number of strikes from January to April 2012, but the figures above were calculated by subtracting the amount of strikes from Jan-April 2011 from the total number of strikes in 2011 and finding the remainder, which can then be subtracted from the 1,137 figure given for May 2011 – April 2012.

[37] Beinin, "The Rise of Egypt's Workers."

[38] Beinin, "Workers, Trade Unions and Egypt's Political Future."

[39] Beinin, "The Rise of Egypt's Workers."

[40] Beinin, "Workers, Trade Unions and Egypt's Political Future."

[41] The other was the sparsely populated western governorate of Matrouh, where Abdel Moneim Aboul Fotouh won 58%.

[42] "Revolutionary Socialists' statement on Egypt's presidential elections," *Socialist Worker* (UK), May 28, 2012, http://socialistworker.co.uk/art.php?id=28595.

[43] Philip Marfleet, "Egypt: The workers advance," *International Socialism* (139), July 4, 2013, http://www.isj.org.uk/index.php4?id=904&issue=139.

[44] Beinin, "Workers, Trade Unions and Egypt's Political Future."

[45] Ali Shariati, *Religion vs. Religion*, (Kazi Publications, Inc., 1993), pg. 15-16.

[46] Dina Bishara, "Who speaks for Egypt's workers?" *Foreign Policy*, September 6, 2012, http://mideast.foreignpolicy.com/posts/2012/09/06/who_speaks_for_egypts_workers.
[47] "2012 Social Protests: Cry of the People," *Egyptian Center for Economic and Social Rights*, January 1, 2013, http://ecesr.com/en/2013/01/01/2012-social-protests-cry-of-the-people/time/.
[48] Quoted in Marfleet, "Egypt: The workers advance."
[49] Ibid.
[50] Bissan Kassab, "Egypt Workers Striking in Record Numbers," *Al-Akhbar English*, September 24, 2012, http://english.al-akhbar.com/node/12592.
[51] Randa Ali, "Egypt's left launches Democratic Revolutionary Coalition," Ahram Online, Wednesday 19, 2012, http://english.ahram.org.eg/News/53304.aspx.
[52] Marfleet, "Egypt: The workers advance." It is important to note that Greek workers in Egypt were some of the first to advance radical political causes at the turn of the 19th century.
[53] Ibid.
[54] Adel Iskandar, *Egypt in Flux: Essays on an Unfinished Revolution*. Cairo: American University in Cairo Press, 2013, pg. 154.
[55] "Egypt: Strike statistics for 2009-2011," *Middle East and North African Solidarity Network*, and Beinin, "Workers, Trade Unions and Egypt's Political Future." As the MENA solidarity network points out: "Egyptian NGO Awlad al-Ard publishes regular reports of strike activity in Egypt. It is not clear exactly what the sources are for this information, but presumably the reports are largely compiled from press coverage of strikes. The distinction between these different categories of collective action is not particularly clear. For example, most sit-ins will necessarily involve the workers concerned being on strike. But in addition to being on strike they are also occupying their workplace or the street outside. These figures don't give a sense of the duration of each episode of collective action, nor the numbers involved (a strike by 10 people appears as one episode alongside a factory occupation involving 20,000 workers), but they do provide a useful index of the levels of strike activity." Joel Beinin's comments on the methodology of calculating labor unrest are also important: "Statistics for the 2000s, for 2011 and for 2012 were compiled by different NGOS, using slightly different methods to classify strikes, factory occupations and other forms of collective action. All depend on reports in the media, not a fully accurate source. Although the precision of the figures is questionable, the orders of magnitude are almost certainly correct."
[56] "The Struggle for Worker Rights in Egypt," Solidarity Center (AFL-CIO), February 2010, http://www.solidaritycenter.org/files/pubs_egypt_wr.pdf.
*Beinin cites *Awlad al-Ard* at "over 600,000" workers taking part in 2011. See "The Rise of Egypt's Workers," http://carnegieendowment.org/2012/06/28/rise-of-egypt-s-workers/coh8#. This seems to be a very conservative estimate, given the sheer number of labor incidents during February of that year and the

organization's own figures of at least 500,000 workers taking part in labor activity during September. The 1.0 to 1.4 million estimate for 2011 does not even factor in labor actions from October to December, so the actual number may be higher. Furthermore, Beinin notes in "The Rise of Egypt's Workers" (2012) that the amount of workers engaged in labor actions in 2011 were "two to three times more than any year in the previous decade," yet the Solidarity Center report (2010) claims that some 540,000 engaged in labor action during 2008 alone. This suggests that the 1.0 to 1.4 million number is likely closer to reality than the conservative 600,000 figure.

[57] For January through June see "Egypt: Strike statistics for 2009-2011," *Middle East and North African Solidarity Network*. For July through September, see the following: "The Labor movement in the month of July 2011," Awlad al-Ard, http://www.e-socialists.net/node/7255, "The Labor movement in the month of August 2011," Awlad al-Ard http://www.anhri.net/?p=39423, "The Labor movement in the month of September 2011," Awlad al-Ard http://www.e-socialists.net/node/7678.

[58] Estimates for March-September Alexander, "The Egyptian workers' movement and the 25 January Revolution." Estimates for January and February based on newspaper reports and other sources compiled in Chapter 6, 7, and 8, combined with a rough estimation based on trends from other months, since no official statistics are provided. No statistics are offered for January and February, but the range estimated for February is a conservative one. Anne Alexander argues that the number of participants in September "were probably lower than February." This may well be true, but without any amalgamation of reports, it is safe to assume a conservative number based on the evidence available. This is the case given the relatively low level of organization and small, wildcat nature of the strikes during February.

[59] "2012 Social Protests: Cry of the People," *Egyptian Center for Economic and Social Rights*.

[60] Abdalla, "Egypt's Workers – From Protest Movement to Organized Labor" and Beinin, "The Rise of Egypt's Workers." *This statistic comes from January 2012, but is likely higher as statistics for October 2012 were unavailable.

Conclusion

The explosion of social conflict in Egypt from the uprising of 2011 through the ouster of Mohammed Morsi in 2013 prompted the Wall Street Journal, historically one of the most honest mouthpieces of the ruling class, to call for a military dictatorship in Egypt. After more or less incorporating Morsi into the US orbit, an embarrassed Obama was forced to call for a review of military aid to Egypt once the coup took place. The coup led by Abdel Fatah al-Sisi harnessed and redirected the popular sentiment against Morsi, thereby appropriating and enervating the energy that could have furthered the revolution. The WSJ editorial proclaimed it would be foolish for the US to suspend aid, explaining that "Egyptians would be lucky if their new ruling generals turn out to be in the mold of Chile's Augusto Pinochet, who took power amid chaos but hired free-market reformers and midwifed a transition to democracy."[1] Pinochet's "midwifing" of democracy included the overthrowing of the democratically-elected and popular Salvador Allende government, the murder of Allende, the killing or disappearing of some 10,000 to 30,000 political opponents, the torture of thousands more, and the implementation of the same economic policies in Chile that utterly destroyed the livelihood of Egyptians. By his death in 2006, Pinochet had amassed a fortune of $28 million and had some 300 criminal charges pending against him in Chile, including human rights violations, tax evasion, and embezzlement. The Wall Street Journal, in all its imperial arrogance, hoped against odds that the Egyptian masses would acquiesce to an Egyptian Pinochet, even after suffering decades of economic neoliberalism and heroically struggling for two and a half years against regimes inimical to their interests.

Egyptians constantly and relentlessly challenged the period of military rule following Mubarak's downfall. These popular challenges to the military establishment laid the groundwork for the deepening of the revolution as Egypt's first relatively free presidential elections brought Morsi to power. One year after Morsi's inauguration, however, it remained clear that the social and economic demands of the revolution remained unfulfilled and the political changes made were mostly superficial. Morsi, Egypt's post-Mubarak, democratically-elected president of Egypt was quite successfully and, perhaps even willingly, absorbed into the regional and world hegemonic power structure; he represented "Mubarak with a *zibiba*." The limits of bourgeois elections, superimposed upon a fundamentally flawed economic system, could not have been more obvious.

In 2008, Mamdouh Habashi and Saber Barakat, two veterans of the Egyptian trade union and socialist movement, gave a talk in Chicago on the emerging class struggle in Egypt. When Habashi was asked about the role of the Muslim Brotherhood by an audience member, he responded with something of a prophetic analysis:

> About the role of the Muslim Brothers… I don't consider the Muslim Brothers anti-imperialist. They are not. Although they may say many things, one of the main properties of the Muslim Brothers in Egypt [is that] they really master in opportunism. They can talk to any political power the discourse they want to hear… They speak to Marxists as if they were Marxists. They speak to the state power as if they are partners in state power. They speak to Islamist fundamentalists, that are even miles to the right of them, as if they are more fundamentalist than them. But, how to evaluate their policies… we only have to stick on what they do, not what they say… They can say they are now with the workers' movement, but they are not. Or they are now with the peasants' movement. We have [had] in the last years many, many revolts of peasants that have been kicked out of their lands that they got in the land reform under Nasser… they are kicked out by a plot from the regime and the former owners of the land, the landlords. So, in such a fight, the Muslim Brothers, with 88 members of parliament, they took the side of the landlords… 'We are for land property, the right to own land is holy, the land belonged to the landlords, and this injustice that happened by Nasser through the land reform law should be corrected.' This is their attitude, and it is declared. In terms of policies against the United States in Iraq, or in Palestine, or whatever, you can see the difference between our attitudes. It is radical, because they accuse the policies of the United States, not because of imperialism and occupation, and perhaps different interests between the Arab countries on one hand and the United States on the other, these are Christians, and these are the people we are fighting against. They are making a war against Islam, which is not true… When we evaluate the policies of the Muslim Brothers, we have to take our scale according to… their policies and attitudes towards imperialism. This is the scale, and if we apply this scale to all policies of the Muslim Brothers, we should find out

very easy... they are neoliberals! And when they come into power one day, or when they realize a political party one day, the first thing they will do is to collaborate with the imperialism of the United States and Israel. And this is one hundred percent what we say.[2]

Habashi's predictions rang "one hundred percent" true. The list of Morsi's betrayals was long. He continued autocratic Mubarak-era policies, "collaborated with the imperialism of the United States and Israel," and pushed a neoliberal economic agenda anathema to the interests of the masses.

From the outset it was evident that Morsi planned to sustain the normalization of relations between Egypt and Israel, contrary to Egyptians' popular support for the Palestinians. This was brazenly illustrated during Israel's most recent assault on Gaza, where he inserted himself as the negotiator between Israel and Hamas, a public relations stunt he then used as a cover to usurp domestic power. Perhaps the most dramatic instance of these policies were seen when his administration used sewage to flood the underground tunnels that serve as lifelines for residents in Gaza.[3] His assurance that the 1979 Camp David Accords, universally unpopular amongst Egyptians, were to remain in place, as well as his bolstering of the so-called "qualified industrial zones" in direct contravention to the Boycott, Divestment, and Sanctions put forward by Palestinian civil society in 2005, reflect Morsi's desire to maintain the geopolitical status quo.[4] Time and again Morsi proved he could act as a faithful ally of Israel and the United States rather than a representative of Egyptian people. Unsurprisingly, the US political elites returned the favor by continuing the annual Mubarak-era $1.3 billion in military aid to the Egyptian government for the year Morsi held office.[5]

Morsi also continued the Sadat-Mubarak era acquiescence to and dependence upon the neoliberal economic order of the world. One of the first decisions he made was to push forward with an attempt to secure a $4.8 billion dollar loan, a plan originally pursued by the SCAF in the form of a smaller $3.2 billion loan, from the International Monetary Fund.[6] The IMF loan, like all other IMF policies, was coupled with and contingent upon an austerity program for the Egyptian population. This included general decreases in state spending and an emphasis on gutting subsidy programs, especially to bread and fuel. This policy, begun under Sadat and furthered under Mubarak, was adopted by Morsi in betrayal of the promises and political positions taken by the Muslim Brotherhood before coming to power. Morsi was eventually forced to renegotiate with the IMF, mostly in fear of the repercussions that wide-scale protests could have if he implemented such a harrowing austerity program immediately after his executive power grab in late 2012. Still, this attempt was representative of the economic trajectory he would pursue throughout his short tenure, one that roughly corresponded with his predecessors.[7] The perpetuation of these economic policies, which had already caused immense misery for much of the Egyptian population, would continue to have the same effect.

Morsi noticeably failed to grasp an opportunity when the Popular Campaign to Drop Egypt's Debt launched an initiative in 2012 for the SCAF to reject the first post-Mubarak IMF loan offered. The campaign argued that debt accumulated under the former regimes was "illegitimate" and Egyptians should not be expected to repay loans to the very same countries and agencies which propped up the former dictators. Implementing a policy of non-payment, however, would require a significant overhaul of the Egyptian economy and a drastic shift away from neoliberal capitalism, a path neither Morsi nor the Muslim Brotherhood were prepared to venture. Thus, Morsi ignored the social and economic demands of the revolution. It should be noted that this policy even went against large segments of his own social base, many of whom viewed the extortionist loans of the IMF as *riba* (usury) and payments on them *haram* (proscribed by Islamic law, or *Shari'a*). "The aura of religious authority which has been essential to the influence of the *Ikhwan* [the Brothers] has been falling away, especially since Mursi was elected. He's seen more and more as just another politician striking dubious deals," one Egyptian academic and activist explained in September of 2012, "The Brotherhood faces big problems as a party that's seen to have power but can't use it for moral purposes."[8] His government failed to initiate any wide-reaching economic programs to ameliorate conditions for the poor, refused to acknowledge the demands of the working class for a livable minimum wage, continued the repression of workers engaging in independent labor activity, and even went so far as to refuse to take state control of companies even when court ordered to do so.

Ultimately, Morsi's replacement of Mubarak did not represent a revolutionary restructuring of Egypt. Thus, two and a half years on Egypt's revolution was half made and the graves of the more than 32 million Egyptians who live on less than $2 a day continued to be dug. Egyptians, who have rapidly developed one of the most profoundly democratic and collective impulses in the world, refused to be swindled. This is the context in which on June 30th of 2013, one year after Morsi assumed office, a protest movement took to the streets even larger than the one that ousted Mubarak. The opposition to Morsi's rule, a complex and contradictory convergence of social forces, gathered some 22 million signatures demanding Morsi's resignation under the umbrella *Tamarod* (Rebel) movement. Even if these numbers are inflated, as some commentators suggest, it was this mass movement that compelled the military, without a doubt for their own economic and political purposes, to remove Morsi from office on July 3rd. Thus, in less than 30 months, Egyptians had overthrown two regimes in what seemed like a historic achievement of prodigious magnitude.

As with the anti-Mubarak movement, the opposition forces were a mixed bag that could remain cohesive just so long as Morsi was the enemy. The ephemeral nature of the movement was congenital due in large part to its contradictory class character. It did not represent a sustainable and long-lasting coalition based on mutual economic interests and solidarity between oppressed groups. "The bill of indictment against Morsi included complaints about Islamism, but otherwise looked rather like the list of grievances against Mubarak," the editors at MERIP explain, arguing the Brotherhood's message after elections was "We won fair and square, so the rest of you should quiet down and trust us to protect your prerogatives."9 The leadership of the Muslim Brothers successfully alienated and marginalized a wide and disparate cross-section of Egypt's population: workers (both secular and religious), liberals, Coptic Christians, women (including many who wear hijab), and even some unaffiliated Islamists. Politically, the movement against Morsi was composed primarily of three elements: segments of the old regime fragmented and in disarray after the dissolution of the NDP, the liberal political opposition, and labor and left elements whose demands largely converged. The coalescence of this opposition movement could only be short-lived, as the liberals who despised Morsi and the Muslim Brothers primarily for political differences largely agreed with the group's neoliberal economic program. Meanwhile, elements of the old regime, attempting to capitalize on the upsurge against the government which replaced them, opportunistically attached themselves to and helped orchestrate the movement in hopes of regaining lost ground while continuing to remain opposed to any fundamental political or economic change.

Working class and leftist elements in the *Tamarod* movement stood in stark opposition to the neoliberal economic doctrine, as well as the political and social policies of the Morsi government. The independent labor movement network responded to this campaign enthusiastically. Heba El-Shazli expands on the role workers played:

> …workers collected hundreds of thousands of signatures, endorsing the call for early presidential elections. The Center for Trade Union and Worker Services, a mainstay in the independent labor movement since its establishment in 1990, used its six offices around the country to collect

> the Tamarod petitions. The Egyptian Federation of Independent Trade Unions (EFITU) and the Egyptian Democratic Labor Congress (EDLC) both actively encouraged their members to come out and protest on 30 June. Meetings were held at their respective headquarters, provincial trade union federations, and local union offices, all to encourage members to show their support for Tamarod Campaign principles and protest former President Morsi's rule.[10]

In some cities, such as al-Mahalla al-Kubra, the Tenth of Ramadan, and Sadat City, workers were both the majority and the leading organizers of the anti-Morsi campaign, while in Daqahiliyya and Beheira municipal workers successfully shut down local government institutions. Support from labor and the left could also be evidenced when EFITU and the Revolutionary Socialists embraced the movement, releasing a joint statement in support of the protests.

While these three disparate elements came together as the National Salvation Front, other alternatives were in the process of developing. Concrete steps towards providing a revolutionary alternative were already being taken. In June, a coalition of revolutionary forces briefly merged to form the Revolutionary Alternative Front (*Jabihah al-Badil al-Thawra*) as both a rejection to the Morsi government and as a means of providing an alternative leadership to the liberal-*feloul* NSF alliance. This was particularly important as it brought together members and former members of Hamdeen Sabahi's Egyptian Popular Current, Mohamed ElBaradei's *Destour* Party, Islamist Abdel Moneim Abu al-Futouh's Strong Egypt Party, the April 6 youth movement, the Socialist Popular Alliance, and the Revolutionary Socialists. Noticeably, the RAF rejected any collaboration with elements from the old regime. The RAF was not sustained and never came into a position of leadership over the opposition movement vis-à-vis the NSF, but it did provide a glimpse of how a revolutionary coalition could provide a challenge to the liberal-*feloul* alliance. Many of these same players were involved in the "third square movement" that would go on to develop in July, rejecting the leadership of both Morsi and the generals. The RAF and the third square movement appear to have been precursors to *Thuwwar*, the Way of the Revolution Front (*Gabhet Tareeq al-Thawra*), established in September. Immediately after the coup the Revolutionary Socialists outlined the complex dynamics of the uprising in a statement titled "Four Days That Shook the World"[11]:

> What happened on June 30 was, without the slightest doubt, the historic beginning of a new wave of the

Egyptian revolution, the largest since January 2011…The significance of this surpasses any participation by old regime remnants, or the apparent support of the army and police. Mass demonstrations of millions are exceedingly rare events in human history, and their effect on the consciousness and confidence of the populace in themselves, and in their power to change the course of history, transcend the limitations of the slogans raised and the political alternatives put forward.

Yes, the liberal bourgeois elite wanted to use this mass impetus to overthrow the rule of the Islamist elite, in order to themselves reach power with the endorsement and support of the military establishment. And it is true that the feloul [remnants of the old regime] wanted to return to the political scene by way of this new revolutionary tide. But there is a special logic to popular revolutions that will not submit to the illusions or schemes of the liberals or feloul, even if sections of the masses were temporarily affected by the slogans and promises of that elite, just as they were affected before by the slogans and promises of the Islamist elite….

The masses have not revolted anew out of a desire for military rule or love for the feloul liberal alternative to the Muslim Brotherhood. They have revolted anew because Morsi and the Brotherhood betrayed the revolution. The Brotherhood did not implement even one of the demands of the revolution for social justice, freedom, human dignity or retribution for the martyrs of the revolution, whether they fell at the hands of Mubarak and al-Adly, or the Supreme Council of the Armed Forces (SCAF), or the Brotherhood and the Interior Ministry during the period of Brotherhood rule… Thus, Brotherhood rule became merely an extension on all levels of the Mubarak regime against which the Egyptian people had revolted…[12]

As events developed on June 30th and after, social media outlets, news networks, and even lawmakers in the US Congress debated the nature of the Egyptian revolution. The MERIP editorial frames the debate and correctly dismisses it as the wrong one to be having: "Was the gathering of millions in Egypt on June 30th the continuation of a revolution or the occasion for a coup d'état? The answer is 'both,' but the question is not the right one to ask." As they go on to point out, there is no "necessary contradiction between the two terms," as the overthrow of heads of state by force or the threat of force is present in every revolutionary scenario in human history. This conception of June 30th as a dichotomy pitting the military and the Muslim Brotherhood, "imposed liberalism or elected fundamentalism," remains a "centuries-old trope, of course, rooted in Orientalism, propagated by modern Arab states from Algiers to Riyadh and reprised today by insufferable pundits in service of their own agendas." [13]

Within these debates a dominant paradigm regarding the second mass uprising emerged. Two opposing discourses were of central importance. The first one was what Noura Erakat coined a "reactionary defense of electoral democracy,"[14] usually accompanied by an even more reactionary defense of the Muslim Brotherhood and Morsi. Generally, this line of argument attempted to disparage and traduce any social movement outside the narrow, electoral realm of "official" democracy. Democracy, however, cannot simply be defined as dropping a vote into a ballot box every two or four years and hoping for change, no matter how desperately the ruling order hopes to push this narrative. Indeed, "the events of late June and early July are evidence of both radical democratization and the failure of institutions - including elections - to arbitrate popular demands, much less deliver on them."[15] The Revolutionary Socialists articulate this lucidly:

> The governments and media outlets of the American and European bourgeoisie are trying to describe what has happened in Egypt as if it were only a military coup against a democratically elected president, or a coup against the "legitimacy" of formal democracy. But what has happened in reality far surpasses formal democracy, with its ballot boxes. It is legitimacy via the democracy of the popular revolution--direct democracy creating revolutionary legitimacy. It opens the horizons to new forms of popular power, which dwarf the temporary democracy of the ballot box that results in nothing but sustaining bourgeois rule with its different wings.
>
> The temporary democracy of the ballot box ensures only the continuance of power of the capitalist state apparatus. It ensures the delusions of the people who believe they rule because they choose once every few years who among the bourgeois elite will rule and exploit them--without, of course, getting near to the state apparatus or the sheltered capitalist corporations through the manipulation of the ballot box.

> What has happened in Egypt is the height of democracy, a revolution of millions of people to directly topple a ruler. As for the military displacement of Morsi, this was nothing but a foregone conclusion once the military institution saw that the masses had already settled the issue in the streets and squares of Egypt.[16]

Furthermore, whatever one thinks of Morsi's tenure, it is bewildering to claim that a popular movement forcing him to resign is undemocratic. Morsi won some 13 million votes, about 26% of the total Egyptian voting age population, a narrow margin even by bourgeois electoral standards. The *Tamarod* opposition movement against him collected some 22 million signatures. This is nearly double the amount of votes he passively won in the election, a time when millions of Egyptians were simply voting against Shafiq. Even if these numbers are inflated, the signatures against Morsi were certainly higher than the votes he earned in 2012, revealing the magnitude of displeasure with his governance. Whatever mandate Morsi may have had in June 2012, if he ever had a popular mandate at all, rapidly deteriorated and was negligible a year later.

The other discourse that dominated coverage of June 30th was a complete inability to distinguish between the mass, democratic movement against Morsi and the maneuvering of the military. Wael Gamal explained how June 30th was mostly viewed through the lens of politics being the "monopoly of senior power circles" who "plot for and against" leaders "behind the scenes within state institutions." He juxtaposed the two competing narratives of the proponents and detractors of June 30th, which were actually two sides of the same coin. Mainstream anti-Morsi writers explained with enthusiasm how the overthrow was pre-planned and orchestrated by the army and the leaders of the National Salvation Front, who Gamal pointed out were quickly "waist deep in roadmaps, negotiations over cabinet appointments, and details of the interim phase, which are all negotiations behind closed doors." In contrast, or coming full circle, the Muslim Brotherhood adopted "the exact same approach," except in mirror-image, proclaiming that the revolt was merely a military coup in conjunction with the old regime and propped up by Saudi Arabia and the United Arab Emirates. What both these narratives fail to do is "take into consideration the power that has the final say on matters these days: the power of the masses on the street and in the workplace." This simplistic binary leaves no room for understanding the social conditions and force that invigorated the mass movement on June 30th.[17]

During Morsi's last days in office, oil and gas shortages had rocked the country and affected millions of Egyptians. Conspiracy theories abounded, retroactively accusing the military of hoarding petrol reserves to augment instability and thereby creating cause Morsi's removal. Without the benefit of any evidence, this narrative seems the last thing any rational observer would accuse the military of desiring. If oil and gas "magically appeared" as some commentators suggest, it is likely the same way that bread "magically appeared" in 2008, to offset events that could have spiraled into something akin to the bread riots of 1977. This has less to do with the military trying to sabotage the Muslim Brotherhood government, which we can assume it hoped would normalize Egyptian society, and more to do with avoiding an all-out social conflict. The oil, like the bread, did not magically appear, it appeared at a time where social conflict had reached a precipice, and that is when the Egyptian military utilized its reserves to try and restore "order" and make the "wheel of production turn."

The reality is that even before June 30th, as living conditions continued to decline, the revolutionary activity in the streets never stopped. Millions of Egyptians were not simply manipulated by NSF leaders or military elites. A core of popular anger permeated Egyptian society and fed the mass movement that led to Morsi's removal. This was facilitated by the fact that the alliance between the Muslim Brotherhood and the military was a fragile one, and the failure to work out a functioning formula for normalization meant that the more powerful of the two institutions, the "deep state" or the military, could throw the other under the bus when times got tough. Thus, it is true that the military ousted an unpopular leader. Morsi's downfall was a cause of celebration for millions of Egyptians who felt either betrayed or attacked by him and his administration. On the other hand, it is also clear that for the military elites, this was little more than a calculated political move to keep Egypt's "wheel of production turning." This is not surprising considering that the Egyptian military remains the single largest economic institution in the country. The victory against Morsi, while important, was a relatively small victory insofar as the military remained the owners of Egypt's economy and shapers of Egyptian politics. The convergence of the demands articulated by the mass movement and the interests of the military establishment were to be short-lived, as the former desired a fundamental social transformation while the latter desired a return to order and stability. To try and accomplish this, they drowned the uprising in blood, skillfully utilizing anti-Morsi and anti-*Ikhwaan* sentiment to try and legitimize their crimes.

Despite its contradictions, the mass movement preceding Morsi's ouster was something to celebrate. The events following the July 2nd coup, however, were not as heartening. Almost immediately the military stormed news offices, closed the Rafah border with Gaza, and rounded up dozens of Muslim Brotherhood leaders and activists as clashes broke out across the country between pro-coup forces and the Muslim Brothers. At the time, the

220

military successfully won over significant portions of the secular liberal camp to their agenda, providing a layer of "revolutionary" legitimacy to their crackdown on the Muslim Brothers. The Revolutionary Socialists, despite their opposition to Morsi, argued that "we must be consistent in opposing all forms of abuse and repression to which the Islamists will be exposed in the form of arrests and closures of satellite channels and newspapers, for what happens today to the Islamists will happen tomorrow to the workers and the leftists."[18]

Tension increased through July and August, with clashes erupting all over the country. Coptic Christians often found themselves on the receiving end of political backlash by Morsi supporters. On August 14th, the military moved against two camps of pro-Morsi protesters at al-Nahda square and the Rabaa al-Adawiya mosque. According to protestors, the military closed off all exits and attacked the occupations, securing their coup through intense state violence. The National Alliance to Support Legitimacy, a broad Muslim Brother-led Islamist coalition brought together in the aftermath of the coup, estimate the number of dead at over 2,600 of their supporters.[19] In contrast, the Egyptian Health Ministry registered the deaths of 595 civilians and 43 police officers[20] while other NGOs and human rights organizations suggest a number of deaths closer to 1,000.[21] Whatever the actual number, August 14th was the single deadliest day since the 2011 uprising began. The brutal manner in which anti-coup forces were met show how little concern the military establishment has for democracy and social justice.

Perhaps the greatest irony is that the Muslim Brotherhood was the last political movement to enter the 2011 revolution and the first to start negotiating with the Supreme Council of the Armed Forces when they came to power. That the same establishment so quickly turned on the Muslim Brothers for the sake of political expediency, in the same way the Muslim Brothers turned on the revolution, is telling. After all, while the Egyptian military released their communiqués and public denunciations condemning workers for trying to win a living wage via strikes after Mubarak's downfall, it was the leadership of the Muslim Brotherhood who lent them their infrastructure to create an anti-labor echo chamber for the SCAF. The "wheel of production must turn," especially when the military controls so much of it, and much of the rest remained in the hands of the "Brothers of the 1%," as Business Week so aptly referred to the MB leadership.[22] While the military regime initiated the legislation sentencing strikers with prison time and fines well over a workers' yearly income, it was the Muslim Brothers who supported and provided political and religious legitimacy to the law. Likewise, it was the Brotherhood who perpetuated these and other Sadat-Mubarak era policies of social control once they came to power.

Another telling sign of the nature of the Muslim Brotherhood is that for the first time in nearly four decades the US seriously debated and then actually decided to reduce aid to the Egyptian military. As Habashi suggested they would, Morsi and the Muslim Brotherhood had shown how willing they were to "collaborate with the imperialism of the United States and Israel." In turn, a cautious Obama administration was positioned between a military regime they had propped up for decades and a political opposition they had successfully coopted. The administration deliberated on how to handle the new turn of events, debating whether or not what happened was regarded as a "coup," and then finally decided to take steps to punish the Egyptian military, presumably for getting out of line. In October the Obama administration announced it would withhold the delivery of important military equipment, including Apache helicopters, Harpoon missiles, F-16 warplanes, tank parts, and $260 million of the normal budget. This was largely a symbolic gesture, however, as they continued to provide aid for "counterterrorism programs" and military operations in Sinai. As one administration official explained, "This is not meant to be permanent; this is meant to be the opposite. It is meant to be continually reviewed," adding that "it's fair to say that holding up hundreds of millions of dollars of assistance is a pretty clear message."[23] It appears the "clear message" was that once the US has successfully incorporated a political organization into its orbit, the Egyptian military should not independently act to remove it. Indeed, a façade of independence and legitimacy is sometimes more conducive to ensuring the long-term interests of the US ruling class than outright military rule. Even this limited move to punish the Egyptian military had a cost, however, as in November military leaders announced they had opened up negotiations to purchase $1 billion in weapons from Russia.[24]

While it is clear that the military establishment needs to be challenged, the Muslim Brothers would not have been the ones to so in power. Rank-and-file Muslim Brothers may have a part to play in any future challenge, but this will be difficult due to how dramatically the leadership augmented disdain for the organization during its short period in power. The future of the Muslim Brotherhood rests largely on two factors: the amount of legal and political repression they face from the military and the outcome of the social conflict in Egypt. While the legacy of state repression against the Muslim Brotherhood is long, it has never been successful in doing away with the organization entirely. The recent crackdown, however, suggests that the "deep state" is willing to intensify its repression of the organization. The other factor that will potentially expand or delimit the space in which the organization can function is the social and economic realm. If there is a resolution of the class conflict in Egypt resulting in fundamental social and economic change, including a rejection of neoliberal dogma and the imperial powers which facilitate it, it is likely that the importance and influence of the Muslim Brotherhood would decline. If a government came to power that implemented serious social and economic reforms, including massive state investment in direct improvements to the lives of ordinary Egyptians, it follows that the social base of the Muslim Brotherhood would likely deteriorate. This could conceivably occur as social services provided by the state supplant the ad hoc networks currently provided by the Brothers. The vast majority of Muslim Brotherhood activists are middle class professionals, while the financial backers are among the wealthiest in the country. Even if their rhetoric and vernacular have a long reach, their political ideology represents the interests of a relatively small portion of the population. Despite this, the organization's social base is largely drawn from the poor who benefit from the social services controlled by the Muslim Brotherhood. If economic change is brought about by a new wave of revolutionary activity, it is conceivable that the result would be a significantly reduced space for the organization to operate once as its social base shrinks. On the contrary, if conditions remain the same or worsen, it is likely that the Muslim Brotherhood will continue to play an important role in Egyptian society. In this case, however, they may remain relegated to a position where they cannot impose their vision on the rest of Egypt.

Although the military positioned a judge, Adly Mansour, as the acting civilian president, it became increasingly clear that Abdel Fatah al-Sisi was calling the shots. Sisi had been Commander-in-Chief of the Egyptian Armed Forces since August 2012, but quickly became the face of the coup. It was Sisi who appeared on television, gave speeches and called for rallies defending the military's legitimacy, and actively engaged in splitting the social forces of June 30th. By mid-July, major media outlets such as Foreign Policy, Reuters, and Al-Arabiya were all running articles with titles proclaiming to hear "echoes of Nasser" in Sisi,[25] clumsily superimposing Egypt's historical past onto its current context. Nasser, who did indeed give speeches rallying ordinary Egyptians while implementing repressive policies, also captivated the Egyptian street with a political ideology and economic program far more akin to the late Chavez in Venezuela. Sisi lacks any such commitment to the social content which Nasser elevated and, subsequently, the only real echo found between Nasser and Sisi is their conflict with the Muslim Brotherhood. Although it is true that Nasser's commitment to economic reform did not develop immediately after the Free Officer coup of 1952, Sisi has given no signs that he will propose any social or economic program in the direction of Nasser's. Thus, while the comparisons between the two are almost entirely without basis, and while Morsi is certainly no Allende, the *Wall Street Journal* appeared to be getting their Pinochet in Sisi.

From the outset the military successfully exploited already existing schisms within the June 30th movement. The *Tamarod* movement behind the petition drive to oust Morsi gave a figurative blank check to the military regime, supporting whatever repression they wanted to dish out to the Islamists. Meanwhile, the April 6th Movement and the Revolutionary Socialists, both organizations which supported the June 30th uprising, broke with *Tamarod* on the issue of providing ideological cover for the military. For them, once Morsi was gone the military was the primary enemy of the people.

As the political parties split over the military's role in the ouster, so too did the unions. The professional syndicates, especially the doctors and pharmacists organizations, "have been and still are actively mobilizing their forces against the June 30th movement, and in support of Morsi."[26] This was to be expected, given both the activist-base of the Muslim Brotherhood and the method by which they took control of the professional syndicates. It was not entirely clear whether the Brotherhood would use the full force of their syndicates, or even if they could. The conservative nature of the group's leadership was evidenced in mid-July when, according to member Abdallah al-Keryoni, the Brotherhood was "deliberating whether or not it should resort to syndicate strikes as part of their campaign of resistance against this military coup." While "the idea of strikes" had been proposed, Keryoni noted that "our position has not yet been determined."[27] The Brotherhood, which engaged in the process of criminalizing strikes while it was in power, was hesitant to use a form of social protest that could set a precedent for others to move beyond the organization's ability to control. Combined with this ambivalence there was a contentious battle for control within the professional syndicates between leftist factions and the Muslim Brotherhood. This was most notable in the doctors' union, where left-wing doctors were organized around the Doctors without Rights group and challenged the Islamist right-wing which oriented toward a "service union" mode of operation.

While a sharp distinction between the professional syndicates and the working-class unions emerged, there was a simultaneous disintegration of the coalition between the independent unions. Despite the confirmation of solidarity reaffirmed at the EDLC's founding conference, immediately following the coup an attempt to co-opt the independent labor movement began. Less than two weeks after the joint RS-EFITU statement, independent labor union leader Kamal Abu 'Aita revealed his opportunism by endorsing a military statement calling on workers to suspend any strike activity. Resigning as president of EFITU, he was quickly rewarded for his acquiescence and granted a position in the ministry that oversees labor affairs.[28] The EFITU leadership followed in step, releasing a statement that while workers were the "heroes of the strikes against the previous two governments," they were now to "be the heroes of hard work and production for the nation."[29] The transition from independent labor unionism to accepting the nationalist "wheel of production" rhetoric was a rapid one, but not everyone in EFITU was giving in so easily. EFITU council member Fatma Ramadan issued a rebuttal to Abu 'Aita, insisting that "Egypt's workers must never sacrifice their right to strike," and warning that June 30th may represent "an uprising-turned-coup. It lacks both a unified leadership and clear aims. SCAF, along with right-wing elements and remnants of the Mubarak regime, appear to be taking over this movement, and may turn June 30th from an uprising to a counter-revolution."[30] The leadership of EDLC, while supportive of the June 30th uprising, was more cautious in its appraisal of the military than Abu 'Aita and gave no indication that it sanctioned the cessation of strikes. Thus, two schisms began to clearly emerge, one within EFITU as a reformist leadership clashed with a more militant base, and another between the leadership of EFITU and the EDLC. The leaders of the state-sponsored yellow trade union, the ETUF, condemned the appointment of Abu 'Aita for their own opportunistic reasons.

Given the balance of forces, it is perhaps unlikely but not impossible that a fundamental restructuring of Egyptian society will take place in the future. As EFITU and the Revolutionary Socialists argued in their joint statement during the days leading up the June 30th protests:

> What is happening now brings to mind the days before the fall of Mubarak: striking unions everywhere, protests against the decisions made by the government, and our situation is going from bad to worse with the ongoing fuel and electricity crisis. What are we waiting for? Egyptian labour workers are an organised productive force, and alone are capable of moderating the balance of power on 30 June and onwards.[31]

While it is not true that workers are the only force capable of moderating Egyptian politics, they are the only force capable of engaging in the radical, emancipatory project of transforming society into one where social justice and democratic control of the economy are the foundations upon which all else is built. At the moment, the Egyptian labor movement faces obstacles that enervate its ability to achieve this task.

In late September 152 activists and revolutionaries of different stripes came together to form a new coalition, the Way of the Revolution Front (*Gabhet Tareeq al-Thawra*, or *Thuwwar*), which aimed to remain independent of both the pro-Morsi and pro-military camp. They positioned themselves as an alternative to the polarizing enmity between the Muslim Brothers and the pro-coup forces. In its founding statement, *Thuwwar* summarized itself by the following five principles: the redistribution of wealth, the end of political dictatorship, the implementation of complete equality before the law, the establishment of a clear path for transitional justice, and the adoption of a foreign policy based on the interests of the people.[32] It announced the immediate launch of three campaigns: one for "Egyptian Bill of Rights" guaranteeing civil, economic, political, and cultural rights for Egyptians, the second a long-term campaign dealing with a broader set of social and economic rights, and the third an anti-debt campaign titled "Don't Borrow in Our Name."[33] Some of the founding members included activist Alaa Abdel-Fattah, April 6 founding member Ahmed Maher, renowned novelist Ahdaf Soueif, leftist writer and economist Wael Gamal, student activist Wesam Atta of the Justice and Freedom Youth, as well as the labor lawyer and Revolutionary Socialist Haitham Mohamadein.[34] Other founding members included rights lawyer Gamal Eid, Hossam El-Hamalawy, Basma Al-Husseiny, and Saud Omar. The front was meant to be non-sectarian and open only to individuals, not representatives of organizations, even if individuals already held membership in another group. While it was unclear at the time of writing if *Thuwwur* would prove different than the previous ad hoc attempts at united fronts in response to particular developments, activists at the founding conference expressed their intention of maintaining a long-term front.

This development is encouraging. However, the Egyptian left, like much of the left worldwide, is infinitesimally small. Despite its recent importance the coordination of economic actions and political organizing, the Egyptian left does not maintain hegemony over the entirety of the working class, let alone all of Egyptian society. The Revolutionary Socialists acknowledge this in their July statement:

> The dilemma of the Egyptian revolution today is the political weakness of revolutionary forces espousing the demand of continuing the revolution, with the social demands at its heart. For these forces, the ballot box will not suffice, and they will not accept the continuance of capitalist policies of impoverishment. They will not abandon the demand for retribution for the blood of the revolutionary martyrs. They will continue to insist upon the overthrow of Mubarak's state, including its security, military and judiciary institutions. These institutions still control the country and still protect the interests of the big businessmen and Mubarak's feloul. They remain a great swamp of corruption, plunder and despotism.
>
> It is incumbent upon the revolutionary forces today to unite their ranks and put themselves forward as a

> convincing revolutionary alternative for the masses--an alternative to the liberal forces who are ascendant today on the shoulders of the military, and to the forces of political Islam which have dominated over broad swaths of the population for decades. We must create a platform to unite the economic and social struggle among the ranks of the workers and the poor, to unite all of the oppressed sections of society...
>
> So we begin from this moment preparations for the third Egyptian revolution inevitably to come, to be ready to lead this revolution to final victory. For the masses have proven anew that their revolutionary energy is endless, that their revolution is truly a permanent revolution. Let us rise to the task of this historical responsibility, and let us work together for the success of the revolution.[35]

The first step, uniting the ranks of revolutionary forces and putting forward an alternative, came to fruition in the form of *Thuwwur*. It remains to be seen whether *Thuwwur* will become a vehicle for the masses. The Egyptian working class is a giant with the capacity to control the future of Egypt, but it is not at this time in a hegemonic position where it can fulfill this potential. Still, the struggles of Egyptian workers and the social justice-oriented Egyptian left remain a heroic and valiant one that should inspire class-conscious workers around the world. It is conceivable in the long term, as the Egyptian working class movement continues to engage in the struggle for social justice, that it will develop the political capacity to fulfill its potential. The giant has awoken, and it alone has the social power to transform Egyptian society into one which the oppressed of the world will seek to emulate.

[1] *Wall Street Journal*, July 7, 2013. http://online.wsj.com/news/articles/SB10001424127887324399404578583932317286550

[2] Mamdouh Habashi, "Class Struggle in Egypt," Lecture given at *Socialism 2008* in Chicago.

[3] Fares Akram and David Kirkpatrick, "To Black Gaza Tunnels, Egypt Lets Sewage Flow," *The New York Times*, February 20, 2013, http://www.nytimes.com/2013/02/21/world/middleeast/egypts-floods-smuggling-tunnels-to-gaza-with-sewage.html.

[4] It is safe to assume that the only reason for the annulment of the natural gas giveaway scheme was that "the gas line to Israel was severed 14 times in 12 months by a series of explosions." See Franklin Lamb, "Will Sadat's Camp David and the Zionist Embassy be Next?" *CounterPunch*, May 02, 2012, http://www.counterpunch.org/2012/05/02/will-sadats-camp-david-and-the-zionist-embassy-be-next/.

[5] Nicole Gaouette and Laura Litvan, "Egypt's $1.5 Billion U.S. Aid Questioned Amid Crackdown," *Bloomberg*, January 31, 2013, http://www.bloomberg.com/news/2013-02-01/egypt-s-1-5-billion-u-s-aid-questioned-amid-crackdown.html.

[6] See SCAF loan attempt here: Liam Stack, "Pressed by Unrest and Money Woes, Egypt Accepts I.M.F. Loan," *The New York Times*, February 19, 2012, http://www.nytimes.com/2012/02/20/world/middleeast/egypt-announces-imf-loan.html.

[7] For more on the haggling between Morsi and the IMF, see: "Egypt will not accept emergency IMF loan, says Cabinet spokesman," *Egypt Independent*, March 12, 2013, http://www.egyptindependent.com/news/egypt-will-not-accept-emergency-imf-loan-says-cabinet-spokesman. See also: Bisan Kassab, "Egypt Seeks IMF Loan at Any Cost," *Al-Akhbar English*, April 19, 2013, http://english.al-akhbar.com/node/15577. Last, see: "Egypt: Prime Minister Kandil Says He Expects IMF Loan Deal Within 45 Days," *All Africa*, May 13, 2013, http://allafrica.com/stories/201305140434.html.

[8] Quoted in Marfleet, "Never going back: Egypt's continuing revolution."

[9] "Egypt in Year Three," *Middle East Research and Information Project*, July 10, 2013, http://www.merip.org/mero/mero071013.

[10] Heba F. El-Shazli, "Where Were the Egyptian Workers in the June 2013 People's Coup Revolution?" *Jadaliyya*, July 23, 2013, http://www.jadaliyya.com/pages/index/13125/where-were-the-egyptian-workers-in-the-june-2013-p.

[11] The title of this statement is presumably a reference to *Ten Days that Shook the World* by John Reed, a book documenting the October Revolution of 1917.

[12] Translated by Jess Martin, "Four days that shook the world," *Socialist Worker* (US), July 05, 2013, http://socialistworker.org/2013/07/05/four-days-that-shook-

the-world. Original in Arabic published in *Al-Ishtiraki*, July 4, 2013: http://revsoc.me/politics/rb-ym-hzt-llm.
13 "Egypt in Year Three," *Middle East Research and Information Project.*
14 Noura Erakat, "For the Revolution or Against the Coup? My Two Cents on Egypt & Recommended Readings," *Noura Erakat* (blog), July 04, 2013, http://www.nouraerakat.com/1/post/2013/07/for-the-revolution-or-against-the-coup-my-two-cents-on-egypt-recommended-readings.html.
15 "Egypt in Year Three," *Middle East Research and Information Project.*
16 "Four days that shook the world," *Socialist Worker.*
17 Wael Gamal, "Who really decided in revolutionary Egypt?" *Ahram Online*, July 11, 2013, http://english.ahram.org.eg/News/76234.aspx.
18 Four days that shook the world," *Socialist Worker.*
19 "Egypt's Brotherhood to hold 'march of anger'," *Al-Jazeera English*, August 16, 2013, http://www.aljazeera.com/news/middleeast/2013/08/201381522364486906.html
20 Manar Mohsen, "Health Ministry raises death toll of Wednesday's clashes to 638." *Daily News Egypt*, August 16, 2013, http://www.dailynewsegypt.com/2013/08/16/health-ministry-raises-death-toll-of-wednesdays-clashes-to-638/.
21 "Rights groups urge probe of mass killing in Egypt," *Al-Ahram*, December 10, 2013, http://english.ahram.org.eg/NewsContent/1/64/88788/Egypt/Politics-/Rights-groups-urge-probe-of-mass-killing-in-Egypt.aspx.
22 Suzy Hansen, "The Economic Vision of Egypt's Muslim Brotherhood Millionaires," *Businessweek*, April 19, 2012, http://www.businessweek.com/printer/articles/20938-the-economic-vision-of-egypts-muslim-brotherhood-millionaires.
23 Michael R. Gordon and Mark Landler, "In Crackdown Response, U.S. Temporarily Freezes Some Military Aid to Egypt," *New York Times*, October 9, 2013, http://www.nytimes.com/2013/10/10/world/middleeast/obama-military-aid-to-egypt.html?_r=0
24 Heba Saleh and Kathrin Hille, "Egypt and Russia hail new era of military co-operation," *Financial Times*, November 14, 2013, http://www.ft.com/cms/s/0/8d7c0526-4d48-11e3-bf32-00144feabdc0.html#axzz2nHIh3se6
25 Steven A. Cook, "Echoes of Nasser," *Foreign Policy*, July 16, 2013, http://www.foreignpolicy.com/articles/2013/07/16/echoes_of_nasser_egypt_muslim_brotherhood_history. Also see: Michael Georgy and Tom Perry, "Egypt's new top general stirs echoes of Nasser," *Reuters*, July 29, 2013, http://www.reuters.com/article/2013/07/29/us-egypt-protests-future-idUSBRE96S0KJ20130729. *Al-Arabiya* ran the same article: http://english.alarabiya.net/en/perspective/analysis/2013/07/29/Egypt-s-new-top-general-stirs-echoes-of-Nasser.html
26 Jano Charbel, "And where do the workers stand?" *Mada Masr*, July 15, 2013, http://www.madamasr.com/content/and-where-do-workers-stand.
27 Charbel, "And where do the workers stand?"

[28] "Labour leader Abu Eita to be appointed Egypt's manpower minister," *Ahram Online*, July 15, 2013, http://english.ahram.org.eg/NewsContent/1/64/76509/Egypt/Politics-/Labour-leader-Abu-Eita-to-be-appointed-Egypts-manp.aspx.

[29] In Arabic: EFITU Statement, *Al-Bawaba News*, July 08. 2013, http://www.albawabhnews.com/News/71894#.UdsI3v6uI80.facebook

[30] Charbel, "And where do the workers stand?"

[31] Luiz Sanchez, "Trade Unions call for 30 June Revolution," *Daily News Egypt*, June 25, 2013, http://www.dailynewsegypt.com/2013/06/25/trade-unions-call-for-30-june-revolution/.

[32] "A revolutionary front in Egypt," *Socialist Worker*, October 10, 2013, http://socialistworker.org/2013/10/10/a-revolutionary-front-in-egypt

[33] "'We will not ally with the Brotherhood or the Army': The Way of the Revolution Front," Daily News Egypt, Setemeber 24, 2013, http://www.dailynewsegypt.com/2013/09/24/we-will-not-ally-with-the-brotherhood-or-the-army-the-way-of-the-revolution-front/

[34] "New 'anti-Brotherhood, anti-military' front launched to 'achieve revolution goals'," *Ahram Online*, September 24, 2013, http://english.ahram.org.eg/News/82400.aspx.

[35] "Four days that shook the world," *Socialist Worker*.

Resources

What follows is by no means a complete bibliography for the book. For those interested, all the sources I have utilized for the book are cited in the footnotes. Instead of a full works cited section here, what follows here is a list of useful media outlets, journals, and organizations that will help guide an individual to useful material regarding Egyptian politics. Also, a list of suggested readings organized broadly by topic is provided. Not every book or article cited here was utilized in my work, for reasons of space or content. However, they are all readings that will help unravel the complexities of modern Egypt in one way or another. Finally, it should be noted that there are probably resources that should have been included in this list but were not. This was most likely not intentional, as there are certainly other articles, books, journals, media outlets, and organizations which are useful. Despite their absence, it is my hope that this list will help direct readers in the right direction.

Newspapers, blogs, periodicals, and other news outlets

Arabic
Al-Jazeera
Al-Ahram
El-Badil
Al-Bawaba
Al-Dostor
Al-Ishtiraki (*The Socialist*)
Al-Masry al-Youm
Al-Shorouk
Al-Wafd
Tadamon Masr (blog)

English (from Egypt)
3arabawy (blog)
Ahram Online
Daily News Egypt
Egypt Independent (formerly Al-Masry al-Youm)
Egyptian Streets

Mada Masr

English (Other)
Al-Jazeera English
Al-Akhbar English
Egypt Workers Solidarity (blog)
Informed Comment (blog)
Middle East Online
Middle East and North Africa Solidarity Network
Jadaliyya

Journals
Arab Studies Quarterly
British Journal of Middle Eastern Studies
International Labor and Working Class History
International Journal of Middle East Studies
International Socialism
International Socialist Review
Journal of Developing Areas
Journal of Third World Studies
Khamsin
The Middle East Journal
Middle Eastern Studies
Middle East Research and Information Project
Radical History Review
Review of African Political Economy

Organizations
Awlad al-Ard
Center for Economic and Social Rights
Center for Research on Globalization
Egyptian Center for Economic and Social Rights
International Labor Organization
The Hampton Institute

Further Reading

Arab Socialism and Gamal Abd al-Nasser
Abdel-Malek, Anouar. *Egypt: Military Society, the Army Regime, the Left, and Social Change under Nasser*. New York: Random House, 1968.

Abu-Laban, Baha. "The National Character of the Egyptian Revolution." *The Journal of Developing Areas.* Vol. 1, no. 2 (1967): 179-98.

Alexander, Anne. *Nasser: His Life, His Times.* Cairo: American University in Cairo Press, 2005.

Alexander, Anne. "Suez and the high tide of Arab Nationalism." *International Socialism.* No. 112 (2006).

Ginat, Rami. *Egypt's Incomplete Revolution: Lutfi al-Khuli and Nasser's Socialism in the 1960s.* Boulder: Lynne Rienner, 1997.

Hanna, Sami A. and George H. Gardner. *Arab Socialism: A Documentary Survey.* Salt Lake City, University of Utah Press, 1969.

Kerr, Malcolm H. *The Arab Cold War: Gamal 'Abd al-Nasir and His Rivals, 1958-1970.* London: Oxford University Press, 1971.

Said, Abdul Moghny and Samir Ahmed. *Arab Socialism.* Little Hampton Book Services, 1972.

The Egyptian Communist Movement

Agwani, Mohammad Shafi. *Communism in the Arab East.* New York: Asia Publishing House, 1969.

Akhavi, Shahrough. "Egypt's Socialism and Marxist Thought: Some Preliminary Observations on Social Theory and Metaphysics." *Comparative Studies in Society and History.* Vol. 17, no. 2 (1975): 190-211.

Beinin, Joel. "Henri Curiel and the Egyptian Communist Movement." *Radical History Review.* No. 45 (1989): 157-163.

Beinin, Joel. "Exile and Political Activism: The Egyptian-Jewish Communists in Paris, 1950-59." *Diaspora: A Journal of Transnational Studies.* Vol. 2, No. 1 (1992): 73-94.

Beinin, Joel. "The Communist Movement and Nationalist Political Discourse in Nasirist Egypt." *Middle East Journal,* Vol. 41, no. 4 (1987): 568-584.

Beinin, Joel. *Was the Red Flag Flying There? Marxist Politics and the Arab-Israeli Conflict in Egypt and Israel, 1948-1965.* Berkeley: University of California Press, 1990.

Botman, Selma. "Women's participation in radical Egyptian politics, 1939-1952." *Khamsin* (1987): 12-25.

Botman, Selma. "The Experience of Women in the Egyptian Communist Movement, 1939-1954." *Women's Studies International Forum,* Vol. 11, No. 2 (1988): 117-126.

Flores, Alexander. "The Arab CPs and the Palestine Problem." *Khamsin.* No. 7 (1979).

Ginat, Rami. *A History of Egyptian Communism: Jews and Their Compatriots in Quest of Revolution.* Boulder: Lynne Rienner, 2011.

Ginat, Rami. "The Egyptian Left and the Roots of Neutralism in the Pre-Nasserite Era." *British Journal of Middle Eastern Studies*, Vol. 30, no. 1 (2003): 5-24.

Gorman, Anthony P. "Egypt's Forgotten Communists: The Postwar Greek Left." *Journal of Modern Greek Studies*, Vol. 20, No. 1 (2002): 1-27.

Ismael, Tareq Y. *The Arab Left*. New York: Syracuse University Press, 1976.

Ismael, Tareq Y. and Rifa'at El-Sa'id. *The Communist Movement in Egypt, 1920-1988*. New York: Syracuse University Press, 1990.

Shamir, Shimon. "Marxism in the Arab World: The Cases of the Egyptian and Syrian Regimes." *The Van Leer Jerusalem Foundation Series*. Vol. 2 (1977): 271-278.

The Political Economy of Modern Egypt

Abdel-Khalek, Gouda. *Stabilization and Adjustment in Egypt: Reform or De-industrialization*. Northampton: Edward Elgar Publishing, 2001.

Ayubi, Nazih N. *Over-stating the Arab State: Politics and Society in the Middle East*. London: I.B. Tauris & Co Ltd., 2008.

Beinin, Joel. "Labor, Capital, and the State in Nasserist Egypt, 1952-1961." *International Journal of Middle East Studies*. Vol. 21, no. 1 (1989): 71-90.

Botman, Selma. *Egypt from Independence to Revolution, 1919-1952*. Syracuse: Syracuse University Press, 1991.

Bradley, Clive. "State capitalism in Egypt – a critique of Patrick Clawson." *Khamsin*. No. 10 (1983): 73-99.

Clawson, Patrick. "The Development of Capitalism in Egypt." *Khamsin*. No. 9 (1981): 77-116.

Cooper, Mark N. *The Transformation of Egypt*. New York: Routledge, 1982.

Harik, Iliya, and Denis Sullivan. *Privatization and Liberalization in the Middle East*. Bloomington: Indiana University Press, 1992.

Ja'far Mohammad. "National formation in the Arab region: a critique of Samir Amin." *Khamsin*. No. 6 (1979): 60-86.

Mabro, Robert and Samir Radwan. *The Industrialization of Egypt, 1939-1973: Policy and Performance*. Oxford: Oxford University Press, 1978.

Mitchell, Timothy. *Colonising Egypt*. London: Cambridge University Press, 1988.

Mitchell, Timothy. *Rule of Experts: Egypt, Techno-Politics, Modernity*. Berkeley: University of California Press, 2002.

Posusney, Marsha Pripstein. *Labor and the State in Egypt: Workers, Unions, and Economic Restructuring*. New York: Columbia University Press, 1997.

Vitalis, Robert. *When Capitalists Collide: Business Conflict and the End of Empire in Egypt*. 1995.

Political Islam and Egypt

Dreyfuss, Robert. *Devil's Game: How the United States Helped Unleash Fundamentalist Islam.* New York: Henry Holt and Company, 2005.

El-Hamalawy, Hossam. "Comrades and Brothers." *Middle East Research and Information Project*, no. 242, http://www.merip.org/mer/mer242/comrades-brothers (accessed July 17, 2013).

Hallaq, Wael B. *The Impossible State: Islam, Politics, and Modernity's Moral Predicament.* New York: Columbia University Press, 2013.

Kumar, Deepa. *Islamophobia and the Politics of Empire*, (Chicago: Haymarket Books, 2012).

Lia, Brynjar. *The Society of the Muslim Brothers in Egypt: The Rise of an Islamic Mass Movement, 1928-1942.* Reading: Garnet Publishing Limited, 1998.

Mitchell, Richard P. *The Society of Muslim Brothers.* Oxford: Oxford University Press, 1969.

About the Author

Derek Ide received degrees in both Education and History at the University of Toledo. He was a co-founder of and community adviser to UT's "Students for Justice in Palestine" chapter on campus. He is currently a graduate student at UT studying Middle Eastern history and serves as chair of the Social Movement Studies Department at the Hampton Institute.

www.ingramcontent.com/pod-product-compliance
Lightning Source LLC
Chambersburg PA
CBHW071112160426
43196CB00013B/2549